REVIEW COPY

Price $ *7.20*

(includes mailing)

We would appreciate three copies
of any notice.

SALES SECTION
BRITISH INFORMATION SERVICES
845 THIRD AVENUE
NEW YORK, N.Y. 10022

Agents for Her Majesty's Stationery Office

BOARD OF TRADE

Competition, monopoly and restrictive practices

A select bibliography

LONDON   HER MAJESTY'S STATIONERY OFFICE
1970

©Crown copyright 1970

Published by
Her Majesty's Stationery Office

To be purchased from
49 High Holborn, London WC1
13a Castle Street, Edinburgh EH2 3AR
109 St. Mary Street, Cardiff CF1 1JW
Brazennose Street, Manchester M60 8AS
50 Fairfax Street, Bristol BS1 3DE
258 Broad Street, Birmingham 1
7 Linenhall Street, Belfast BT2 8AY
or through any bookseller

SBN 11 510211 6

Contents

Introduction

The Board of Trade has the responsibility within the Government for the formulation and administration of policy concerning competition and monopoly. The Board's Economic Research Unit, as part of its programme of research into various aspects of competition, with the assistance of the staff of the Economics Division of the Board of Trade Library, has compiled an annotated select bibliography of the subject. While this was undertaken primarily for internal use within the Government, the absence of a comparable published work has led the Board to offer it to a wider audience.

The literature relating to competition and monopoly is vast. A comprehensive list could be taken to embrace a large part of the whole field of economics; such a list would be of limited practical value to prospective users. Even within the narrower field of specialisation in the theory and practice of competition, the literature is too large to constitute a manageable bibliography. Therefore the scale of interest in the subject, as expressed in the written word, forced the compilers to be selective.

Selection of entries

For the user, the principles of selection are clearly important. Four criteria for inclusion have been applied:
1 Publications based on or which contribute to the pursuit of empirical study in the field of competition, which combine theory and empirical study or which represent an important development in the theory;
2 Publications which discuss problems of methodology, measurement, and definition or which provide important sources of relevant data;
3 Publications which are applicable especially to conditions in Britain. A good number of publications pertaining to United States or Canadian conditions have been included also, since many important aspects such as problems of concentration, diversification, integration, the implications of bigness, barriers to entry, have been more extensively explored in those countries than in the United Kingdom, and much of the experience is relevant to British conditions.
4 Publications which have appeared since 1st January, 1950 or which are considered to be so important that the date of publication is immaterial. The closing date for entries was the end of 1967. It was possible in a few cases to incorporate in existing entries references to related publications which appeared during 1968.

The application of these criteria involved some personal judgment, and not everyone would agree with the actual selection. With a few exceptions, publications by organisations such as the Bow Group, the Fabian Society, the TUC, and the CBI, have been omitted. Acts of Parliament and subordinate legislation concerned with the distribution of industry, with patents, monopolies and restrictive practices, have also been excluded. They can be identified in *Index to the statutes in force* (annually), and in *Index to Government orders in force* (latest edition 1966), supplemented by the annual and monthly *List of statutory instruments* (all published by HMSO). The Economic Research Unit would be glad, of course, to learn of any glaring errors or omissions, or if it is thought that the judgments have been misplaced.

Annotations

It was thought likely to be valuable, given the variety of potential users in the Government service, if some brief description or summary could be given in addition to the usual bibliographical details. This could save much time in identifying the particular publications of greatest relevance to the user. Again, the choice lay between comprehensive and selective annotation.

For practical reasons selective annotation was chosen. Publications annotated contain some particular contribution, under any given heading, on some special aspect important to the understanding of the subject, or of significance for future empirical research. Of course it is impossible to do justice to an argument or analytical study by means of a short annotation, but an effort has been made to present the essence of the principal points which the author was putting forward.

In addition, headings and major sub-headings have been provided with a short introduction drawing attention to the scope of the works included and to major contributions in the respective fields of research.

Classification

The bibliography has been classified into seven main classes and 21 sub-classes in a manner thought to be most convenient and intelligible to economists and others interested in the general range of topics. In several cases the contents of publications belong to several classes or sub-classes and where thought necessary, cross references have been provided. The subject index will help in tracing publications on any given topic.

In the sub-divisions headed 'General' have been placed those publications which go beyond the scope of any

specific sub-class, but it should be borne in mind that
frequently they will also contain material relevant for
sub-classes.

Name index

This provides entries for the names of authors, whether
individuals or corporate bodies, of every item in the
bibliography. In many cases, annotations to entries in the
bibliography for conference proceedings, symposia, etc.
provide full or partial contents lists of papers included ;
their authors are also indexed. Index entries have also been
made under corporate bodies in respect of works published
or sponsored by those bodies. Where two or more entries
appear under the name of a corporate body, the titles of the
works have been added.

Subject index

The purpose of this index is to facilitate a search for, and to
reveal the presence in the bibliography of, items dealing
with very specific topics. It contains entries based not only
on the subject matter suggested by the titles of items, but
also on the annotations accompanying the entries in the
bibliography. It serves also to collect together references to
items dealing with a particular country or industry.

Conventions

The following conventions have been used in entries in the
bibliography :
Authors' Names. Forenames have been abbreviated to
initials, regardless of authors' own usage.

Place of Publication. Omitted for works published in
London.

Publishers' Names. Omitted for works published directly by
the person or organisation cited as author. Commercial
publishers' names have been abbreviated to a form readily
identifiable in standard directories of publishers.

Journal Articles. Titles of journals have been abbreviated in
accordance with the British Standard *Recommendations
for the abbreviation of titles for periodicals* (BS 4148 : 1967).
The full titles of journals cited in the bibliography are given
in Appendix 1, pages 89-93. Citations are made in the form
volume number (issue number), date of issue, inclusive
pagination, e.g. 18(4), Nov. 1956, pp 373-386.

Acknowledgements

The principal work involved in selecting, arranging and
annotating the items in the bibliography was undertaken by
Mr S. Moos, of the Board of Trade Economic Research Unit.
The staff of the Board of Trade Library, and particularly
Mr G. E. Hamilton, contributed both technical advice and
practical assistance with the preparation of entries,
checking of bibliographical details and the compilation of
indexes.

1 Competition and monopoly: general and general theoretical

See also items 78, 324, 564, 800, 805, 873, 901.

In this section of the bibliography mainly those works have been listed which deal with general aspects of competition and monopoly or which cannot be allocated to other headings. Of the great number of publications raising general questions of competition and monopoly the better known have been selected to provide a cross section in particular of the interpretation and definition of the terms used, the assessment of competitive situations, the relation between competition and welfare, the significance of patterns of competitive and monopolistic forces and methods, etc. They include some of the inter-war publications which have remained standard works, such as those by A. R. Burns, J. M. Clark, E. H. Chamberlin, A. F. Lucas, E. A. G. Robinson, J. A. Schumpeter and P. Sraffa. Of the post-war works amongst the outstanding contributions are J. S. Bain's *Industrial organization* (item 78) and *Barriers to new competition* (item 324). M. Shubik's *Strategy and market structure* (item 61) applies, for the first time, the game theory to problems of market organisation.

Additional references to standard works on the theory of the firm, competition and monopoly, can be found in *A bibliography in economics for the Oxford Honour School of Philosophy, Politics and Economics* (2nd ed. Oxford Univ. Pr., 1959). Authors whose works are listed there include : E. H. Chamberlin, R. F. Harrod, J. R. Hicks, M. Kalecki, N. Kaldor, F. Machlup, J. Robinson, K. W. Rothschild, P. Sraffa, G. J. Stigler, R. Triffin. A new publication, *A bibliography for students of economics* (Oxford Univ. Pr., 1968) lists many, but not all, of these works. Each of these bibliographies is also a source for publications concentrating on general fiscal and monetary policy, which have been omitted from the present bibliography. However, a number of entries refer to the implications of these policies for competition and monopoly policy, e.g. T. Balogh (items 935, 957, 1057, 1058), C. A. R. Crosland (item 85), J. C. R. Dow (item 87), Y. C. Koo (item 33), G. D. A. MacDougall (items 956-960, 1016), G. D. N. Worswick (item 115).

1
Abbott, L. Quality and competition ; an essay in economic theory. New York, Columbia Univ. Pr., 1955. ix, 229 p.

Study of non-price competition. Discusses whether differences in quality should be interpreted as monopolistic imperfection or as a competitive element. Suggests that price theory should be supplemented by a quality theory. Bibliography.

2
Adams, W. Competition, monopoly and countervailing power. *Q. j. econ.*, 67 (4), Nov. 1953, pp 469–492. (Correction 68 (3), Aug. 1954, p 481).

Critical examination of Galbraith's thesis that monopoly is kept in check by countervailing power (see item 23).

3
Allen, G. C. Economic fact and fantasy : a rejoinder to Galbraith's Reith lectures. Institute of Economic Affairs, 1967. 34 p. (IEA occasional papers, no. 14).

Criticism of item 95.

4
Allen, G. C. A note on monopoly and economic progress. *Economica,* new ser. 20, 1953, pp 359–361.

Criticism of item 29.

5
Archibald, G. C. Monopolistic competition and returns to scale. *Econ. j.,* 77 (306), June 1967, pp 405–412.

Controversy about the validity of the theory of monopolistic competition. A reply by H. Demsetz, pp 412–420.

6
Bain, J. S. The theory of monopolistic competition after thirty years : the impact on industrial organisation. *Am. econ. rev.,* 54 (3), May 1964, pp 28–32.

Discusses Chamberlin's theory (item 13).

7
Bain, J. S. Workable competition in oligopoly : theoretical considerations and some empirical evidence. *Am. econ. rev.,* 40 (2), May 1950, pp 35–47.

Distinguishes between : oligopolies with blockaded or very difficult entry and a high concentration of sellers ; oligopolies with moderately difficult entry and moderate concentration ; oligopolies with easy entry, high or moderate concentration. Believes that there may be logically explicable association between oligopoly market structure and workability of competition. Finds strong relation between concentration ratio and annual profit rate in 39 industries examined.

8

Bernhard, R. C. Competition in law and in economics. *Antitrust bull.*, 12, Winter 1967, pp 1099–1163.

A short history of thought on competition from Adam Smith to J. K. Galbraith. Of special interest is the account (pp 1125–1129) of Marshall's concept of 'economic biology' and its relation to concepts used in anti-monopoly law. Many footnote references.

9

Bernhard, R. C. The law and the economics of market collusion in Europe, Great Britain, and the United States : an American point of view. *J. ind. econ.*, 14 (2), April 1966, pp 101–123.

10

Brewster, K. Enforceable competition : unruly reasons or reasonable rules ? *Am. econ. rev.*, 46 (2), May 1956, pp 482–489.

Discusses the *Report* of the US Attorney General's National Committee to study the antitrust laws, 1955 (item 631 A). Raises questions of relationship between economic power and economic effects ; consequences of enforced competition ; concept of 'workable competition' ; principles of administrative process. The discussion (pp 496–507) includes an important contribution by G. J. Stigler.

11

Burns, A. R. The decline of competition : a study of the evolution of American industry. New York, McGraw-Hill, 1936. xiv, 619p.

12

Can the American economy be made more competitive ? *Am. econ. rev.*, 40 (2), May 1950, pp 67–104.

Contents: On the alleged ubiquity of oligopoly, by C. Wilcox (pp 67–73) ; The influence of size of firms on the functioning of the economy, by A. D. H. Kaplan (pp 74–84) ; Product heterogeneity and public policy, by E. H. Chamberlin (pp 85–92) ; The orientation of antitrust policy, by J. M. Clark (pp 93–99) ; discussion.

13

Chamberlin, E. H. The theory of monopolistic competition : a re-orientation of the theory of value. 8th ed. Cambridge (Mass.), Harvard Univ. Pr., 1963. 396 p.

First published 1933, the pioneer work creating this theory. Contains an international bibliography of some 1500 publications 'related in any important way' to the theory of monopolistic competition. (See also item 6).

14

Clark, J. M. Competition as a dynamic process. Washington, Brookings Institution, 1961. 501p.

Valuable extension of item 15. Useful discussion of spatial competition ; does not adopt J. S. Bain's analytical framework (see item 78).

15

Clark, J. M. Towards a concept of workable competition. *Am. econ. rev.*, 30(2), June 1940, pp 241–256.

States that where one of the conditions of perfect competition is absent, the presence of others may lead to greater rather than less imperfection. With standardised products, a chaotic market tends towards ruinous competition. Pure oligopoly is rare. Important case : openly quoted prices, with varying deviations. Moderate quality differentials may be 'workably competitive' especially with growth of closer substitutes and better buyers' knowledge.

16

Devons, E. Essays in economics. Allen & Unwin, 1961. 203 p.

Most relevant : chap. 3, pp 47–60, 'The case for investment and productivity' (first published in *Lloyds Bank rev.*, Oct. 1955). Interesting observations on problems of competition and monopoly are in chap. 1, pp 13–32, 'Applied economics—the application of what ?' (paper read at the 1958 Annual Conference of the Association of Teachers of Economics) and chap. 2, pp 33–46, 'The role of the economist in public affairs' (first published in *Lloyds Bank rev.*, July 1959). Part II of the book, comprising 5 essays, examines the reliability of economic statistical data for measuring economic phenomena.

17

Downie, J. The competitive process. Duckworth, 1958. 199 p.

A theoretical analysis of the way in which the working of the market may be affected by industrial concentration and restrictive practices.
Uses census data for 1935 and 1948. Chooses a sample of 30 trades out of the total of 156 census trades, selecting industries with different degrees of concentration (high, medium, low) ; industries with and without restrictive agreements ; industries selling consumer, intermediate and capital goods. Samples establishments. The author believes that without greater understanding of nature of competitive process Restrictive Practices Court cannot fulfil its function.

18

Edwards, C. D. Maintaining competition : requisites of a governmental policy. New York, London, McGraw-Hill, 1949. xi, 337 p.

Examines anti-competitive forces at work and 'how they may be checked or destroyed'. Valuable introductory chapter, 'The Objective'. Also comments on use and misuse of given trade practices, and on the difficulty of establishing a permissible size of firm ; advocates attack on excessive concentration. Lists defects in administration of antitrust policy and administrative requisites for success. Important section, 'Difficulties in preventing restrictive agreements' deals with the problem of 'tacit collusion'.

19
Einhorn, H. A. Competition in American industry, 1939–1958. *J. political econ.*, 74 (5), Oct. 1966, pp 506–511.

Extends G. W. Nutter's study of monopoly in the USA (item 47) to the period 1939–1958. Concludes that monopoly concentration has not significantly increased in this period and is more likely to have declined.

20
Fellner, W. J. Competition among the few : oligopoly and similar market structures. 1st ed. reprinted. Cass, 1965 (i.e. 1966). xv, 328 p.

Originally published New York, Knopf, 1949.

21
Fortman, B. de Gaay. Theory of competition policy : a confrontation of economic, political and legal principles. Amsterdam, North Holland Pub. Co., 1966. 351p.

A survey-type compilation of theories of competition and of monopoly policy. A 20 page bibliography includes Dutch, French and German publications.

22
Frisch, R. Monopoly-polypoly : the concept of force in the economy. *Int. econ. pap.*, (1), 1951, pp 23–36.

Translation of 'Monopole-polypole : la notion de force dans l'économie', first published in *Festschrift til Harald Westergaard*, supplement to *Nationaløkonomisk tidsskrift*, April 1933.

23
Galbraith, J. K. American capitalism : the concept of countervailing power. Rev. ed. Hamish Hamilton, 1957. xvi, 208 p.

Main thesis : not a firm's competitors but the power exercised by economically strong customers and suppliers (including trade unions) effectively checks misuse of monopoly power. Argues that this 'countervailing power' is a substitute for competition and makes protection of the public by the State unnecessary. A long essay rather than a theoretical or empirical study. For criticism see items 2, 27.

24
Gosse, R. The enforcement of competition in the United Kingdom. *Can. bar rev.*, 38, May 1960, pp 163–196.

25
Harrod, R. F. (Sir Roy Harrod). Economic essays. Macmillan, 1952. vii, 241 p.

Part II deals with competition, including chapters on the law of decreasing costs, equilibrium of duopoly, imperfect competition, theory of profit, and (Chap. 10) 'Profiteering, an ethical study'. Sir Roy Harrod makes considerable use of empirical studies, comparing their results with relevant theory.

26
Heflebower, R. B. Recent American anti-trust experience. *Three banks rev.*, June 1960, pp 3–23.

27
Hunter, A. Notes on countervailing power. *Econ. j.*, 68 (269), March 1958, pp 89–103.

A critical examination of the concept of countervailing power in a British context.

28
International Economic Association. Monopoly and competition and their regulation : papers and proceedings of a conference held by the . . . Association ; edited by E. H. Chamberlin. Macmillan, 1954. xvi, 549 p.

The Conference was held in 1951. Among the contributors : G. C. Allen ; J. S. Bain ; E. H. Chamberlin ; J. M. Clark ; R. B. Heflebower ; Joan Robinson ; K. W. Rothschild ; E. Schneider ; I. Svennilson. Comparative analysis of problems of competition and monopoly in ten countries. Discussion of forces making for or against monopoly. Questions of measurement, of market and industrial structure, of control. Many references.

29
Jewkes, J. Monopoly and economic progress. *Economica*, new ser. 20 (79), August 1953, pp 197–214.

Discusses the effect of monopoly on innovation. For criticism see item 4.

30
Kaplan, A. D. H. Big enterprise in a competitive system. Washington, Brookings Institution, 1954. xii, 269 p.

A summary of this report, *Big business in a competitive society*, by A. D. H. Kaplan and A. E. Kahn, is in *Fortune*, Feb. 1953, Section 2, pp 1–14. See also item 178.

31
Kaysen, C., *and* **Turner,** D. F. Antitrust policy : an economic and legal analysis. Cambridge (Mass.), Harvard Univ. Pr., 1959. xxiii, 345 p. (Harvard Univ. series on competition in American industry, 7).

Contains an interesting classification of market structure, according to degree of concentration, size of industry, extent of market (local, regional, national) and type of industry (consumer durable and non-durable, investment goods, material inputs). A methodological appendix explains some of the procedure.

32
Kefauver, E. In a few hands : monopoly power in America. Harmondsworth, Penguin Books, 1966. 255 p.

Comments on Hearings before the US Senate Sub-committee on antitrust and monopoly, of which the author was chairman. Examines undesirable effects of monopoly on prices, wastefulness, small business and the community at large. Chap. I quotes evidence about excessive advertising by pharmaceutical firms.

33
Koo, Y. C. Market structure and the differential effects of restrictive monetary policy. *Kyklos,* 20 (4), 1967, pp 924–934.

Discusses how oligopolistic and competitive sectors will react to monetary policy. Valuable references.

34
Kuenne, R. E., *ed.,* Monopolistic competition theory : studies in impact ; essays in honor of Edward H. Chamberlin. New York, London, Wiley, 1967. x, 387 p.

Includes contributions by Bain, Harrod, Heflebower, H. G. Johnson, Samuelson, Tinbergen and others. Of special interest : Harrod's contribution on 'Increasing returns' ; Bain's on 'Chamberlin's impact on microeconomic theory'. E. T. Grether surveys pre- and post-Chamberlin literature of marketing.

35
Lanzilotti, R. F. Market structure and antitrust vulnerability. *Antitrust bull.,* 8 (5–6) Sept.–Dec. 1963, pp 853–871.

Tries to identify conditions which make firms liable to antitrust action. Discusses size, market power, integration, price-discrimination, identical bids. Advocates that structural considerations should be given priority in anti-monopoly policy.

36
Lucas, A. F. Industrial reconstruction and the control of competition : the British experiments. Longmans, 1937. xi, 384 p.

An early standard work ; empirical and historical approach to monopolistic developments in Britain, with case studies of coal, iron and steel, shipbuilding, flour milling, cotton textiles, chemicals, agriculture. Discusses four basic issues of control : determination of prices ; regulation of output ; maintenance of industrial efficiency ; economic and legal safeguards.

37
Lydall, H. F. Aspects of competition in manufacturing industry. *Bull. Oxf. Univ. Inst. Statist.,* 20 (4), Nov. 1958, pp 319–337.

Describes sampling method for choosing 876 manufacturing firms employing 10–499 persons. Discusses problem of assessing competitive situation. Questionnaire included questions about opinions on competition in the particular trade, knowledge of competitors' prices, competition from new entrants, pricing methods, variations in the 'mark-up', price leadership, time-lag between rise in wage costs and rise in prices. The study divided the firms into 'jobbers' (working mainly on customers' specification orders) and 'marketers' (producing mainly their own specifications) and found significant differences between these two types of firms on almost every issue.

38
Lynch, D. The concentration of economic power. New York, Columbia Univ. Pr., 1946. x, 423 p.

A summary and critical appraisal of the unique pre-war investigations into concentration of economic power undertaken by the US Temporary National Economic Committee (TNEC). Although the magnitudes involved and other parts of the information are out of date, some of the chapters, especially chap. 8 on the implementation of monopoly, remain a valuable source.

39
Machlup, F. The political economy of monopoly : business, labor and government policies. Baltimore, Johns Hopkins Pr., 1952. xvi, 543 p.

40
Mackay, I., *and* **Lythe,** C. M. The theory of bilateral monopoly : some aspects of its application to the labour market. *J. econ. studies,* 1 (1), Winter 1965, pp 72–87.

41
Mansfield, E., *ed.* Monopoly power and economic performance : the problem of industrial concentration. New York, Norton, 1964. xiii, 174 p. (Problems of the modern economy).

A well-chosen anthology of 20 pieces by various authors reprinted from their original sources. Part 1, Market structure, resource allocation, and economic progress (7 pieces) ; pt 2, Industrial concentration, collusion, and the social responsibility of big business (4 pieces, plus 4 on the steel price controversy, 1962) ; pt 3, The antitrust laws : provisions, effectiveness, and standards (5 pieces).

42
Marris, R. L. The economic theory of 'managerial' capitalism. Macmillan, 1964. xviii, 347 p.

43
Mason, E. S. Monopoly in law and economics. *Yale law j.,* 47 (1), Nov. 1937, pp 34–49.

44
Massel, M. S. Competition and monopoly : legal and economic issues. Washington, Brookings Institution, 1962. xiii, 477 p.

Is concerned about confused pattern of anti-monopoly policy. Emphasises need to evaluate competitive conditions (price and non-price), to improve methods and use of economic analysis and to research into trends. Pleads for more market studies. Chapters on 'indicators of competition' and 'definition of market'. 126 pages of references.

45
Miller, J. P., *ed.* Competition, cartels and their regulation. Amsterdam, North-Holland Pub. Co., 1962. 428 p. (Studies in industrial economics, 4).

Ten studies of different aspects of this theme. Topics discussed : the role of competition, of monopoly, of restrictive practices (T. Wilson), patents, US anti-trust policy, European anti-cartel policy. Some extensive bibliographies.

46
Modigliani, F. New developments on the oligopoly front. *J. political econ.,* 66, Jun. 1958, pp 215–232.

A comment by D. E. Farrar and C. F. Phillips, and a reply by Modigliani, are in *J. political econ.,* 67, Aug. 1959, pp 414–419.

47
Nutter, G. W. The extent of enterprise monopoly in the United States, 1899–1939 : a quantitative study of some aspects of monopoly. Chicago, Univ. of Chicago Pr., 1951. xvi, 169 p.

Excluding monopolies of the cartel type, concludes that competition in the USA had not declined in the period examined. For a continuation of this study see item 19.

48
Organisation for Economic Co-operation and Development. Economic surveys . . . United Kingdom. 1962+ Paris.

Continues *Economic conditions in . . .United Kingdom,* published by the Organisation for European Economic Co-operation. Annual survey of major current economic problems and the organisation's recommendations for meeting them. Of special interest : 1962 report reviewing cyclical developments, investments and profits in the 1950s and comparing the record of the UK with that of the Common Market countries. The 1967 report includes a chapter on competitiveness with sub-sections on costs and prices and on productivity.

49
Papandreou, A. G. *and* **Wheeler,** J. T. Competition and its regulation. New York, Prentice Hall, 1954. viii, 504 p.

50
Papandreou, A. G. Market structure and monopoly power. *Am. econ. rev.,* 39 (5) part 1, Sept. 1949, pp 883–897.

On definition and measurement of monopoly power.

51
Phillips, A. Policy implications of the theory of interfirm organisation. *Am. econ. rev.,* 51 (2), May 1961, pp 245–254.

Author's hypothesis : some form of interfirm organisation inevitably appears in every market. Objects to courts ignoring good effects of groups' behaviour, such as avoiding excess competition, and reserving the term 'agreement' for unfavourable effects of group action.

52
Robinson, E. A. G. Monopoly. Nisbet, 1941. xvi, 298 p. (Cambridge economic handbooks, 11).

53
Robinson, J. The economics of imperfect competition. Macmillan, 1933. xii, 352 p.

54
Schumpeter, J. A. Capitalism, socialism and democracy. 3rd ed. Allen & Unwin, 1950. xviii, 412 p.

First published 1942. Part 2, 'Can capitalism survive ?', including chap. 8 on monopolistic practices. Argues that, in judging monopoly one must distinguish between 'bad' practices which sabotage economic progress, and positive effects ('creative destruction') of large scale enterprise. See also item 901.

55
Schumpeter, J. A. The theory of economic development : an inquiry into profits, capital, credit, interest, and the business cycle. Cambridge (Mass.), Harvard Univ. Pr., 1934. xii, 255 p. (Harvard economic studies, vol. 46).

Translation of German edition, first published in 1911 and revised in 1926. A theoretical work. Of special interest is chap. IV on entrepreneurial profit, discussing the role of profit and of the entrepreneur in the rise and decline of firms and products. See also item 901.

56
Schwartzman, D. The burden of monopoly. *J. political econ.,* 68, 1960, pp 627–630. (Correction, 69, 1961, p 494).

57
Schwartzman, D. The effect of monopoly on price. *J. political econ.,* 67, 1959, pp 352–362. (Correction, 69, 1961, p 494).

58
Scitovsky, T. Ignorance as a source of oligopoly power. *Am. econ. rev.,* 40 (2), May 1950, pp 48–53.

Also published in *Papers on welfare and growth* by T. Scitovsky (Allen & Unwin, 1964).

59
Scitovsky, T. Monopoly and competition in Europe and America. *Q. j. econ.,* 69 (4), Nov. 1955, pp 607–618.

Also published in *Papers on welfare and growth* by T. Scitovsky (Allen & Unwin, 1964).

60
Scitovsky, T. Welfare and competition : the economics of a fully employed economy. Allen & Unwin, 1952. xvi, 457 p. (Library of economics, section 2 : new works, 5).

61
Shubik, M. Strategy and market structure : competition, oligopoly and the theory of games. New York, Wiley ; London, Chapman & Hall, 1960. xix, 387 p.

Application of games theory to oligopolistic competition and explanation of von Neumann's and Morgenstern's treatment of monopoly and monopsony. Critical survey of current theories of monopolistic competition. (Chamberlin, Robinson, Triffin, Brem, Fellner). Role of product differentiation, advertising, information. Problems of entry, innovation. Structure of several US industries. Bibliography.

62
Singh, A., *and* **Whittington,** G. Growth, profitability and valuation : a study of United Kingdom quoted companies. Cambridge Univ. Pr., 1968. 323 p. (Univ. of Cambridge Dept of Applied Economics occasional papers, 7).

An important empirical study of relationship between size, growth, profitability and valuation of quoted companies in four industries—shipbuilding and non-electrical engineering, food, clothing and footwear, and tobacco— during the periods 1948–1954 and 1954–1960. 150 tables give much factual information and the result of extensive regression and correlation analysis. Useful references.

63
Sosnick, S. H. A critique of concepts of workable competition. *Q. j. econ.*, 72 (3), Aug. 1958, pp 380–423.

64
'Spartacus'. Growth through competition : an alternative to the national plan. Institute of Economic Affairs, 1966. 70 p. (Hobart paper, 35).

Advocates unilateral abolition of all import duties and import restrictions, to make British industry more competitive.

65
Sraffa, P. The laws of return under competitive conditions. *Econ j.*, 36 (144), Dec. 1926, pp 535–550.

Reprinted in *Readings in price theory*, selected by a committee of the American Economic Association (Allen & Unwin, 1953).

66
Stigler, G. J. The statistics of monopoly and merger. *J. political econ.*, 64 (1), Feb. 1956, pp 33–40.

67
Stocking, G. W., *and* **Watkins,** M. W. Cartels or competition ? The economics of international controls by business and government ; with the report and recommendations of the Committee on cartels and monopoly. New York, Twentieth Century Fund, 1948. xiv, 516 p. (International cartels survey of the Twentieth Century Fund).

68
Sylos-Labini, P. Oligopoly and technical progress . . . trans. from the Italian by Elizabeth Henderson. Cambridge (Mass.), Harvard Univ. Pr., 1962. xv, 206 p. (Harvard economic studies, v. 19).

Deals mainly with theory of oligopoly ; one chapter deals with subject suggested in the title of the book.

69
United States. *Congress. Temporary National Economic Committee.* Investigation of concentration of economic power . . .Monograph no. 27, The structure of industry. Washington, Gov't. Print. Off., 1941. xv, 759 p.

A study made under the auspices of the Department of Commerce ; monograph prepared under the direction of W. L. Thorp and W. F. Crowder. *Contents:* Part 1, Trends in the scale of manufacturing operations, by W. L. Thorp, D. D. Humphrey, M. H. Porter ; pt 2, The integration of manufacturing operations, by W. F. Crowder ; pt 3, The merger movement, by W. L. Thorp ; pt 4, The history of concentration in seven industries, by W. L. Thorp, G. W. Knott ; pt 5, The concentration of production in manufacturing, by W. F. Crowder ; pt 6, The product structures of large corporations, by W. F. Crowder, A. G. Abramson, E. W. Staudt. (See also note to item 264).

70
Weinrich, J. E. Market structure and competition, with special reference to the electrical machinery industry in the US. 1964. (Ph.D. Thesis, Univ. of London).

Examines critically the operational significance of present-day theories on competition. Author questions real economic advantages of giant size in view of L-shaped average cost curve and of multi-plant operations. Discusses difficulties of using profit performance as indicator of workable competition. Argues that competition is more favourable to progress and diffusion of economic gain than market domination by giant enterprise. 16 page bibliography.

71
Weintraub, S. Revised doctrines of competition. *Am. econ. rev.*, 45 (2), May 1955, pp 463–479.

Paper discusses Harrod's, J. Robinson's and E. H. Chamberlin's approach. Argues against complacency about progressive role of monopoly and about competitive structure of industry. Contributions to discussion by F. Machlup and others.

72
Wilcox, C. Competition and monopoly in American industry. Washington, Gov't. Print. Off., 1941. xi, 344 p. (Temporary National Economic Committee. Investigation of concentration of economic power, Monograph no. 21).

73
Williams, B. R. Some conditions of useful competition.
Yorks. bull. econ. social res., 11 (2), Dec. 1959, pp 71–78.

Important condition of useful competition : opportunity to
innovate. Yet, this opportunity is not created by competition
but by system of education and by provision for
fundamental scientific activity. Monopoly matters in
science-based industry. Competitive pressure needed :
(a) for choosing the right projects for research and
development ; (b) for giving a chance to the 'outsider'.
Common pricing may or may not protect the inefficient,
it may provide stability which may encourage 'long views'
and innovation.

74
Wright, J. F. Some reflections on the place of
discrimination in the theory of monopolistic competition.
Oxf. econ. pap., 17 (2), July 1965, pp 175–187.

2 Industrial structure

2.1 Industrial structure: General

Publications listed under this heading are those covering several aspects of the very wide field known as industrial structure. Among contributions of special importance are J. S. Bain's *Industrial organisation* (item 78), the three volumes edited by R. S. Edwards and H. Townsend (items 89–91), A. Maddison's *Economic growth in the West* (item 99) and the two volumes on the British economy edited by G. D. N. Worswick and P. Ady (items 115, 116).

Only a small part of the publications on general problems of growth has been selected. Because many factors enter the relation between competition and growth, several entries under other headings of the bibliography contribute to this field of study.

75
Adams, W., *ed*. The structure of American industry : some case studies. 3rd ed. New York, Macmillan, 1961. xi, 603 p.

76
Allen, G. C. British industries and their organization. 4th ed. Longmans, 1959. xi, 332 p.

Industrial change 1914–1958 in the coal, iron and steel, engineering, shipbuilding and marine engineering, and motor vehicles industries.

77
Allen, G. C. The structure of industry in Britain : a study in economic change. Longmans, 1961. x, 236 p.

78
Bain, J. S. Industrial organization. New York, Wiley ; London, Chapman & Hall, 1959. xviii, 643 p.

Although based exclusively on US data, an important study of monopolistic and competitive behaviour of groups of firms rather than of individual firms or industries. Examines patterns of market structure, market conduct of sellers and buyers, and market performance, also their inter-relation. Surveys changes in concentration 1870–1950, product differentiation, conditions of entry, oligopolistic industries, determination of costs, prices and products ; significance of selling cost ; definition and measurement of profits. Wants existing public policies strengthened to preserve competition and prevent monopoly. An extensively revised second edition (xv, 678p.) was published in 1968.

79
Baran, P. A. Monopoly capital : an essay on the American economic and social order. New York, London, Monthly Review Pr., 1966. xiv, 402 p.

'The first serious attempt to extend Marx's model of competitive capitalism to the new conditions of monopoly capitalism' (H. J. Sherman, in *Am. Econ. Rev.*, 56 (4, part 1), Sept. 1966, p. 919).

80
Beckerman, W. The British economy in 1975, by W. Beckerman and associates. Cambridge Univ. Pr., 1965. xxiv, 631 p. (National Institute of Economic and Social Research. Economic and social studies, 23).

Contains relevant chapters on demand, exports and growth ; Britain's visible trade ; pattern of growth of output ; employment and productivity ; investment requirements ; energy industries ; transport industries.

81
Burn, D., *ed*. The structure of British industry : a symposium. Cambridge Univ. Pr., 1958. 2v. (National Institute of Economic and Social Research. Economic and social studies, 15).

Contents: Vol. 1, Agricultural production and marketing ; building industry ; inland carriage by road and rail ; coal industry ; oil industry ; chemical industry ; steel ; building materials industry ; machine tools industry ; v.2, motor industry ; aircraft industry ; shipbuilding industry ; electronics industry ; cotton and rayon textile industry ; woollen and worsted industry ; man-made fibres industry ; pottery industry ; pharmaceuticals industry ; cutlery trade. The volumes contain bibliographies for each industry. The concluding chapter discusses the effect on efficiency of competition, restrictive practices, expansion, research, size and ownership.

82
Cairncross, A. K. Factors in economic development. Allen & Unwin, 1962. 346 p.

Part II deals with investment, technical progress and development.

83
Carter, A. P. Changes in the structure of the American economy, 1947 to 1958 and 1962. *Rev. econ. statist.*, 49 (2), May 1967, pp 209–224.

Part of a Harvard research project using input-output

analysis to examine the impact of the growth of new materials, and the decline of old materials, on the structure of industry, specialisation, diversification and demand for groups and sub-groups of commodities.

84
Comanor, W. S. Market structure, product differentiation and industrial research. *Q. j. econ.*, 81 (4), Nov. 1967, pp 639–657.

Distinguishes between industries with product-directed and process-directed research, between industries producing investment goods and producing 'material-inputs'. Examines effects of barriers to and ease of entry on research effort. Includes an examination of the relationship between firm size and research.

85
Crosland, C. A. R. Britain's economic problem. Cape, 1953. 224 p.

86
Department of Economic Affairs. The national plan. HMSO, 1965. xix, 204, 239, 31 p. (Cmnd. 2764).

87
Dow, J. C. R. The management of the British economy, 1945–60. Cambridge Univ. Pr., 1964. xix, 439 p. (National Institute of Economic and Social Research. Economic and social studies, 22).

Concerned mainly with macro-economic phenomena : fiscal, monetary and other control policies ; demand and price inflation. Important part IV on effects of economic fluctuations, and on the rate of economic growth.

88
Dunning, J. H. *and* **Thomas,** C. J. British industry : change and development in the twentieth century. 2nd ed. Hutchinson, 1963. 236 p. (Hutchinson university library : economics).

Specially useful chapter II on changes in size-structure, ownership pattern and location of industry. In chapter V the impact of new materials and processes is discussed. Chapter VI comments on the role of the state and of monopoly legislation.

89
Edwards, R. S. *and* **Townsend,** H., *eds*. Business enterprise : its growth and organisation. Macmillan, 1958. xvii, 607 p.

Based on papers given at the London School of Economics seminar on problems in industrial administration, Oct. 1946 to May 1957. Includes several case-studies. The discussion of general problems such as new entries, specialisation, integration, growth, size, centralisation, research, location, innovation, includes a chapter (XXIV) on the economic and social background, with a few pages on 'restrictionism and competition'.

90
Edwards, R. S. *and* **Townsend,** H., *eds*. Business growth. Macmillan, 1966. xxiv, 410 p.

Based on papers given at the London School of Economics seminar on problems in industrial administration. Includes case-studies of the aircraft industry, British Oxygen Co, United Steel Co, GEC, etc. Special chapters on marketing, advertising, contracting and sub-contracting, research and innovation.

91
Edwards, R. S. *and* **Townsend,** H., *eds*. Studies in business organisation : a supplement to 'Business enterprise'. Macmillan, 1961. xxiii, 160 p.

Studies prepared for the London School of Economics seminar on problems in industrial administration, 1957–59. Includes studies of Elliott Automation, Vauxhall Motors, Boots, and HMSO.

92
Florence, P. S. Investment, location and size of plant : a realistic inquiry into the structure of British and American industries. Cambridge Univ. Pr., 1948. xiii, 211 p. (National Institute of Economic and Social Research. Economic and social studies, 7).

93
Florence, P. S. The logic of British and American industry : a realistic analysis of economic structure and government. 2nd rev. ed. Routledge, 1961. xxiv, 368 p.

Based on an earlier book, *Logic of industrial organisation* (Routledge, 1933). Thesis : the structure and character of firms is logically determined by the materials, methods of production and markets for a firm's products. This logic leads to an overall similarity of structural development in any given British and American industry. Chapters on size and efficiency, integration and dispersion, costs of distribution, pros and cons of monopolistic structure.

94
Florence, P. S. Post-war investment, location and size of plant. Cambridge Univ. Pr., 1962. viii, 51 p. (National Institute of Economic and Social Research. Occasional papers, 19).

95
Galbraith, J. K. The new industrial state. *Listener,* 17 Nov. 1966, pp 711–714 ; 24 Nov. 1966, pp 755–758 ; 1 Dec. 1966, pp 793–795, 812 ; 8 Dec. 1966, pp 841–843, 853 ; 15 Dec. 1966, pp 881–884 ; 22 Dec. 1966, pp 915–918.

Reith Lectures, 1966. For criticism of Galbraith's views on big corporations see *Puppets or masters ? With Galbraith towards statism*, by P. Bareau (*Statist*, 6 Jan. 1967, pp 13–14). Galbraith's view of the consumer's role in the economy dominated by large corporations is criticised by C. Fulop in *Consumers. 1—Puppets or masters* (*Statist*, 6 Jan. 1967, pp 28–29), *2—Why products fail* (*Statist*, 3 Feb. 1967, pp 167–168). For general criticism see item 3.

96

Galbraith, J. K. The new industrial state. H. Hamilton, 1967. xi, 427 p.

The work, some chapters of which correspond to author's Reith Lectures 1966 (item 95), provides an impressionist, controversial, survey of modern technology's impact on America's economic organisation and social behaviour (not necessarily of general validity). The author challenges present day economic theory and monopoly legislation and argues that the market mechanism has been replaced by planning activities of giant corporations ; these determine prices and consumer wants and aim at growth and power rather than maximisation of profits. Important postscript on values beyond industrial performance. Galbraith's ideas have been challenged by J. E. Meade in 'Is "The new industrial state" inevitable ?' (*Econ. j.*, 78 (310), June 1968, pp 372–392). See also annotation to item 95.

97

Harrod, R. F. (Sir Roy Harrod). The British economy. New York, London, McGraw-Hill, 1963. 240 p.

Chapter 4, on industry, deals with the problem of monopoly. The author believes that the high degree of specialisation in modern science–based industry requires more mutual agreement between firms.

98

House of Commons. *Select Committee on Nationalised Industries.* Reports.

These reports, of which at least one has been published in each Parliamentary session since 1956/57, provide valuable information on a variety of problems such as costs, pricing, productivity, profitability, investment, size, research and development, and advertising. Of special interest is the evidence on purchasing procedures, contracts, tenders, etc. The reports contain minutes of evidence, memoranda and appendices, and summaries of the Committee's findings, which are cross-referenced to the minutes of evidence. For reports on individual industries, see items 445, 446 447, 448, 449, 450, 459, 482, 512, 513, 514, 566 in this bibliography. Of broader scope is the investigation made during the 1966/67 and 1967/68 sessions into ministerial control of the nationalised industries, and published as :

House of Commons. *Select Committee on Nationalised Industries* (*1967/68*). First report from the Select Committee. . .Ministerial control of the nationalised industries. HMSO, 1968. 3v. (HC 371–I–II–III, sess. 1967/68).

Vol. 1, *Report and proceedings of the Committee* (v, 235 p). Of special interest : chap. V, The economic and financial framework ; chap. VI, Problems and principles of economic control ; chap. IX, Implementation of economic and financial policy ; chap. X, Control of investment ; chap. XI, Capital structure and borrowing ; chap. XIV on social costs and benefits ; chap. XV on the importance of efficiency studies by the National Board for Prices and Incomes.

Vol. 2, *Minutes of evidence* (v, 730 p). Includes memoranda dealing with problems of borrowing, investment, pricing, financial objectives, unremunerative services, unfair competition, etc. Several of these memoranda, and the related evidence, were first published as separate daily parts, with House of Commons paper numbers as shown below. Session 1966/67 : electricity supply industry (HC 440–I) ; National Coal Board (HC 440–II) ; British Railways (HC 440–III) ; BOAC (HC 440–IV) ; London Transport (HC 440–V) ; gas (HC 440–VI) ; BEA (HC 440–VII) ; fuel industries (HC 440–IX) ; transport industries (HC 440–X). Relationships of nationalised industries with Government departments were dealt with in HC 440–VIII, XI and XII. Memoranda by D. L. Munby, J. R. Sargent and J. Wiseman were first published in HC 440–XIII ; see item 750. Memoranda by the Rt. Hon. Aubrey Jones, *Public sector price references made to the National Board for Prices and Incomes*, and *Some problems of nationalised industries in Britain* (pp 677–687) were first published in HC 183–I, sess. 1967/68 ; these emphasise the importance of efficiency studies for judging price levels, the importance of social costs and benefits for investment appraisals, and the dependence of pricing policies of public enterprise on governmental fiscal and financial policies. A memorandum by the Treasury, *The role of the Government—and in particular the Treasury—in relation to the nationalised industries* (pp 1–22), refers to problems of the appraisal and control of investment, to pricing policy and financial objectives.

Vol. 3, *Appendices and index* (iv, 267 p). Includes statistics on rates of return, investment and exchequer financing ; procedures for investment appraisal ; types of investment reviews ; test discount rate ; examples of cost-benefit analysis ; examples of pricing policies ; techniques for forecasting demand ; efficiency audits ; relevant legislation 1957–1966. There is also a section of miscellaneous memoranda, among them *Financial objectives and investment appraisal*, by R. L. Meek (pp 248–250). He suggests that the application of average rates of return for evaluating individual investment projects, and the use of target rates of return for determining the discount rate, can lead to wrong investment decisions.

99

Maddison, A. Economic growth in the West : comparative experience in Europe and North America. New York, Twentieth Century Fund ; London, Allen & Unwin, 1964. 246 p. (A Twentieth Century Fund study).

Original attempt at analysis of growth, based on data on investment, output and employment for twelve countries, from 1870 (with descriptions of methods used for comparing data and with sources of data). Argues that the main driving force for growth is maintenance of high demand, and for economies of scale high income elasticity of demand for mass-produced goods ; i.e. innovation, investment, reduction of trade barriers emerge as effects mutating into secondary causes.

100

Meier, G. M. *and* **Baldwin,** R. E. Economic development : theory, history, policy. New York, Wiley ; London, Chapman & Hall, 1957. 588 p.

101

National Economic Development Council. The growth of the economy. HMSO, 1964. v, 127 p.

102

National Economic Development Council. Growth of the United Kingdom economy, 1961-1966. HMSO, 1963. viii, 149 p.

103

Phillips, A. Market structure, organisation and performance : an essay on price fixing and combinations in restraint of trade . . . Cambridge (Mass.), Harvard Univ. Pr. 1962. xiii, 257 p.

Based on five US antitrust cases. Believes that the inconsistencies in the application of antitrust legislation can be explained partly by alternative theories of competition, and partly by alternative objectives of policy, but that these inconsistencies have been exaggerated. Examines critically the assumption of profit maximisation and replaces behaviour of the individual firm by the market-group and inter-firm organisation.

104

Political and Economic Planning. Growth of the British economy : a study of economic problems and policies in contemporary Britain. Allen & Unwin, 1960. xii, 256 p.

Comments on many aspects of growth, among them productivity, private and public investment, pricing policies of public enterprise, planning. Also some international comparisons for the mid-1950s.

105

Political and Economic Planning. Industrial trade associations : activities and organisation. Allen & Unwin, 1957. xiii, 340 p.

106

Political and Economic Planning. Thrusters and sleepers : a study of attitudes in industrial management . . . Allen & Unwin, 1965. 295 p.

Reprinted by Penguin Books, 1967, as *Attitudes in British management* (334 p.). Interviews with 47 (out of 128 firms approached) of the most and the least progressive firms in six industries (wool textiles, machine tools, shipbuilding, electronics, domestic appliances, earth moving equipment) which were to represent a cross section of different types of industry : old and new, science and non-science based, contracting and expanding, capital and consumer goods, craft and mass-production, localised and non-localised, American influenced and wholly British. Lists 59 main thrusting and sleeping qualities, e.g. sleepers believe that competition should not hurt.

107

Purdy, C. R. Industry patterns of capacity or volume choice : their existence and rationale. *J. accounting res.,* 3 (3), Autumn 1965, pp 228–241.

Empirical study. Describes sampling method for choosing 400 firms in 5 US industries (motor-car, steel, petroleum, timber, aircraft). Gives selected sources of data. Concludes that, in future investigations, industries studied should have high degrees of internal homogeneity. The author investigated how capacity is determined and how this affects calculation of overhead costs per unit of given product.

108

Richardson, H. W. The new industries between the wars. *Oxf. econ. pap.,* new ser. 13 (3), Oct. 1961, pp 360–384.

Argues that the orthodox view of unsatisfactory progress in these industries is refuted by the available evidence. Raises questions about lessons for post-war II period. Bibliography, including PEP reports on selected industries.

109

Robinson, E. A. G. The structure of competitive industry. [3rd ed.]. Nisbet ; Cambridge Univ. Pr., 1953. xiv, 191 p. (Cambridge economic handbooks, 7).

Standard textbook on the optimum firm. Of special interest, situation when optima of the contributing factors— production, management, finance, market—do not balance.

110

Shonfield, A. Modern capitalism : the changing balance of public and private power. Oxford Univ. Pr., 1965. xvi, 456 p.

Chapter 15 : the changing style of private enterprise. See also item 950.

111

Svennilson, I. Growth and stagnation in the European economy. Geneva, United Nations Economic Commission for Europe, 1954. xvi, 342 p.

Sponsored by the United Nations Economic Commission for Europe and the Rockfeller Foundation.

112

United States. *National Resources Committee.* The structure of the American economy. Washington, Gov't. Print. Off., 1939-40. 2 v.

Part 1, Basic characteristics : a report prepared . . . under the direction of G. C. Means (vii, 396 p.). Deals with structure of production, tariffs, prices and controls. Data on concentration ; interlocking directorships ; industrial and financial alliances (by P. M. Sweezy). Part 2, Towards full use of resources : a symposium (v, 48 p.), issued by National Resources Planning Board. Contents of special relevance : *Economic policy and the structure of the American economy* by M. Ezekiel, discussing corporate price policies, the effects of restriction of competition, and possible counter-measures ; *Price flexibility and the full employment of resources* by A. H. Hansen, who argues that prices of different commodities should be adjusted to changes in the structure of the economy rather than to economic fluctuations, and that price policy should be integrated with monetary and fiscal policies. Other contributors are J. M. Clark, G. C. Means and D. E. Montgomery.

113
Vance, S. Industrial structure and policy. Englewood Cliffs (N.J.), Prentice-Hall, 1961. 529 p.

114
Weiss, L. W. Economics and American industry. New York, London, Wiley, 1961. xi, 548 p.

115
Worswick, G. D. N. *and* **Ady,** P. H., *eds.* The British economy in the nineteen-fifties. Oxford, Clarendon Pr., 1962. xii, 564 p.

Contains chapters on government and industry, capital market and the finance of industry, wages and productivity.

116
Worswick, G. D. N. *and* **Ady,** P. H., *eds.* The British economy, 1945-1950. Oxford, Clarendon Pr., 1952. viii, 621 p.

Contains chapters on the structure of the British economy (based on work of Leak and Maizels—see item 207), trade associations, location of industries, productivity, monopoly policy. Bibliography, pp 574–605.

2.2 The firm

See also items 208, 210, 214, 221, 227, 721

Problems of competition, monopoly and industrial structure to a large extent relate to the behaviour of the firm. Publications relevant for studying the behaviour of firms will, therefore, be found under many headings, especially under *Competition and Monopoly: General and General Theoretical* (page 3), *Concentration and Size* (page 17), *Specific Industries* (page 32), *Prices and Costs* (page 55).

This special section on the firm contains only those publications which are concerned with individual firms and which concentrate on 'the theory of the firm'. Representative of the lively controversy about the firm in the mid-thirties are articles by R. H. Coase (item 123) and N. Kaldor (item 126). Useful leads into post-war literature are provided by A. G. Papandreou (item 132) and by H. A. Simon's article (item 134). Among other important works are those by E. Penrose (item 221), R. L. Marris (item 130) and P. W. S. Andrews (item 721).

117
Andrews, P. W. S. *and* **Brunner,** E. Capital development in steel : a study of the United Steel Companies Ltd. Oxford, Blackwell, 1951. x, 374 p.

118
Baumol, W. J. On the theory of expansion of the firm. *Am. econ. rev.,* 52 (5), Dec. 1962, pp 1078–1087.

119
Boulding, K. E. Implications for general economics of more realistic theories of the firm. *Am. econ. rev.,* 42 (2), May 1952, pp 35–44.

120
Buckner, H. How British industry buys : an enquiry. Hutchinson, 1967. 100 p. (Hutchinson marketing library).

Study sponsored by the Institute of Marketing and Industrial Market Research Ltd. An interesting survey of 924 companies and 9 groups of manufacturing industry relating to purchasing procedures in ordering plant, materials and components. The study consists largely of tables ; among the topics examined are the relative importance of price, technical specification and the qualifications of those responsible for ordering:

121
Cadbury Brothers Ltd. Industrial challenge : the experience of Cadburys of Bournville in the post-war years. Pitman, 1964. 91 p.

122
Cadbury Brothers Ltd. Industrial record, 1919-1939 ; a review of the inter-war years. Bournville, 1947. 84 p.

Together with item 121, gives interesting details of the working of a large scale enterprise between 1919 and 1962, with regard to buying and selling, costs, efficiency, finance and growth.

123
Coase, R. H. The nature of the firm. *Economica,* new ser. 4 (13-16), Nov. 1937, pp 386–405.

An important article on definition and on the growth of firms.

124
Hale, L. Hedley of Newcastle, from the accession of Queen Victoria, 1837, to the coronation of Queen Elizabeth II, 1953. Newcastle upon Tyne, Hedley, [1954]. 40 p.

Manufacturers of soaps and other cleaning compounds.

125
Hickman, C. A. *and* **Kuhn,** M. H. Individuals, groups and economic behavior. New York, Dryden Pr., 1956. 266 p.

Investigation into managerial motives.

126
Kaldor, N. The equilibrium of the firm. *Econ. j.,* 44 (173), March 1934, pp 60–76.

127
Lewis, W. A. Overhead costs : some essays in economic analysis. Allen & Unwin, 1949. 200 p.

A collection of essays on themes with a link to overhead costs. Problems discussed : competition between road and rail transport ; peak demand and peak costing ; quantity discounts and tying contracts ; differential freight rates for tramp shipping ; competition in retail trade ; anti-monopoly measures ; administrative and pricing policy of public enterprise.

128

Mackintosh, A. S. The development of firms : an empirical study with special reference to the economic effects of taxation. Cambridge Univ. Pr., 1963. 305 p.

Thirty-six case studies of firms, with the relevant questionnaire as appendix. Covers roughly post-war period up to 1955. Questions and answers refer to size, rate of growth, rate of profit, output, liquidity, sources of finance, investment, price and dividend policy. Effects of taxation are strongly emphasized.

129

Malmgren, H. B. Information, expectations and the theory of the firm. *Q. j. econ.*, 75 (3), Aug. 1961, pp 399–421.

130

Marris, R. L. A model of the managerial enterprise. *Q. j. econ.*, 77 (2), May 1963, pp 185–209.

131

Monsen, R. J. *and* **Welsch,** D. E. A theory of large managerial firms. *J. political econ.*, 73, June 1965, pp 221–236.

Discusses relation between owners (too distant from the firms' affairs to organise profit maximisation), top management (aiming at rapid promotion), and managerial bureaucracy (with its red tape effects). Profit maximisation replaced by policy of steady growth (of earnings and stock prices) ; risk taking replaced by caution.

132

Papandreou, A. G. Some basic problems in the theory of the firm [with comments by R. B. Heflebower and E. S. Mason]. In *A survey of contemporary economics*, ed. by B. F. Haley, vol. 2, pp 183–222 (Homewood (Illinois), Irwin, 1952).

133

Rice, A. K. The enterprise and its environment ; a system theory of management organisation. Tavistock Publications, 1963. 364 p.

134

Simon, H. A. New developments in the theory of the firm. *Am. econ. rev.*, 52 (2), May 1962, pp 1–27.

Paper on contribution of operational research, aided by high-speed digital computers, to the testing of theories about behaviour of firms with regard to profit maximisation, pricing, uncertainty, decision-taking. Recommends combination of empirical research, observation, and laboratory experiments. Discussion.

135

Williamson, O. E. The economics of discretionary behavior : managerial objectives in a theory of the firm. Englewood Cliffs (NJ), Prentice-Hall, 1964. 182 p.

136

Wilson, C. The history of Unilever : a study in economic growth and social change. Cassell, 1954. 2 v.

2.3 Ownership and control

See also items 42, 187, 209, 1078

The relationships under modern capitalism between ownership and control and their influence on the power, finance, structure, price and profit policies of large companies have been widely studied. Apart from the work of A. A. Berle (items 137-139), articles by R. J. Larner (item 152), C. Kaysen (item 151) and S. Peterson (item 158) should be mentioned. *The Directory of directors* (item 146) is useful for tracing interlocking directorships ; the directory *Who owns whom* (item 167) provides valuable information on ownership. In addition, chapters 4 and 5 of M. L. Lindahl's book *Corporate concentration and public policy* (item 209) deal with the problems of ownership and control of large corporations.

137

Berle, A. A. The impact of the corporation on classical economic theory. *Q. j. econ.,* 79 (1), Feb. 1965, pp 25–40.

Comments on *Corporate control and capitalism,* by S. Peterson (item 158).

138

Berle, A. A. *and* **Means,** G. C. The modern corporation and private property. New York, Macmillan, 1948. xii, 396 p.

Discusses change of large companies from a private business device to a 'series of huge industrial oligarchies', 'a collective hopper'. Problems of ownership and control ; position of stockholders and directors. Data on concentration and dispersion of stock ownership, referring to period 1900-1930, valuable for comparison.

139

Berle, A. A. The twentieth-century capitalist revolution. Macmillan, 1955. ix, 157 p.

Title of the book refers to modern giant corporation which, according to author, is not only an economic phenomenon, but a quasi-political and social institution, 'chief heir of the explosion of technical progress' and a force in international affairs (a quarter of the book is dedicated to this issue). Outlines potential dangers which should be met by new moral and philosophical system.

140

Board of Trade. Acquisitions and amalgamations of quoted companies 1954-1961. *Econ. trends,* (114), April 1963, pp ii–xi. (Also published in : Central Statistical Office. *New contributions to economic statistics, 3rd series,* pp 61–70. HMSO, 1964).

Includes statistical appendix for 22 industry groups. Supplementary information is contained in *Acquisitions and amalgamations of quoted companies, 1954–1961: summary and industrial group tables,* by the Statistics Division of the Board of Trade (1963. 26 leaves).

141

Board of Trade. Acquisitions and amalgamations of quoted companies 1962-1963. *Econ. trends,* (145), Nov. 1965, pp xx–xxvi. (Also published in : Central Statistical Office. *New contributions to economic statistics, 4th series,* pp 103–109. HMSO, 1967).

Supplementary information is contained in *Expenditure by quoted companies on acquiring subsidiary companies,* by the Statistics Division of the Board of Trade (1962+).

142

Boyle, A. J. The sale of controlling shares : American law and the Jenkins committee. *Int. comparative law q.,* 13, Jan. 1964, pp 185–202.

Discusses possible conflict of interests and aims between controlling firm and taken-over firm. Examines recommendations of Jenkins Committee (item 281) with regard to the effect conversion of majority shareholder (in old company) to minority shareholder (in new parent company) can have on a firm's behaviour.

143

British Iron and Steel Federation. Steel today ; who owns the steel industry ? 1957. 8 p.

144

Copeman, G. H. Leaders of British industry : a study of the careers of more than a thousand public company directors. Gee and Co., 1955. 173 p.

Contains two tables on number of subsidiary, associated and independent directorships. Based on a London School of Economics Ph.D. thesis, *Leadership in the public joint stock company,* 1953.

145

Cox, E. B. Trends in the distribution of stock ownership. Philadelphia, Univ. of Pennsylvania Pr. ; London, Oxford Univ. Pr., 1963. xiii, 221 p.

Describes various methods of measurement and its problems. Five-page bibliography.

146

The Directory of directors. 1880+Skinner.

147

Dobrovolsky, S. P. Corporate income retention. New York, National Bureau of Economic Research, 1951. xviii, 122 p. (Financial research programme : studies in business financing).

Study based on primary business records. Examines relation between ploughed-back profit, firm's size and rate of growth.

148

Edwards, G. W. Evolution of finance capitalism. Longmans, 1939. xvi, 429 p.

149

Eells, R. S. F. The government of corporations. New York, Free Press of Glencoe, 1962. 338 p.

150

Goyder, G. The responsible company. Oxford, Blackwell, 1961. x, 192 p.

Discusses the social responsibility of industry, with special reference to big business. Group personality of big business can lead to inhuman, anti-social behaviour. Author pleads for legislation determining companies' responsibilities to the various interests of consumers, employees, shareholders, etc. Of special interest chapter 16 on profits and dividends, with examples of successful firms which had voluntarily limited dividends and had used surplus for incentive schemes and price reductions.

151

Kaysen, C. Another view of corporate capitalism. *Q. j. econ.,* 79 (1), Feb. 1965, pp 41–51.

Comments on *Corporate control and capitalism,* by S. Peterson (item 158).

152

Larner, R. J. Ownership and control in the 200 largest non-financial corporations, 1929 and 1963. *Am. econ. rev.,* 56 (4) part 1, Sept. 1966, pp 777–787.

Includes a short bibliography.

153

Levy, A. B. Private corporations and their control. Routledge & Kegan Paul, 1950. 2 v. (International library of sociology and social reconstruction).

Contents: Pt 1, Historical and economic background ; pt 2, Legal problems of private corporations. Describes past and present legal and economic aspects of private corporations in various countries, especially Britain, France, Germany and USA. A few chapters deal with the disposal of share ownership, the role of shareholders, the problems connected with management and control. Extensive bibliography, mainly of historical and legal publications.

154

Morgan, E. V. The structure of property ownership in Great Britain. Oxford, Clarendon Pr., 1960. xi, 207 p.

155

O'Neal, F. H. Squeeze-out in American corporations. *J. bus. law,* 1962, pp 210–216.

Deals with a rarely treated aspect of ownership and control. Is in large part a summary of *Expulsion or oppression of business associates: 'squeezeouts' in small enterprises,* by F. H. O'Neal and J. Derwin (xii, 263 p. Durham (N.C.), Duke Univ. Pr. ; London, Cambridge Univ. Pr., 1961), reporting research financed by US Small Business Administration.

156

Paish, F. W. Company profits and their distribution since the war. *Dist. Bank rev.,* (114), June 1955, pp 3–26.

157
Parkinson, H. Ownership of industry. Eyre &
Spottiswoode, 1951. 129 p.

An analysis of amounts of industrial capital held by small,
medium sized, and large investors. Ten per cent sample
enquiry based on Board of Trade lists of shareholders in
1941-42.

158
Peterson, S. Corporate control and capitalism. *Q. j. econ.,*
79 (1), Feb. 1965, pp 1–24.

For comments see items 137, 151. A reply by Peterson is in
Q. j. econ., 79 (3), Aug. 1965, pp 492–499.

159
Profit sharing. *Dist. Bank rev.,* (115), Sept. 1955, pp 31–40.

160
Revell, J. *and* **Moyle,** J. The owners of quoted ordinary
shares : a survey for 1963. Chapman & Hall, 1966. xii, 82 p.
(A programme for growth, 7).

Pub. for Univ. of Cambridge Department of Applied
Economics. A valuable publication, based on an analysis of
176 share registers in companies' transfer offices. One table
on comparison with US.

161
Robertson, *Sir* D. H. *and* **Dennison,** S. R. The control of
industry. New ed. Digswell Place (Herts.), Nisbet ;
London, Cambridge Univ. Pr., 1960. xiii, 161 p. (Cambridge
economic handbooks).

162
Tew, B. *and* **Henderson,** R. F., *eds.* Studies in company
finance ; a symposium on the economic analysis and
interpretation of British company accounts. Cambridge
Univ. Pr., 1959. xx, 301 p. (National Institute of Economic
and Social Research. Economic and social studies, 17).

Survey of 2549 continuing quoted companies grouped into
21 industries for period 1949-1953 ; based on published
consolidated company accounts. First part gives general
data on the sources of finance. S. J. Prais writes on the
effect of finance on size, growth and concentration, and
vice versa, including data and observations on the 'death'
of companies. Also discussion of the problem of classifying
firms according to industry. The second part contains case
studies of the finance of industries : S. R. Dennison on
brewing and cotton ; C. F. Carter on building ; B. R. Williams
on building materials and pottery ; T. Wilson on electrical
engineering and electrical goods ; R. Evely on retail
distribution. Some of the case studies refer to problems of
mergers, prices, profits.

163
The Times
During 1959 and 1960 *The Times* published a series of
articles on share ownership, comprising :
Widening ordinary share ownership, by G. Cummings :
1, Nearly 250,000 steel shareholders (8 Jan. 1959, p 15) ;
2, 3m. investors in Britain ? (9 Jan. 1959, p 16). Ordinary
share ownership analysed : revival in personal investment,

by E. V. Morgan (2 March 1959, p 14). Who owns the
capital of Unilever Ltd. ? Growing spread of share
ownership, by G. Cummings (2 June 1959, p 14). Who
holds ordinary shares in Britain ? Further data from
companies (18 June 1959, p 16). Who owns the Midland
Bank's share capital ? What the latest figures show, by
G. Cummings (4 Aug. 1959, p 12). A new inquiry into
ordinary share ownership, by P. S. Florence : 1, How
inequality has declined (11 Aug. 1959, p 12) ; 2, Measuring
shareholders' control (12 Aug. 1959, p 12). More company
facts about share ownership : individual holdings analysed
(20 April 1960, p 17). Who owns ordinary share capital ?
A new Cambridge analysis, by C. H. Feinstein and J. R. S.
Revell (23 June 1960, p 19).

164
United States. *Congress. House. Select committee on
small business* (85th Cong., 1st sess.). Interlocking
directors and officials of 135 large financial companies of
United States. Part 1 of a preliminary report of the . . .
committee . . . Washington, Gov't. Print. Off., 1957.
xxi, 176 p.

165
United States. *Federal Trade Commission.* Report of
the . . . Commission on interlocking directorates.
Washington, Gov't. Print. Off., 1951. xiv, 510 p.

166
United States. *Congress. Temporary National Economic
Committee.* Investigation of concentration of economic
power . . . Monograph no. 29, distribution of ownership in
200 largest non-financial corporations. Washington, Gov't.
Print. Off., 1940. xviii, 1557 p.

167
Who owns whom : a directory of parent, associate and
subsidiary companies. 1958+ O. W. Roskill and Co.
(Reports).

Includes an appendix listing and classifying selected
companies which have diversified far outside the main
activity with which they are commonly associated.

2.4 Concentration and size

See also items 19, 32, 38, 47, 257, 261, 303, 420, 629, 712,
715, 716, 724, 774, 850, 851, 878, 880, 886, 890, 900,
1034, 1052, 1089

Developments in the concentration of industry have led to
a number of noteworthy studies. Publications by J. S. Bain
(item 171), E. S. Mason (item 213), C. Pratten and R. M.
Dean (item 223), W. G. Shepherd (items 231–234) and
L. W. Weiss (items 249–251) are of special importance for
investigating the relation between concentration and
competition. Concentration in British industry has been
studied by H. Leak and A. Maizels (item 207), R. Evely and
I. M. D. Little (item 185), W. G. Shepherd (item 231) and
K. D. George (item 189). In view of the considerable
problems which arise in the measurement of size and of
concentration several contributions to this discussion,
including those by J. M. Blair (item 175) and P. E. Hart
(items 196–199), have been selected for the bibliography.

The hearings before the US Senate Sub-committee on anti-trust and monopoly (item 241) contain statements by many leading economists specialising in this field. See also entries under the heading *Mergers* (page 25).

168
Adelman, M. A. The measurement of industrial concentration. *Rev. econ. statist.,* 33, Nov. 1951, pp 269–296.

169
Armstrong, A. *and* **Silberston,** A. Size of plant, size of enterprise and concentration in British manufacturing industry, 1935–1958. *J. R. Statist. Soc.,* ser. A 128 (3) 1965, pp 395–420.

170
Bain, J. S. International differences in industrial structure : eight nations in the 1950s. New Haven, London, Yale Univ. Pr., 1966. xiv, 209 p. (Studies in comparative economics, 6).

Tries to compare the structure of 10–34 individual manufacturing industries in US, Canada, UK, Sweden, France, Italy, India, Japan. Is concerned with the comparative degree of concentration, with comparative incidence of monopolies, oligopolies, and atomistic industries. Plant size, plant concentration, plant efficiency, and company concentration are compared. Latest data used for the UK 1951 and 1954. A 17 page bibliography for the eight countries. Emphasises the tentative nature of and sketchy evidence for the findings. Pleads for more empirical research on comparative structure and on performance of industry.

171
Bain, J. S. Relation of profit rate to industry concentration : American manufacturing, 1936-1940. *Q. j. econ.,* 65(3), Aug. 1951, pp 293–324. (Erratum, Nov. 1951, p 602).

172
Bates, J. A. The activities of large and small companies. *Bus. ratios,* 1 (2), 1967, pp 3–14.

Gives 1961 data on share of small enterprise (with under 100 employees) in total number of firms and total number of employed. Compares small and large establishments with regard to shares of various cost items in total costs. Examines differences in financial behaviour between large and small firms and financial obstacles to the small firm's expansion. About twenty references.

173
Benishay, H. Concentration and price-cost margins : a comment. *J. ind. econ.,* 16 (1), Nov. 1967, pp 73-74.

An important note on the relevance of the sale-assets ratio (output-capital ratio) for measuring the rate of profit ; also on problem of using groupings of four-digit or three-digit industries.

174
Blair, J. M. Does large scale enterprise result in lower costs ? Technology and size. *Am. econ. rev.,* 38 (2), May 1948, pp 121–152. (Discussion, pp 165–171).

Suggests that many new technological developments favour smaller rather than larger size of plant. Examines cases where aggregate pre-merger earnings exceeded post-merger earnings.

175
Blair, J. M. Statistical measures of concentration in business : problems of compiling and interpretation. *Bull. Oxf. Univ. Inst. Statist.,* 18 (4), Nov. 1956, pp 351-372. (Rejoinder by S. J. Prais and further rejoinder by J. M. Blair in 19 (3), Aug. 1957, pp 249–252).

A pioneer contribution to the problem, with useful references. (See also item 196).

176
Board of Trade. Export and size of firms. *Brd Trade j.,* 180 (3354), June 1961, pp 1515-1516.

177
Collins, N. R. *and* **Preston,** L. E. Concentration and price-cost margin in food manufacturing industries. *J. ind. econ.,* 14 (3), June 1966, pp 226–242.

Authors survey work on relation between concentration and rate of return. Report on their own research into US food manufacturing firms. Find curvi-linear relationships ; above a certain level, concentration accounts for about one half of variations in price-cost margin. Other factors : capital/output ratio, location, etc.

178
Collins, N. R. *and* **Preston,** L. E. The size structure of the largest industrial firms 1909-1958. *Am. econ. rev.,* 51 (5), Dec. 1961, pp 986–1011.

Study based on an analysis of the 100 largest US firms. Authors argue against Kaplan's findings (item 30), and state that over the last half century equality of opportunity in the upper reaches of the US economy has significantly declined.

179
Crowder, W. F. The concentration of production in manufacturing. *In:* United States. *Congress. Temporary National Economic Committee.* Investigation of concentration of economic power ... Monograph no. 27, The structure of industry (Washington, Gov't. Print. Off., 1941), pp 265–573.

180
Crum, W. L. Corporate size and earning power. Cambridge (Mass.), Harvard Univ. Pr., 1939. 418 p. (Harvard studies in monopoly and competition, no. 1).

181
de Jong, H. W. Concentration in the common market : a comment on a memorandum of the EEC commission. *Common mkt law rev.,* 4 (2), Sept. 1966, pp 166–179.

Discusses the Memorandum on the concentration of enterprises in the Common Market, submitted to member states 1 Dec. 1965.

182
Edwards, C. D. Big business and the policy of competition. Cleveland, Press of Western Reserve Univ., 1956. x, 180 p.

Four lectures given in 1955, dealing with issues and standards in the appraisal of, and the case for and against big business, and with problems of public policy. Two appendices : US Department of Justice cases and US Federal Trade Commission cases, giving offences charged, methods of decision, and penalties or remedies recommended.

183
European Economic Community. *Commission.*
La problème de la concentration dans le marché commun. (Luxembourg), Services de Publications des Communautés Européennes, 1966. 26 p. (Etudes : série concurrence, 3).

184
Evely, R. Concentration in American industry. *Cartel,* 8 (1), Jan. 1958, pp 18–23.

185
Evely, R. *and* **Little,** I. M. D. Concentration in British industry : an empirical study of the structure of industrial production, 1935–51. Cambridge Univ. Pr., 1960. xvi, 357 p. (National Institute of Economic and Social Research. Economic and social studies, 16).

Discusses concept and measurement of concentration. 14 case studies, dealing with coke-ovens, razors, mineral ore refinery, watches, mines, lead, bricks, metal, bones, tinplate, cinematographic film printing, sugar, wrought iron and steel tubes, bread and flour, confectionery, soap. Authors examine changes in concentration, 1935–1951, and factors leading to high concentration. Although high concentration not identical with monopoly power, most cases of monopoly power found in trades with high concentration ratios. Obstacles to new entry contribute substantially to the maintenance of high concentration. Latest data used for the study : 1951 Census of production. For the continuation of the study to 1958 see item 231.

186
Florence, P.S. New measures of the growth of firms. *Econ. j.,* 67 (266), June 1957, pp 245–248.

187
Florence, P.S. Ownership, control and success of large companies : an analysis of English industrial structure and policy, 1936–1951. Sweet & Maxwell, 1961. xiv, 279 p.

Analyses 109 very large companies with over £3m. issued capital and sample of some 1,600 companies with issued capital between £2,000,000 and £3,000,000. Gives details of individual firms. Discusses the concentration of voting shares, changes in the role of directors and boards of directors, the problem of directors' share holding, dividend policy. Concludes that beyond a certain size of firm, control by personal or family ownership is not possible. Bibliography and extensive appendices.

188
The Fortune directory : the 500 largest US industrial corporations, and the 50 largest banks, merchandising, transportation, life-insurance and utility companies, and the 200 largest industrial corporations outside the US. 1954+ New York.

Sub-title varies. Published annually, in an issue of *Fortune;* subsequently issued as a reprint. The 1967 reprint is in two parts : part 1, The 500 largest US industrial corporations : part 2, The 200 largest industrial corporations outside the US. The issues for 1954 to 1965 have been reprinted in a single volume as Part 5A of *Economic concentration: hearings before the Sub-committee on antitrust and monopoly of the Committee on the judiciary,* US Senate, 89th and 90th Congresses (Washington, Gov't. Print. Off., 1967).

189
George, K. D. Changes in British industrial concentration, 1951–1958. *J. ind. econ.,* 15 (3), July 1967, pp 200–211.

Examines whether a negative association exists between an industry's rate of growth and change in concentration. Discusses W. G. Shepherd's findings (item 231) and the applicability to the UK of Nelson's conclusions (item 219) from US data.

190
Grossack, I. M. Towards an integration of static and dynamic measures of industry concentration. *Rev. econ. statist.,* 47 (3), Aug. 1965, pp 301–308.

191
Haldi, J. *and* **Whitcomb,** D. Economies of scale in industrial plants. *J. political econ.,* 75 (4) pt 1, Aug. 1967, pp 373–385.

Authors approach determination of economies of scale via engineering studies and engineering literature. Comment on shortcomings of accounting approach and of neglecting importance of economies in transport and marketing. Refers to a Ph.D. dissertation by H. B. Chenery, *Engineering bases of economic analysis* (Harvard Univ., 1949).

192
Hall, M. *and* **Tideman,** N. Measures of concentration. *J. Am. Statist. Ass.,* 62 (317), March 1967, pp 62–68.

193
Hamberg, D. Size of firm, monopoly and economic growth. In : United States. *Congress. Joint economic committee (86th Cong., 1st sess.).* Employment, growth and price levels : hearings . . . Part 7, Effect of monopolistic and quasi-monopolistic practices (Washington, Gov't. Print. Off., 1959), pp 2337–2358.

194
Hamberg, D. Size of firm, oligopoly, and research : the evidence. *Can. j. econ. political sci,.* 30 (1), Feb. 1964, pp 62–75.

195
Harris, R. *and* **Solly,** M. A survey of large companies. 2nd ed. Institute of Economic Affairs, 1961. [5], 27, [46] p.

Results of a questionnaire sent to 512 leading companies (from the NIESR list—item 218), 151 of which answered most or all of the questions (1st edition 1959) and another 30 companies answered in the 2nd edition. Authors discuss the criteria of size—capital, employment, turnover—and some characteristics of large-size companies—structure, control and ownership, and fringe benefits. Some of the 21 tables give analysis of directorships and of share ownership.

196
Hart, P. E. *and* **Prais,** S. J. The analysis of business concentration : a statistical approach. *J. R. Statist. Soc.,* ser. A 119 (2), 1956, pp 150–191.

Examines concentration between 1885 and 1950, based on the London Stock Exchange market valuation of firms' assets. The authors analyse size-distribution, with the help of Lorenz curves and the log-normal hypothesis. Conclude that over the last half century changes in business concentration in the economy as a whole may not be very great. Discussion by Champernowne, C. Clark, Kendall, Mason, Barna, and others. For further discussion see items 175, 200 and 201.

197
Hart, P. E. Business concentration in the United Kingdom. *J. R. Statist. Soc.,* ser. A 123 (1), 1960, pp 50–58.

A sequel to item 196.

198
Hart, P. E. On measuring business concentration. *Bull. Oxf. Univ. Inst. Statist.,* 19 (3), Aug. 1957, pp 225–248.

199
Hart, P. E. Statistical measures of concentration vs. concentration ratios. *Rev. econ. statist.,* 43 (1), Feb. 1961, pp 85–86.

200
Horowitz, I. A note on the Hart-Prais measure of changes of business concentration. *J. R. Statist. Soc.,* ser. A 127 (2), 1964, pp 234–237.

Discusses item 196.

201
Hymer, S. *and* **Pashigian,** P. Firm size and rate of growth. *J. political econ.,* 70 (6), Dec. 1962, pp 556–569.

Critically examines the work of Hart and Prais (item 196).

202
Ijiri, Y. *and* **Simon,** H. A. Business firms growth and size. *Am. econ. rev.,* 54 (2) part 1, March 1964, pp 77–89.

203
International Chamber of Commerce. The problem of concentration in Europe. [Paris, 1965]. 16 p. (Brochure 240).

Tries to summarize the main problems connected with concentration and integration of firms, optimum size and mergers, with special reference to the European Common Market.

204
Jacoby, N. H. The relative stability of market shares : a theory and evidence from several industries. *J. ind. econ.,* 12 (2), March 1964, pp 83–107.

205
Kaplan, A. D. H. The influence of size of firm on the functioning of the economy. *Am. econ. rev.,* 40 (2), May 1950, pp 74–84.

206
Kaplan, A. D. H. Small business : its place and problems. New York, McGraw-Hill, 1948. xiv, 281 p. (Committee for Economic Development research study).

207
Leak, H. *and* **Maizels,** A. The structure of British industry. Royal Statistical Society, 1945. 59 p. (Also published, with discussion, in *J. R. Statist. Soc.,* ser. A 108 (1-2), 1945, pp 142–207).

Authors use census data to measure concentration in British industry.

208
Leyland, N. H. Growth and competition. *Oxf. econ. pap.,* 16 (1), March 1964, pp 3–8.

Reports on an inquiry on business policy in an expanding economy undertaken by the Oxford Economic Research Group. Sixteen interviews of growth firms, including firms expanding into new fields.

209
Lindahl, M. L. *and* **Carter,** W. A. Corporate concentration and public policy. 3rd ed. Englewood Cliffs (N.J.), Prentice-Hall, 1959. vi, 698 p.

Contents: I, The modern corporation (observations on development of large corporations with special reference to period 1937–57 ; problems of ownership and control) ; II, Industrial monopoly and oligopoly (eight US case studies, with two summary chapters on relevance of case studies for theory) ; III, Public regulation of monopoly, oligopoly and competitive practices (limitations and possibilities of strengthening competition by Government action). Many references.

210
Lydall, H. F. The growth of manufacturing firms. *Bull. Oxf. Univ. Inst. Statist.,* 21 (2), May 1959, pp 85–111.

211

Lydall, H. F. The impact of the credit squeeze on small and medium-sized manufacturing firms. *Econ. j.,* 67 (267), Sept. 1957, pp 415–431.

A sample enquiry.

212

Mandy, P. L. La structure de la dimension des entreprises dans les pays du marché commun. *Rev. écon.,* 11 (3), May 1960, pp 395–413.

213

Mason, E. S. Economic concentration and the monopoly problem. Cambridge (Mass.), Harvard Univ. Pr., 1957. xvi, 411 p. (Harvard economic studies, vol. 100).

Contents: Pt 1, The large firm and the structure of industrial markets ; pt 2, Wage-price problems ; pt 3, Raw materials, security and economic growth ; pt 4, Antitrust policy. Argues that monopolistic position in the USA has not changed over last half century. Stresses the lack of sufficient information, the dangers in interpreting concentration ratios, and warns against generalising.

214

Miller, H. The way of enterprise : a study of the origins, problems and achievements in the growth of post-war British firms. Deutsch, 1963. xii, 274 p.

Pub. for the Institute of Economic Affairs. 21 case studies of enterprising and innovating firms in traditional and science based industries.

215

Moore, F. T. Economies of scale : some statistical evidence. *Q. j. econ.,* 73 (2), May 1959, pp 232–245.

Divides expansion of plant into several classes, from new plant at new locations to removal of bottlenecks in old plant. Discusses problems of indivisibilities and of the '.6 rule' (Δ cost $= \Delta$capacity raised to .6 power). Surveys several enquiries into continuous process, capital intensive industries with homogeneous products. Pleads for more enquiries 'process by process' in various plants belonging to different industries to establish relationships. For a comment see item 230.

216

National Bureau of Economic Research, *New York.* Business concentration and price policy ; a conference of the Universities—National Bureau Committee for Economic Research. Princeton, Princeton Univ. Pr., 1955. x, 511 p. (Special conference series, no. 5).

Partial contents: Introduction, by G. J. Stigler (pp 3–14 ; summarises the twelve papers included in the volume) ; Census principles of industry and product classification, manufacturing industries, by M. R. Conklin and H. T. Goldstein (pp 15–55) ; Measures of concentration, by G. Rosenbluth (pp 57–95. A comment by O. C. Herfindahl is on pp 95–99) ; Economic theory and the measurement of concentration, by T. Scitovsky (pp 101–118) ; Measures of monopoly power and concentration ; their economic significance, by J. P. Miller (pp 119–140).

217

National Industrial Conference Board. Economic concentration measures : uses and abuses. A session of the 41st annual meeting of the Conference Board, held ... May 1957. New York, 1957. 55 p. (Studies in business economics, no. 57).

218

National Institute of Economic and Social Research. A classified list of large companies engaged in British industry, December 1955. 1956. 39 p.

219

Nelson, R. L. Concentration in the manufacturing industries of the United States : a midcentury report. New Haven, London, Yale Univ. Pr., 1963. xv, 288 p. (Social Science Research Council. Economic census studies, 2).

See also item 189.

220

Niehans, J. An index of the size of industrial establishments. *Int. econ. pap.,* 8, 1958, pp 122–132.

Translation of "Eine Messziffer für Betriebsgrössen", from *Zeitschrift für die gesamte Staatswissenshaft,* v. 111, no. 3, 1955.

221

Penrose, E. T. The theory of the growth of the firm. Oxford, Blackwell, 1959. viii, 272 p.

Deals with problems of size, diversification, mergers, concentration, with strong emphasis on problems of growth and innovation.

222

Prais, S. J. The financial experience of giant companies. *Econ. j.,* 67 (266), June 1957, pp 249–264.

A study of the implications of statistics given in *Company income and finance, 1949–53,* issued by the National Institute of Economic and Social Research (item 1105).

223

Pratten, C. *and* **Dean,** R. M. The economics of large-scale production in British industry ; an introductory study. Cambridge Univ. Pr., 1965. 105 p. (University of Cambridge Dept of Applied Economics. Occasional papers, 3).

Four case studies. Authors discuss meaning and measurement of economies of scale. Distinction made between single product and multi-product plants, and between single and multi-plant firms. Difficult to compare data in view of great diversity of firms operating within one industry. Care needed in rationalisation procedures if old works can earn profits although prices determined by modern large-scale plant. When there is a long-run conflict between maintenance of competition and full economies of scale, difficult to assess best compromise. How to assess impact on efficiency of presence of competition.

224
Quandt, R. E. On the size distribution of firms. *Am. econ. rev.,* 56 (3), June 1966, pp 416–432.

Demonstrates difficulty of finding good fits for size distribution of firms. Warns against results based on small samples of firms.

225
Quinn, T. K. Giant corporations : challenge to freedom. New York, Exposition Pr., 1956. 198 p. (A Banner book).

Author was Director General of US war production drive during World War II. Argues against pro-big corporation school of thought ; highly critical of present-day concentration of economic power, of the concentration of research and of firms' excess size, beyond what is necessary for efficiency.

226
Ray, G. F. Size of plant : a comparison. *Natn. Inst. econ. rev.,* (38), Nov. 1966, pp 63–66.

Compares British and German size of plant and net-output per head.

227
Richardson, G. B. The limits to a firm's rate of growth. *Oxf. econ. pap.,* 16 (1), March 1964, pp 9–23.

228
Rosenbluth, G. Concentration in Canadian manufacturing industries. Princeton (NJ), Princeton Univ. Pr., 1957. xv, 152 p. (National Bureau of Economic Research. General series, no. 61).

229
Samuels, J. M. Size and growth of firms. *Rev. econ. stud.,* 32 (90), April 1965, pp 105–111.

230
Schuman, S. C. *and* **Alpert,** S. B. Economies of scale : some statistical evidence ; comment [and reply by F. T. Moore]. *Q. j. econ.,* 74 (3), Aug. 1960, pp 493–500.

Discusses item 215.

231
Shepherd, W. G. Changes in British industrial concentration, 1951-1958. *Oxf. econ. pap.,* new ser. 18 (1), March 1966, pp 126–132.

An important contribution. Brings Evely's and Little's study (item 185) up to 1958, based on the census of production for 1958. Suggests that, contrary to findings relating to other countries, concentration in Britain has tended to increase during the 1950's. Concentration has been measured by the share in output and employment of the top three firms in each industry. Suggests industry-by-industry analysis to discover whether measures against collusive action have strengthened tendency towards concentration. For discussion see item 189.

232
Shepherd, W. G. A comparison of industrial concentration in the United States and Britain. *Rev. econ. statist.,* 43 (1), Feb. 1961, pp 70–75.

233
Shepherd, W. G. On appraising evidence about market power. *Antitrust bull.,* 12, 1967, pp 49–64.

Discusses limitations of market share approach and emphasises problem of asymmetry in size among leading oligopoly firms.

234
Shepherd, W. G. Trends of concentration in American manufacturing industries, 1947-1958. *Rev. econ. statist.,* 47 (2), May 1964, pp 200–212.

Examines critically J. S. Bain's and G. J. Stigler's theories about oligopolistic behaviour, on basis of 1958 data (published in item 239). Concludes that declining concentration has not been prevailing pattern for oligopolies in post-war US industry.

235
Simon, H. A. *and* **Bonini,** C. P. The size distribution of business firms. *Am. econ. rev.,* 48 (4), Sept. 1958, pp 607–617.

236
Steindl, J. Small and big business : economic problems of the size of firms. Oxford, Blackwell, 1945. v, 66 p. (Oxford University Institute of Statistics. Monograph no. 1).

Important contribution to problem of size of firm. Surveys factors influencing relative position of large and small firms ; difficulty of measuring efficiency and capital intensity ; concept of relative and absolute concentration ; doubts generalisations about relation between size and technological progress.

237
Stigler, G. J. Economies of scale. *J. law econ.,* 1, Oct. 1958, pp 54–71.

Attempts to apply the technique of the 'survivor principle'.

238
The Times 500 : leading companies in Britain and overseas. 1965+ Times Pub. Co. Ltd.

Published annually, to 1967 as *The Times 300*. Gives capital, profit, turnover, number of employees of 500 manufacturing firms and major nationalised industries ; also information relating to banks, top 50 building societies, 50 insurance companies, 50 unit trusts, 50 investment trusts and 100 leading European companies. Information on leading US, Australian and South African companies is included from 1967, and on Canadian and Japanese companies from 1968.

239
United States. *Bureau of the Census.* Concentration ratios in manufacturing industry, 1958. Report prepared . . . for the Sub-committee on antitrust and monopoly . . ., together with individual views. Washington, Gov't. Print. Off., 1962. 2 v. (xi, 510 p.).

Concentration ratios for about 440 industry classifications and 1,000 product class categories. Classification of different types of concentration ratios : value of shipments, by product class and product group, value added by manufacture, share of total manufacturing value added, and employment. The tabulation distinguishes between industries, industry-groups, product groups and product classes, between identical and non-identical four largest companies, between local, regional and national industries.

240
United States. *Congress. Senate. Committee on the judiciary (85th Cong., 1st sess.).* Concentration in American industry ; report of Sub-committee on antitrust and monopoly . . . to study antitrust laws of United States, and their administration, interpretation and effect. Washington, Gov't. Print. Off., 1957. viii, 756 p.

241
United States. *Congress. Senate. Committee on the judiciary (88th and 89th Cong.).* Economic concentration ; hearings before the Sub-committee on antitrust and monopoly . . . Washington, Gov't. Print. Off., 1964-1968. 7 v. (3438 p.).

Contents: Pt 1, Overall and conglomerate aspects (including statements by Adelman, Blair, Means, Nelson and others) ; pt 2, Mergers and other factors affecting industry concentration (including statements by Blair, Gort, Heflebower, Shepherd, Weiss and others) ; pt 3, Concentration, invention and innovation (including statements by Blair, Nelson and others) ; pt 4, Concentration and efficiency (including statements by Blair, Oxenfeldt and others) ; pt 5, Concentration and divisional reporting ; pt 5A, Appendix to part 5 : The *Fortune Directory* of the 500 largest US industrial corporations, 1954-1965 ; pt 6, New technologies and concentration.

242
United States. *Congress. Temporary National Economic Committee.* Investigation of concentration of economic power ; final report and recommendations of Temporary National Economic Committee transmitted to Congress . . . Washington, Gov't. Print. Off., 1941. ix, 783 p.

Includes verbatim testimony of public sessions to consider recommendations, and brief history of TNEC.

243
United States. *Congress. Temporary National Economic Committee.* Investigation of concentration of economic power . . . Monograph no. 13, Relative efficiency of large, medium-sized, and small business. Washington, Gov't. Print. Off., 1941. xv, 449 p.

Study made under the auspices of the Federal Trade Commission.

244
United States. *Federal Trade Commission.* Report of the Federal Trade Commission on changes in concentration in manufacturing, 1935-1947 and 1950. Washington, Gov't. Print. Off., 1954. v, 153 p.

245
United States. *Federal Trade Commission.* Report . . . on concentration of productive facilities, 1947 : total manufacturing and 26 selected industries. Washington, Gov't. Print. Off., 1949. iv, 96 p.

246
United States. *Federal Trade Commission.* Report . . . on industrial concentration and product diversification in the 1000 largest manufacturing companies, 1950. Washington, Gov't. Print. Off., 1957. viii, 656 p.

247
Verloren van Themaat, P. Problems of scale and mergers in the Common Market. *In:* Federal Trust for Education and Research. *Problems of scale in Europe: report on a two-day conference* (1966), pp 16–18.

248
Wedervang, F. Development of a population of industrial firms : the structure of manufacturing industries in Norway, 1930-1948. Oslo, Universitetsforlaget, 1965. 275 p. (Skrifter fra Norges Handelshøyskole, 9).

Based on Norwegian census data. Of special interest chapters 7 and 8, where the author examines rates of entry and exit of firms and whether they are influenced by age and size of firms. Also chapters on concentration and relation of capital and labour productivity to size of firm.

249
Weiss, L. W. Average concentration ratios and industrial performance. *J. ind. econ.,* 11 (3), July 1963, pp 237–254.

Discusses weakness of usual concentration ratios and suggests new method. Short bibliography.

250
Weiss, L. W. Factors in changing concentration. *Rev. econ. statist.,* 45 (1), Feb. 1963, pp 70–77.

251
Weiss, L. W. The survival technique and the extent of sub-optimal capacity. *J. political econ.,* 72 (3), June 1964, pp 246–261. (Correction in 73 (3), June 1965, pp 300–301).

252
Wellisz, S. H. The coexistence of large and small firms : a study of the Italian mechanical industries. *Q. j. econ.,* 61 (1), Feb. 1957, pp 116–131.

Argues that small firms do not necessarily waste resources, e.g. if closure would render these resources idle.

253
Winsten, C. B. *and* **Hall,** M. The measurement of economies of scale. *J. ind. econ.,* 9 (3), July 1961, pp 255–264.

2.5 Diversification and integration

See also items 167, 181, 183, 203, 221, 246, 247

Concentration, diversification, integration are closely linked, so that many works concerned with concentration also deal with questions of diversification and integration, e.g. R. Evely (items 184, 185), P. E. Hart (items 196, 197), H. Leak and A. Maizels (item 207), E. T. Penrose (item 221), M. Gort (item 262). Although it has become so marked a feature of modern industry not many outstanding publications can be found specialising in diversification and its impact on the competitive situation. Among the few studies in this field those by L. R. Amey (item 254), M. R. Fisher (item 259) and M. Gort (item 262) are of special interest. On problems of vertical integration the work of M. Gort and V. Fuchs (item 261) should prove of great value.

254
Amey, L. R. Diversified manufacturing businesses. *J. R. Statist. Soc.*, ser. A 127 (2), 1964, pp 251–290.

Discusses problems of measuring diversification in terms of enterprises, industries, markets or product classes on the basis of census of production data. Difficult to establish which diversified activities do not involve related functions. Neglects diversification of manufacturing enterprises into non-manufacturing industries. Examines relation between diversification, size of firm and industry groups ; also relation between a firm's organised research and diversification ; relation between concentration (via mergers) and diversification. Tries to test various theories about the scope of diversification.

255
Board of Trade. Size and diversification of industrial enterprises. *Brd Trade j.*, 184 (3442), Mar. 1963, pp 553–558.

256
Comanor, W. S. Vertical mergers, market powers, and the antitrust laws. *Am. econ. rev.*, 57 (2), May 1967, pp 254–265. (Discussion, by J. S. McGee, pp 269–271).

Discusses the effects of vertical integration by merger as against a firm's integration (forward or backward) by creating new facilities in competition with existing suppliers or customers. Also examines consequences of vertical mergers on barriers to entry.

257
Crowder, W. F. The integration of manufacturing operations. In : United States. *Congress. Temporary National Economic Committee.* Investigation of concentration of economic power … Monograph no. 27, The structure of industry (Washington, Gov't. Print. Off., 1941) pp 99–226.

258
Enrick, N. L. Product diversification : where to draw the line. *Mgmt decision*, 1 (3), Autumn 1967, pp 16–19.

Argues that firms are forced to diversify by the pressure of increasing consumers' purchasing power and competitors' new lines of product. Suggests application of mathematical programming to avoid failures in diversification. For this purpose tabulates thirteen types of production, marketing and sales costs involved in product diversification.

259
Fisher, M. R. Towards a theory of diversification. *Oxf. econ. pap.*, new ser. 13, Oct. 1961, pp 293–311.

Discusses factors influencing diversification such as imperfections of competition, uncertainty, rise of new wants. Conflict for firms : economies of specialisation versus risk spreading.

260
Foulke, R. A. Diversification in business activity. New York, Dun and Bradstreet, 1956. 79 p.

261
Fuchs, V. R. Integration, concentration, and profits in manufacturing industries. *Q. j. econ.*, 75 (2), May 1961, pp 278–291.

Classifies industry into : a) single unit establishments ; b) multi-unit single-industry establishments ; c) multi-unit multi-industry establishments. Compares size-distribution and value added per employee and per payroll. Examines relation between ease of entry, concentration and rates of profit, taking the regional scatter into account. Uses Stigler's method for measuring rates of returns and of concentration.

262
Gort, M. Diversification and integration in American industry. Princeton (NJ), Princeton Univ. Pr., 1962. xxi, 238 p. (National Bureau of Economic Research. General series, no. 77).

First comprehensive inter-industry study of large, diversified enterprise. Examines 111 US companies 1929-1954. Discusses concepts and measures of diversification, and examines its patterns, sources and trends. Also examines relations between size and diversification ; diversification, growth and profit rates ; size and integration ; integration and diversification ; product addition and industry size.

263
Nelson, R. L. Market growth, company diversification and product concentration, 1947-1954. *J. Am. Statist. Ass.,* 55, Dec. 1960, pp 640–649.

264
Thorp, W. L. The integration of industrial operation : a statistical and descriptive analysis of the development and growth of industrial establishments and of the size, scope and structure of combinations of industrial establishments operated from central offices. 277 p. Washington, 1924. (US Department of Commerce. Census monographs, no. 3).

One of the two important early American studies on diversification which give a detailed breakdown of the nature of relations between commodities produced under common ownership, at a given point of time. Thorp distinguishes five types of relationship between plants owned by one firm. (The other important early study is Monograph 27 of the US Congress Temporary National Economic Committee—see item 69).

International aspects of integration

The growing importance of international integration in some sectors such as the oil industry, international capital movements, customs unions, and the trend towards closer links between Western European countries, is reflected in a small number of studies, e.g. those by M. G. de Chazeau and A. E. Kahn (oil, item 265), H. O. Lundstroem (capital movements, item 268), P. Streeten (European integration, item 271), J. Vanek (customs unions, item 272).

265
de Chazeau, M. G. *and* **Kahn,** A. E. Integration and competition in the petroleum industry . . . New Haven (Conn.), Yale Univ. Pr., 1959. xviii, 598 p. (Petroleum monograph series, vol. 3).

266
Frankel, P. H. Integration in the oil industry. *J. ind. econ.,* 1 (3), July 1953, pp 202–211.

Argues the case for integration and supervision.

267
League of Nations. Customs unions : a . . . contribution to the study of customs union problems. Lake Success (NY), United Nations, 1947. ix, 98 p.

268
Lundstroem, H. O. Capital movements and economic integration : a study of the role of international long term capital movements in international economic integration, with particular reference to Europe. Leyden, Sijthoff, 1961. 232 p. (European aspects, series B, economics, no. 4).

269
Political and Economic Planning. Aspects of European integration : an Anglo-French symposium. [1962]. [5], 140 p.

Prepared in collaboration with the Institut de Science Economique Appliquée, Paris.

270
Scitovsky, T. Economic theory and Western European integration. Allen & Unwin, 1958. 154 p.

271
Streeten, P. Economic integration : aspects and problems. Leyden, Sijthoff, 1961. 151 p. (European aspects, series B, economics, no. 5).

272
Vanek, J. General equilibrium of international discrimination : the case of customs unions. Cambridge (Mass.), Harvard Univ. Pr., 1965. xi, 234 p. (Harvard economic studies, vol. 123).

Examines effects of discriminating trade practices on general equilibrium. Distinguishes between customs unions among countries with similar and with dissimilar structures.

273
Viner, J. The customs union issue. Stevens, 1950. viii, 221 p. (Carnegie Endowment for International Peace. Studies in the administration of international law and organization, no. 10).

List of conventions, decrees, etc., concerning customs unions, pp 141–169. Extensive 40 page bibliography, covering mainly the history of customs unions.

2.6 Mergers

See also item 66

Works listed here refer to case studies of mergers, the mechanism of merger transactions, and the effect of mergers. No outstanding work can be quoted, but among the enquiries (mostly American) the books by J. C. Narver (item 309), J. F. Weston (item 323) and R. L. Nelson (item 311), and the articles by H. G. Manne (item 304) and L. W. Weiss (item 322) are of particular interest. Publications relating to the neighbouring fields of concentration and integration in general will be found in sections 2.4 and 2.5 of the bibliography (pages 17-25).

274
Acton Society Trust. The human effects of mergers : the impact on managers, by Rosemary Stewart [and others]. 1963. [3], 87 p. (Mergers, 2).

275
Acton Society Trust. The human effects of mergers : the impact on the shopfloor, by Dennis Brooks and Randall Smith. 1966. [5], 166 p. (Mergers, 3).

276
Acton Society Trust. Mergers, past and present, by Randall Smith and Dennis Brooks. 1963. [7], 84 p. (Mergers, 1).

277
Adelman, M. A. The antimerger act, 1950-60. *Am. econ. rev.,* 51 (2), May 1961, pp 236–244. (Discussion, pp 263–270).

Stresses the possible advantages of vertical integration.

278
Alberts, W. W. *and* **Segall,** J. E., *eds.* The corporate merger. Chicago, London, Univ. of Chicago Pr., 1966. xviii, 287 p.

Proceedings of a seminar sponsored by the Univ. of Chicago Graduate School of Business. Among the topics : evaluation of proposed mergers, relation between profitability and size.

279
Blair, J. M. *and* **Haughton,** H. F. The Lintner-Butters analysis of the effect of mergers on industrial concentration, 1940-1947 : a reply. *Rev. econ. statist.,* 33, Feb. 1951, pp 63–67.

Discusses item 286.

280
Bo, D. Del. ECSC and the merger. European Community Information Service, 1964. 7 p. (Community topics, 14).

281
Board of Trade. Report of the company law committee. HMSO, 1962. ix, 223 p. (Cmnd. 1749).

Chairman of committee : Lord Jenkins. See also item 142.

282
Brady, R. A. Rationalization movement in German industry ; a study in the evolution of economic planning. Berkeley, Univ. of California ; London, Cambridge Univ. Pr., 1933. xxi, 466 p.

283
Brecher, I. Combines and competition : a re-appraisal of Canadian public policy. *Can. bar rev.,* 38, Dec. 1960, pp 523–593.

284
Bull, G. *and* **Vice,** A. Bid for power. 3rd ed. Elek books, 1961. 299 p.

An account of 'take-over-bids' for business enterprises, including interesting case studies of Clore, Fraser, Wolfson, Rank, etc.

285
Bushnell, J. A. Australian company mergers, 1946-1959. Parkville, Melbourne Univ, Pr., 1961. xii, 223 p.

286
Butters, J. K. *and* **Lintner,** J. Effect of mergers on industrial concentration, 1940-1947. *Rev. econ. statist.,* 32, Feb. 1950, pp 30–48.

For discussion see item 279.

287
Butters, J. K., **Lintner,** J. *and* **Cary,** W. L. Effects of taxation : corporate mergers. Boston, Harvard Univ. Graduate School of Business Administration, 1951. xix, 364 p.

288
Conard, A. F. Corporate fusion in the common market. *Am. j. comparative law,* 14 (4), 1965/66, pp 573–602.

289
Cook, P. L. *and* **Cohen,** R. Effects of mergers ; six studies ... Allen & Unwin, 1958. 458 p. (Cambridge studies in industry).

Contents: 1, The cement industry ; 2, The calico printing industry ; 3, The soap industry ; 4, The flat-glass industry ; 5, The motor industry, by G. Maxcy ; 6, The brewing industry, by J. Vaizey.

290
De Montmorency, S. F. G. Take-over bids. *J. bus. law,* 1963, pp 246–253.

291
Dewey, D. Mergers and cartels : some reservations about policy. *Am. econ. rev.,* 51 (2), May 1961, pp 255–262. (Discussion, pp 263–270).

292
Dewing, A. S. A statistical test of the success of consolidations. *Q. j. econ.,* 36, Nov. 1921, pp 84–101.

Pioneer statistical study of profits, expected and realised, as result of horizontal mergers.

293
Dirlam, J. B. Recent developments in the anti-merger policy : a diversity of standards. *Antitrust bull.,* 9 (3), May-June 1964, pp 381–413.

The open pro-con approach of some courts versus the primarily structural standards approach of others, the latter being based on the prevention of excessive concentration and of substantial lessening of competition.

294
Goyder, D. G. Public control of mergers. *Mod. law rev.,* 28 (6), Nov. 1965, pp 654–674.

Discusses difference between US and UK criteria for judging desirability of mergers. Comments on the conflict between the time limit imposed on Monopolies Commission for reporting back and the time required for examining the relevant facts.

295
Hammond, R. E. Growth through mergers. *Antitrust bull. ,* 10 (5-6), Sept.-Dec. 1965, pp 779–794.

296
Heath, J. B. Mergers and the public interest. *Guardian,* 6 Feb. 1962, p 8.

297
Heath, J. B. Mergers policy in Europe and US. *Guardian,* 7 Feb. 1962, p 10.

298
Heflebower, R. B. Corporate mergers : policy and economic analysis. *Q. j. econ.,* 77 (4), Nov. 1963, pp 537–558.

Author takes a US Supreme Court decision (Brown Shoe Co. vs. US, 1962) as a case study for testing standards used for appraising effects of mergers on competition. Discusses the problems facing monopoly investigators in marginal cases.

299
Issuing Houses Association. Revised notes on company amalgamations and mergers. 1963. [1], 6 p.

Very useful notes on purpose, principles and procedures of amalgamations. Revised edition of *Notes on amalgamations of British businesses* (1959).

300
Kitching, J. Why do mergers miscarry ? *Harv. bus. rev.,* 45 (6), Nov./Dec. 1967, pp 84–101.

Results of interviews with 25 American top level executives whose companies had acquired and managed 181 companies during 1960-1965. Assumes need for 2 to 7 years' experience after merger for drawing valid conclusions. Analyses types of expectations in the field of finance, markets and economies of scale ('highly overrated') and compares failure rates of different types of mergers. Tabulation of types and results of mergers.

301
Korah, V. Restrictive trade practices : the BMC/Pressed Steel merger. *J. bus. law,* April 1966, pp 160–165.

302
Lockwood, B. B. Guides to mergers : legal considerations. *Can. chartered accountant,* 85, Aug. 1964, pp 99–102.

303
McGowan, J. J. The effect of alternative anti-merger policies on size distribution of firms. *Yale econ. essays,* 5 (2), 1965, pp 423–474.

304
Manne, H. G. Mergers and the market for corporate control. *J. political econ.,* 73 (2), April 1965, pp 110–120.

Describes different types of mergers. Problem of finding statistical methods to distinguish between mergers motivated by monopoly profit and those motivated by efficiency.

305
Markham, J. W. Survey of the evidence and findings on mergers. In : National Bureau of Economic Research, *New York. Business concentration and price policy* (Princeton Univ. Pr., 1955), pp 141–212.

306
Maule, C. J. Mergers in Canadian industry. 1966. (London School of Economics Ph.D. thesis).

307
Mennell, W. Takeover ; the growth of monopoly in Britain, 1951–61. Lawrence & Wishart, 1962. 212 p.

A marxist approach. Describes concentration in various industries. Appendix B lists mergers in the 1950's and early 1960's.

308
Moon, R. W. Business mergers and take-over bids . . . 3rd ed. Gee, 1968. 238 p.

'A study of the post-war pattern of amalgamations and reconstructions of companies'. Useful textbook, with chapters on the pros and cons, types and techniques, of mergers.

309
Narver, J. C. Conglomerate mergers and market competition. Berkeley, Univ. of California Pr. ; Cambridge Univ. Pr., 1967. x, 155 p. (Univ. of California Institute of Business and Economic Research. Publications).

An important study. Refers to mergers of firms which are neither competitors nor vertically related but work in separate products and/or markets. The author estimates the magnitude of conglomerate mergers in the US (1958), analyses the factors determining conglomerate mergers, and attempts to assess under what conditions and in what ways conglomerate market power is likely to affect the competitive situation. Also history and review of relevant US legislation. Bibliography.

310
National conference on company mergers and acquisitions, *1967, Glasgow.* Company mergers and acquisitions : proceedings of a national conference . . . Edited by R. V. Arnfield. [Glasgow, Univ. of Strathclyde], 1967. 1 v. (various pagings).

Of special interest among the twelve papers read to the conference (organised by the University of Strathclyde and the Financial Times) : *The economic background,* by K. J. W. Alexander ; *Mergers and monopoly—the public interest,* by P. W. Carey (of the Board of Trade) ; *Managing a diversified holding company,* by P. N. M. Rudder ; *Recent trends in company acquisitions,* by N. A. H. Stacey. The papers contain much valuable factual information on causes and effects of the merger movement.

311
Nelson, R. L. Merger movements in American industry, 1895-1956. Princeton (NJ), Princeton Univ. Pr., 1959. xxi, 176 p. (National Bureau of Economic Research. General series, no. 66).

An attempt to analyse the American merger movement. The statistical basis of the analysis is open to criticism.

312
Norris, W. G. Prescription for mergers. *Dir.,* Sept. 1966 pp 416–417.

313
Rahl, J. A. Anti-merger law in search of a policy. *Antitrust bull.,* 11 (1 and 2), Jan./April 1966, pp 325–349.

314
Rahl, J. A. Current antitrust developments in the merger field. *Antitrust bull.,* 8 (3), May/June 1963, pp 493–515.

315

Rice, D. G. Good and bad take-over bids. *J. bus. law,* 1960, pp 308–321.

316

Stacey, N. A. H. Mergers in modern business. Hutchinson, 1966. xiii, 138 p.

Stresses advantages of and need for more research. Appendix : Concentration ratios in UK, 1951, 1948. Bibliography.

317

United States. *Federal Trade Commission.* Report on corporate mergers and acquisitions. Washington, Gov't. Print. Off., 1955. vii, 210 p.

318

United States. *Federal Trade Commission.* Report on the merger movement : a summary report. Washington, Gov't. Print. Off., 1948. vi, 134 p.

319

The Urge to merge. *Times rev. ind. technol.,* 3, Aug. 1965, pp 12–16.

320

Vice, A. Balance-sheet for take-overs. Barrie and Rockliff, 1960. 36 p. (Hobart paper, 3).

Published for the Institute of Economic Affairs. Examines the case for and against take-over bids. The author concludes that they perform a useful function provided shareholders are given sufficient information.

321

Weinberg, M. A. Take-overs and amalgamations. 2nd ed. Sweet & Maxwell, 1967. xxvi, 371 p.

Deals mainly with the legal background and mechanism of take-overs and amalgamations in Britain, with details of the legislation up to July 31 1967 (i.e. including Monopolies and Mergers Act 1965 and Companies Act 1967). Important chapters on definition, causes of and defences against take-overs ; also on control of companies, and financial and fiscal implications.

322

Weiss, L. W. An evaluation of mergers in six industries. *Rev. econ. statist.,* 47 (2), May 1965, pp 172–181.

323

Weston, J. F. The role of mergers in the growth of large firms. Berkeley (Calif.), Univ. of California Pr., 1952. xvi, 159 p.

An important study of 74 American companies which examines the sources of growth of firms in oligopolistic industries. It extensively discusses the problems of measurement, and the theory and implications of mergers. Concludes that, after the early merger movement at the turn of the century, firms achieved their present-day large size mainly by internal growth.

2.7 Entry

See also items 46, 68, 84

The topics of entry and exit of firms, and of barriers to entry, although so essential for a study of the competitive structure of industry, have not attracted many researchers. J. S. Bain's *Barriers to new competition* (item 324) published in 1956 remains the standard work and has not been followed by any other major study. Important contributions in articles by H. H. Hines (item 326) and H. M. Mann (item 330).

324

Bain, J. S. Barriers to new competition : their character and consequences in manufacturing industries. Cambridge (Mass.), Harvard Univ. Pr., 1956. xii, 329 p. (Harvard Univ. series on competition in American industry, no. 3).

Role of product differentiation, advertising, consumer knowledge, conspicuous consumption, etc. Essential reading. For discussion see item 327.

325

Hawtrey, R. C. Competition from newcomers. *Economica,* new ser. 10 (39), Aug. 1943, pp 219–222.

326

Hines, H. H. Effectiveness of 'entry' by already established firms. *Q. j. econ.,* 71 (1), Feb. 1957, pp 132–150.

Argues that although the threat of established firms entering a new industry may improve the competitive effort of the old firms in that industry, this type of entry is not necessarily as beneficial as entries by newly established firms ; it could lead to an undesirable increase in the economic power of the 'entering' firm.

327

Johns, B. L. Barriers to entry in a dynamic setting. *J. ind. econ.,* 11 (1), Nov. 1962, pp 48–61.

Discusses Bain's three main conditions for free entry (see item 324).

328

Kahn, A. H. Discriminatory pricing as a barrier to entry : the spark plug litigation. *J. ind. econ.,* 8 (1), Oct. 1959, pp 1–12.

329

Mann, H. M., **Haas,** P. *and* **Walgreen,** J. Entry and oligopoly theory. *J. political econ.,* 73 (4), Aug. 1965, pp 381–383.

Authors argue whether Chamberlin or Harrod is right, i.e. whether or not firms charge a price higher than that necessary to exclude new entrants.

330

Mann, H. M. Seller concentration, barriers to entry, and rates of return in thirty industries, 1950-1960. *Rev. econ. statist.,* 48 (3), Aug. 1966, pp 296–307.

331
Mansfield, E. Entry, Gibrat's law, innovation and the growth of firms. *Am. econ. rev.,* 52 (5), Dec. 1962, pp 1023–1051.

Author rejects Gibrat's law. Bases his arguments on small number of observations and on rather crude assumptions.

332
Munthe, P. Freedom of entry into industry and trade. Paris, European Productivity Agency, 1958. 76 p. (EPA project no. 259).

Surveys the various aspects of the problems of freedom of entry and discusses its relationship to productivity. 5 page bibliography.

333
Osborne, D. K. The role of entry in oligopoly theory. *J. political econ.,* 72 (4), Aug. 1964, pp 396–402.

334
Oxenfeldt, A. R. New firms and free enterprise : pre-war and post-war aspects. Washington, American Council on Public Affairs, 1943. 196 p.

335
Sherman, R. *and* **Willett,** T. D. Potential entrants discourage entry. *J. political econ.,* 75 (4 pt 1), Aug. 1967, pp 400–403.

2.8 Location

In spite of extensive governmental measures, the regionally uneven distribution of employment and of economic growth has remained an outstanding feature of Britain's economy. Yet relatively little research has been undertaken into the effects of location and locational policy on size, unit costs and competitiveness, or of their effects on the strength of regional monopoly situations. The studies by M. Beesley (items 337, 338), D. C. Hague (items 348, 349), S. Hirsch (item 352), W. F. Luttrell (items 362, 363), E. Nevin (item 365), and A. P. Thirlwall (items 373, 374) are especially useful. Some bank reviews (District, Lloyds, Three Banks) have published a good number of contributions to the theme.

Further references can be found in *Industrial location: a review and annotated bibliography of theoretical, empirical and case studies,* by B. H. Stevens and C. A. Brackett (Philadelphia, Regional Science Research Institute, 1967).

The subsection *Major Government Reports* contains valuable regional studies, concerned with past and future developments, undertaken in the period 1962-1967.

336
Allen, E. G. W. Regional policies and the North West. *Dist. Bank rev.,* (155), Sept. 1965, pp 25–44.

337
Beesley, M. The birth and death of industrial establishments : experience in the West Midlands conurbation. *J. ind. econ.,* 4 (1), Oct. 1955, pp 45–61.

338
Beesley, M. Changing locational advantages in the British motor car industry. *J. ind. econ.,* 6 (1), Oct. 1957, pp 47–57.

339
Cameron, G. C. *and* **Clark,** B. D. Industrial movement and the regional problem. Edinburgh, London, Oliver & Boyd, 1966. viii, 220 p. (Univ. of Glasgow social and economic studies. Occasional papers, no. 5).

The results of an enquiry covering 100 companies which established manufacturing plant in the development districts between 1958 and 1963.

340
Cameron, G. C. *and* **Reid,** G. L. Scottish economic planning and the attraction of industry. Edinburgh, London, Oliver & Boyd, 1966. iv, 72 p. (Univ. of Glasgow social and economic studies. Occasional papers, no. 6).

341
Clark, C. Industrial location and economic potential. *Lloyds Bank rev.,* (82), Oct. 1966, pp 1–17.

Includes proposals for, and examples of, regional pay-roll taxes and rebates, with comments upon the introduction of the selective employment tax.

342
Cuthbert, N. *and* **Black,** W. Regional policy re-examined. *Scott. j. political econ.,* 9 (1), Feb. 1964, pp 1–16.

An assessment of the Hall Report on the economy of Northern Ireland (item 382).

343
Dennison, S. R. The location of industry and the depressed areas. Oxford Univ. Pr., 1939. vi, 216 p.

344
European Coal and Steel Community. *High Authority.* Arrangements to facilitate the establishment of new economic activities : legal and financial arrangements in force in the member states of the Community and the United Kingdom. Luxembourg, 1962- 1 v. (loose-leaf).

Refers mainly to governmental distribution of industry policy.

345
Fogarty, M. P. Prospects of the industrial areas of Great Britain. Methuen, 1945. xxv, 492 p.

346
Goodman, J. F. B. *and* **Samuel,** P. J. The motor industry in a development district : a case study of the labour factor. *Brit. j. ind. relations,* 4 (3), Nov. 1966, pp 336–365.

347
Greenhut, M. L. Plant location in theory and in practice ; the economics of space. Chapel Hill, Univ. of North Carolina Pr., 1956. xiii, 338 p.

Bibliography.

348
Hague, D. C. *and* **Newman,** P. K. Costs in alternative locations : the clothing industry. Cambridge Univ. Pr., 1952. vii, 73 p. (National Institute for Economic and Social Research. Occasional papers, 15).

Describes methods of investigation. Draws attention to the conceptual statistical difficulties met in the enquiry.

349
Hague, D. C. *and* **Dunning,** J. H. Costs in alternative locations : the radio industry. *Rev. econ. stud.,* 22, 1954–55, pp 203–213.

350
Hall, M. *and* **Winsten,** C. B. Variations in regional averages of census data : a methodological study. *Rev. econ. statist.,* 47 (1), Feb. 1965, pp 54–64.

351
Hart, P. E. *and* **MacBean,** A. I. Regional differences in productivity, profitability and growth : a pilot study. *Scott. j. political econ.,* 8 (1), Feb. 1961, pp 1–11.

352
Hirsch, S. Location of industry and international competitiveness. Oxford, Clarendon Pr., 1967. x, 133 p.

Argument : stage of technology, of economic development, of human and natural resources, and the character of the market should determine the type of industry to be located in a given country. Correctness of choice would be tested by international competitiveness.

353
Holmans, A. E. Restriction of industrial expansion in South-East England : a reappraisal. *Oxf. econ. pap.,* new ser. 16 (2), July 1964, pp 235–261.

Argues against further restrictions on growth in S.E. England, outside conurbations. A reply by A. P. Thirlwall in new ser. 17 (2), July 1965, pp 337–341 ; rejoinder by Holmans pp 343–345.

354
Humphrys, G. Growth industries and the regional economies of Britain. *Dist. Bank rev.,* Dec. 1962, pp 35–56.

355
James, B. G. S. The incompatibility of industrial and trading cultures : a critical appraisal of the growth-point concept. *J. ind. econ.,* 13 (1), Nov. 1964, pp 90–94.

356
Jay, D. Distribution of industry policy and related issues. *Econ. j.,* 75 (300), Dec. 1965, pp 736–741.

357
Klaassen, L. H. Methods of selecting industries for depressed areas : an introduction to feasibility studies. [Paris], Organisation for Economic Co-operation and Development, [1967]. 152 p. (Developing job opportunities, 2).

358
Law, D. Industrial movement and locational advantage. *Manchr sch. econ. social stud.,* 32 (2), May 1964, pp 131–154.

Compares the effects of location in Northern Ireland with those in Great Britain.

359
Loasby, B. J. Making location policy work. *Lloyds Bank rev.,* Jan. 1967, pp 34–47.

360
Lösch, A. The economics of location ; translated from the 2nd revised [German] ed. New Haven (Conn.), Yale Univ. Pr. ; London, Oxford Univ. Pr., 1954. xxviii, 520 p.

Translation of *Die räumliche Ordnung der Wirtschaft,* pub. 1944.

361
Lomax, K. S. The less prosperous areas of the United Kingdom. *Lond. Camb. econ. bull.,* new ser. Sept. 1963, pp xi–xv.

362
Luttrell, W. F. The cost of industrial movement : a first report on the economics of establishing branch factories. Cambridge Univ. Pr., 1952. ix, 104 p. (National Institute of Economic and Social Research. Occasional papers, 14).

Several case studies (shoes and engineering). Comparison of various types of costs in main works and branches. Discussion of methods used.

363
Luttrell, W. F. Factory location and industrial movement : a study of recent experience in Great Britain. National Institute of Economic and Social Research, 1962. 2 v.

Examines the cost of establishing branch factories, with 88 case studies (contained in vol. 2) in shoe manufacture, engineering, hosiery, clothing, textiles, electrical goods, metal goods, scientific equipment, chemicals. Describes methods of comparing costs per unit of output. Raises problem of size of plant.

364
Midland Bank. Old and new industrial areas in Britain. *Midl. Bank rev.,* May 1964, pp 3–10.

An account of official policy towards regional development.

365
Nevin, E. The case for regional policy. *Three banks rev.,* Dec. 1966, pp 30–46.

366
Nicholson, R. J. The regional location of industry ; an empirical study based on the regional tables of the 1948 census of production. *Econ. j.,* 66 (263), Sept. 1956, pp 467–481.

367
Odber, A. J. Local unemployment and the 1958 act. *Scott. j. political econ.,* 6 (3), Nov. 1959, pp 211–228.

Discusses the Distribution of industry (industrial finance) Act and Board of Trade action under the act.

368
Parkinson, J. R. Regional development : policies, programmes or plans. *Scott. j. political econ.,* 9 (1), Feb. 1964, pp 75–82.

369
Robertson, D. J. Scottish Council report on the Scottish economy. *Scott. j. political econ.,* 9 (1), Feb. 1962, pp 73–77.

Discusses item 371.

370
Royal Commission on the Geographical Distribution of the Industrial Population (1937/39). Report. HMSO, 1940. x, 320 p. (Cmd. 6153).

Chairman of the commission : Montague Barlow.

371
Scottish Council (Development and Industry).
Inquiry into the Scottish economy, 1960-1961 : report of a committee . . . Edinburgh, [1961]. 205, lxxiv p.

Chairman of the committee : J. N. Toothill. For discussion, see item 369.

372
Sykes, J. The control of industrial location. *Dist. Bank rev.,* Sept. 1957, pp 1–14.

373
Thirlwall, A. P. A measure of the proper distribution of industry. *Oxf. econ. pap.,* new ser. 19 (1), March 1967, pp 46–58.

Discusses definition of 'proper distribution of industry' and compares industrial structure and growth in the under-employed and overemployed regions of the U.K.

374
Thirlwall, A. P. *and* **Harris,** C. P. Measuring the localization of industry. *Manchr sch. econ. and social stud.,* 35 (1), Jan. 1967, pp 55–68.

375
Warren, K. Steel pricing, regional economic growth and public policy. *Urban studies,* 3 (3), Nov. 1966, pp 185–199.

376
Wilson, T. Finance for regional industrial development. *Three banks rev.,* (75), Sept. 1967, pp 3–23.

Compares capital costs inside and outside development regions and examines usefulness of present financial incentives.

Major government reports on the regions of the United Kingdom

---

377
Board of Trade. The North East : a programme for regional development and growth. HMSO, 1963. 48 p. (Cmnd. 2206).

378
Department of Economic Affairs. The North West : a regional study. HMSO, 1965. xii, 178 p.

379
Department of Economic Affairs. The problems of the Merseyside : an appendix to 'The North West : a regional study'. HMSO, 1965. iv, 83 p.

380
Department of Economic Affairs. The West Midlands : a regional study. HMSO, 1965. xii, 115 p.

381
East Midlands Economic Planning Council. The East Midlands study. HMSO, 1966. x, 120 p.

Published for the Department of Economic Affairs.

382
Joint Working Party on the Economy of Northern Ireland. (*UK and Northern Ireland*). Report . . . HMSO, 1962. vi, 89 p. (Cmnd. 1835).

Chairman of working party : Sir Robert Hall.

383
Northern Economic Planning Council. Challenge of the changing North : a preliminary study. HMSO, 1966. xii, 92 p.

Published for the Department of Economic Affairs.

384
Northern Ireland. Economic development in Northern Ireland, including the report of the economic consultant, Thomas Wilson. Belfast, HMSO, [1965]. 156 p. (Cmd. 479).

385
Scottish Development Department. Central Scotland : a programme for development and growth. HMSO, 1963. 47 p. (Cmnd. 2188).

386
Scottish Office. The Scottish economy 1965 to 1970 : a plan for expansion. Edinburgh, HMSO, 1966. viii, 165 p. (Cmnd. 2864).

387
South East Economic Planning Council. A strategy
for the South East : a first report . . . HMSO, 1967. xii, 100 p.

Published for the Department of Economic Affairs.

388
South West Economic Planning Council. A region
with a future : a draft strategy for the South West. HMSO,
1967. x, 154 p.

Published for the Department of Economic Affairs.

389
Welsh Office. Wales : the way ahead. Cardiff, HMSO,
1967. vii, 137 p. (Cmnd. 3334).

390
West Midlands Economic Planning Council. The
West Midlands : patterns of growth : a first report.
HMSO, 1967. iv, 60 p.

Published for the Department of Economic Affairs.

391
**Yorkshire and Humberside Economic Planning
Council.** A review of Yorkshire and Humberside. HMSO,
1966. x, 130 p.

Published for the Department of Economic Affairs.

2.9 Studies of specific industries

The entries listed below are meant to serve as a guide to
principal sources only. To list publications referring to all
industries would require a separate bibliography. No
attempt has been made to cover extensively agriculture and
raw materials. On the other hand, transport has been
divided into subsections on railways, shipping and air
transport. The subject index should be consulted for
industries entered under the sub-heading 'other industries'
and also for all publications in other sections of the
bibliography which deal with particular industries.

A considerable amount of information on special
industries has accumulated in the reports of the
Monopolies Commission (see Appendix 2, page 94), the
Restrictive Practices Court (see Appendix 3, page 96), the
National Board for Prices and Incomes (item 771), in the
studies of selected industries undertaken by the National
Institute of Economic and Social Research, the Cambridge
University Department of Applied Economics, by
Political and Economic Planning and by authors such as
G. C. Allen, D. Burn, J. H. Dunning, R. S. Edwards and
H. Townsend, supplemented by special studies prepared by
the 'Little Neddies'.

As to transport, the reports commissioned by the Ministry
of Transport (items 465, 466, 468, 484), and the
publications by C. D. Foster (item 458), D. L. Munby
(items 469, 485-487), C. H. Sharp (item 473), J. R.
Sargent (item 471) and G. Walker (items 475, 476)
represent original contributions to an analysis of transport

economics. On shipping S. C. Sturmey's (items 503-505)
and T. Thorburn's (item 507) work, and on air transport
P. G. Masefield's (items 516, 517) and S. F. Wheatcroft's
(items 520-521) studies are of particular value.

Research concerned with one of the major industries—
distribution—has been very limited. The structure of the
distributive system and its significance for a competitive
economy were investigated only after selling costs had
acquired theoretical status. Among the authors who have
specialised in this field, M. Hall (items 535-537) and
J. B. Jefferys (items 542-544) should be mentioned. They
have been joined in the sixties by C. Fulop (items 531-533)
and W. G. McClelland (items 547-549). The Organisation
for Economic Cooperation and Development (formerly
Organisation for European Economic Cooperation) has
also published valuable studies (items 550, 551). Several
reports of the Monopolies Commission contain information
on distribution.

Conditions in a number of problem industries in the
immediate post-war II period have been analysed in reports
of the British (formerly Anglo-American) Productivity
Council (see name index). Most reports of the Board of
Trade Working Parties were published prior to 1950 and
have, therefore, been omitted from the bibliography.
Additional information can be obtained from the annual
reports of nationalised industries and public corporations,
from annual company reports (summarised in Moodies'
British Company service), from directories and trade
journals, from special supplements to quality newspapers ;
also from legislation referring to specific industries
(railways, shipbuilding, shipping, steel).

Chemical industries

392
Anglo-American Council on Productivity.
Ammunition : report of a British productivity team on
ammunition which visited the United States of America in
1952. British Productivity Council, 1953. x, 138 p.

393
Backman, J. Competition in the chemical industry.
Washington, Manufacturing Chemists' Association, 1964.
vi, 90 p.

The author discusses the structure of the industry and the
patterns of competition, inter-product and inter-industry
competition, price and non-price competition in some
selected product groups. Believes that as a result of
test-tube rivalry and of new entries from large established
firms, competition for many chemical products is again on
the increase.

394
Backman, J. Foreign competition in chemicals and
allied products. Washington, Manufacturing Chemists'
Association, 1965. vi, 64 p.

395
British Productivity Council. [A review of productivity
in ammunition production]. [1956]. 22 p. (Productivity
review, 26).

396

British Productivity Council. A review of productivity in the fertilizer industry. [1954]. 29 p.

397

Crum, R. E. The chemicals industry : problems of projection. *Natn. Inst. econ. rev.,* (37), Aug. 1966, pp 39–52.

398

Economic Research Group of the Amsterdam-Rotterdam Bank, Banque de la Société Générale de Belgique, Deutsche Bank, Midland Bank. The chemical industry in some European countries. 1967. 27 p.

Compares structure, growth, prices, costs, capital investment, and international trade.

399

Frankel, P. H. *and* **Newton,** W. L. The state of the oil industry. *Natn. Inst. econ. rev.,* (11), Sept. 1960, pp 16–25.

400

Ministry of Health. *Committee of enquiry into the relationship of the pharmaceutical industry with the National Health Service (1965-67).* Report of the committee ... HMSO, 1967. v, 233 p. (Cmnd. 3410).

Chairman of committee : Lord Sainsbury. Important case study of problems relating to subsidiaries of foreign firms, patents, licence agreements, brand names, promotional expenditure, price and product competition, rates of return, research effort. A critical review of the financial and economic conclusions of the report is given in *Profitability in the pharmaceutical industry: an analysis of the recommendations of the Sainsbury committee,* prepared by Merrett Cyriax Associates for Bayer Products Company (1968. 34 p.).

401

Williams, T. I. The chemical industry, past and present. Penguin Books, 1953. 192 p.

Metal manufacture

See also item 117

402

Anglo-American Council on Productivity. Steel construction : report of a visit to the USA in 1951 of a productivity team on constructional steelwork, fabricated platework [and] mechanical handling plant. 1952. viii, 70 p.

403

Bennett, A. The competitive structure of the aluminium casting industry. *J. ind. econ.,* 14 (2), April 1966, pp 143–163.

Important case study.

404

Bennett, A. The competitive structure of the secondary-aluminium industry. *J. ind. econ.,* 12 (2), March 1964, pp 115–132.

Important case study.

405

British Productivity Council. A review of productivity in the bronze and brass casting industry. [1955]. 40 p.

406

British Productivity Council. [A review of productivity in the iron and steel industry]. [1956]. 47 p. (Productivity review, 27).

407

British Productivity Council. [A review of productivity in the pressure die casting industry]. [1955]. 30 p. (Productivity review, 23).

408

Burn, D. The steel industry, 1939-1959 : a study in competition and planning. Cambridge Univ. Pr., 1961. xvi, 728 p.

409

Crawford, M. Steelmaking : exploiting the spray breakthrough. *Statist,* 191 (4635), 6 Jan. 1967, pp 33–34.

Article on 'potentially Britain's biggest contribution to steel technology'. Process is relevant for size of steel plants.

410

Hart, D. F. W. The metallurgical industry : the economics of product development and marketing. 1953. (M. Sc. thesis, Univ. of London).

411

Iron and Steel Board. Special reports. HMSO.

This series comprises principally four reports on the future development of the iron and steel industry :
Development of the iron and steel industry, 1953-1958. 1955. (iv, 42 p. HC 49, sess. 1954/55).
Development in the iron and steel industry : special report. 1957. (vi, 101 p. HC 214, sess. 1956/57. Covers the period to 1962).
Development in the iron and steel industry : special report. 1961. (v, 153 p. HC 164, sess. 1960/61. Covers the period to 1965).
Development in the iron and steel industry : special report. 1964. (v, 171 p. HC 16, sess. 1964/65. Covers the period to 1970).
Also issued in this series :
Research in the iron and steel industry : special report. 1963. (iv, 63 p.).

412

Shone, R. M. Statistics relating to the UK iron and steel industry. *J. R. Statist. Soc., Ser. A* 113 (4), 1950, pp 464–486.

413
Steel review. Rationalisation : world wide. *Steel rev.,* (45), Jan. 1967, p 9.

414
Steel review. Rationalisation in France. *Steel rev.,* (45), Jan. 1967, pp 10–15.

415
Steel review. Rationalisation in Germany. *Steel rev.,* (45), Jan. 1967, pp 16–25.

416
United Nations. *Economic Commission for Europe.* Aspects of competition between steel and other materials. New York, United Nations, 1966. 121 p.

Engineering and electrical goods

See also items 70, 949, 1059

417
Anglo-American Council on Productivity. Metal working machine tools : report of a productivity team representing the British machine tool industry which visited the United States of America in 1951. British Productivity Council, 1953. xi, 88 p.

418
British Productivity Council. A review of productivity in the diesel locomotive industry. [1954]. 21 p.

419
British Productivity Council. A review of productivity in the valves industry. 1954. 31 p.

420
Corley, T. A. B. Domestic electrical appliances. Cape, 1966. 160 p. (Studies in British industry, no. 1).

Interesting case study of industry with easy entry and low concentration. Describes structure of industry and its effect on costs and prices. Other topics : the chaotic system of distribution and of servicing ; causes of business failures ; likely effects of abolition of RPM ; insufficient market research and investment lowering competitive strength of industry.

421
Dicks-Mireaux, L. A. *and others.* Prospects for the British car industry. *Natn. Inst. econ. rev.,* (17), Sept. 1961, pp 15–47.

422
Economic Research Group of the Amsterdam-Rotterdam Bank, Banque de la Société Générale de Belgique, Deutsche Bank, Midland Bank. The electrical engineering industry in some European countries. 1965. [1], 25 p.

Compares structure, growth, price, costs, capital investment, and international trade.

423
Evans, E. W. The British machine tool industry. *Three banks rev.,* June 1964, pp 25–41.

424
Grossfield, K. The interaction of scientific, technical and economic factors in the cable industry. 1956. (M. Sc. thesis, London School of Economics).

425
Maxcy, G. *and* **Silberston,** A. The motor industry. New York, Macmillan, 1959. 245 p.

426
Ministry of Aviation. *Committee of inquiry into the aircraft industry (1964–65).* Report of the committee . . . HMSO, 1965. iv, 139 p. (Cmnd. 2853).

Chairman of committee : Lord Plowden.

427
National Economic Development Council. *Economic Development Committee for Electronics.* Electronics and the future : a report on the industry. HMSO, 1966. 35 p.

428
Needleman, L. The demand for domestic appliances : the prospects for television sets, refrigerators, washing machines and vacuum cleaners. *Natn. Inst. econ. rev.,* (12), Nov. 1960, pp 24–44.

429
Parkinson, J. R. The economics of shipbuilding in the United Kingdom. Cambridge Univ. Pr., 1960. xi, 227 p. (Univ. of Glasgow. Department of Social and Economic Research. Occasional papers, 6).

Based on the position in the 1950's. Examines : the structure of the industry ; the trend towards concentration ; international competition ; and the factors influencing the competitive position in different countries. Valuable : a table of cost elements in shipbuilding and ship-repairing (using data from 1954 census of production).

430
Political and Economic Planning. Agricultural machinery : a report on the organisation and structure of the industry, its products, and its market prospects at home and abroad. 1949. [4], 110 p. (PEP engineering reports, 1).

431
Political and Economic Planning. Locomotives : a report on the organisation and structure of the industry, its products, and its market prospects at home and abroad. 1951. [5], 75 p. (PEP engineering reports, 3).

432
Political and Economic Planning. Motor vehicles : a report on the organisation and structure of the industry, its products, and its market prospects at home and abroad. 1950. [4], 164 p. (PEP engineering reports, 2).

Textiles and clothing

433
Duxbury, D. The role of man-made fibres. *Dist. Bank rev.,* (121), March 1957, pp 18–32.

434
Hague, D. C. The economics of man-made fibres. Duckworth, 1957. 315 p. (Industrial innovation series).

435
Organisation for Economic Co-operation and Development. Textile industry in OECD countries. 1953+ Paris.

Titles varies. To 1960/61 pub. in the series *Trends in economic sectors* (1953-1959/60 by Organisation for European Economic Co-operation).

436
Robson, R. The cotton industry in Britain. Macmillan, 1957. xx, 364 p.

437
Robson, R. The man-made fibres industry. Macmillan, 1958. viii, 135 p.

438
Vibert, F. Economic problems of the cotton industry. *Oxf. econ. pap.,* new ser. 18 (3), Nov. 1966, pp 313-343.

439
Wray, M. J. The women's outerwear industry. Duckworth, 1957. 318 p. (Industrial innovation series).

Examines the competitive structure of the industry and its effect on innovation in production and marketing.

Fuel and power

440
Anglo-American Council on Productivity.
Electricity supply : report of a visit to the USA in 1949 of productivity teams representing the electricity supply industry. 1950. [4], 8, 129 p.

441
Anglo-American Council on Productivity. Gas : report of a productivity team representing the British gas industry, which visited the United States of America in 1952. British Productivity Council, 1953. xv, 194 p.

442
Brechling, F. P. R. *and* **Surrey,** A. J. An international comparison of production techniques : the coal-fired electricity generating industry. *Natn. Inst. econ. rev.,* (36), May 1966, pp 30–42.

443
Farrell, M. J. *and* **Jolly,** A. R. The structure of the British coal mining industry in 1955. *J. ind. econ.,* 11 (3), July 1963, pp 199–216.

444
Hawkins, E. K. Competition between the nationalised electricity and gas industries. *J. ind. econ.,* 1 (2), April 1953, pp 155–173.

445
House of Commons. *Select committee on nationalised industries (1956/57).* Report from the Select committee ... together with the proceedings of the Committee, minutes of evidence and appendices. HMSO, 1957. xxiv, 212 p. (HC, 304 sess. 1956/57).

The report deals with ministerial control of the nationalised industries, South of Scotland Electricity Board, North of Scotland Hydro-Electric Board, National Coal Board.

446
House of Commons. *Select committee on nationalised industries (1957/58).* Report from the Select committee ... together with the proceedings of the Committee, minutes of evidence and appendices. HMSO, 1958. xxxiv, 169 p. (HC 187-I, sess. 1957/58).

Report on the National Coal Board. See also items 445, 448, 450.

447
House of Commons. *Select committee on nationalised industries (1961/62).* Report from the Select committee ... The gas industry. HMSO ,1961. 2 v. (HC 280, 280-I, sess. 1961/62).

Vol. 1, Report and proceedings ; v. 2, Minutes of evidence, appendices and index, including 56 memoranda by area gas boards, Ministry of Power, Treasury, Gas Council and National Coal Board. Includes statements on competition with electricity and petroleum. Observations of the Gas Council and of the Minister of Power are in *Special report from the Select committee . . .,* 1962 (HC 218, sess. 1961/62) ; further observations of the Minister of Power are in *Second special report from the Select Committee . . .,* 1964 (HC 150, sess. 1963/64).

448
House of Commons. *Select committee on nationalised industries (1961/62).* Report from the Select committee ... together with the proceedings of the Committee, minutes of evidence and appendices. Reports of former Select committees : outcome of recommendations and conclusions. HMSO, 1962. xxxiii, 76 p. (HC 116, sess. 1961/62).

Studies the reports on the North of Scotland Hydro-Electric Board (item 445), the National Coal Board (items 445, 446) and the air corporations (item 512). Appendices contain replies by the Boards and a summary table of recommendations of the Select committees and of observations of the Boards and Ministries concerned.

449

House of Commons. *Select committee on nationalised industries (1962/63).* Report from the Select committee . . . The electricity supply industry. HMSO, 1963. 3 v. (HC 236-I, 236-II, 236-III, sess. 1962/63).

Vol. 1, Report and proceedings ; v. 2, Minutes of evidence ; v. 3, Appendices and index, including 84 memoranda submitted by Central Electricity Generating Board (some dealing with nuclear power and other topics) ; area electricity boards ; Electricity Council ; Ministry of Power and other Government departments ; and trade organisations. Observations of the Electricity Council and of the Minister of Power are in *First special report from the Select committee . . .,* 1964 (HC 67, sess. 1963/64).

450

House of Commons. *Select committee on nationalised industries (1965/66).* Second report from the Select committee . . . together with the proceedings of the Committee, minutes of evidence and an appendix : gas, electricity and coal industries. HMSO, 1966. vii, 59 p. (HC 77, sess. 1965/66).

One day's hearings per industry on current problems.

451

Lingard, P. A. The electricity supply industry. *Steel rev.,* (44), Oct. 1966, pp 16–20.

452

Millar, R. Oil cartel. *Cartel,* 6 (4), Oct. 1956, pp 119–121.

A criticism of the international oil cartel.

453

Ministry of Fuel and Power. *Committee of inquiry into the electricity supply industry.* Report of the committee . . . HMSO, 1956. viii, 189 p. (Cmd. 9672).

Chairman of committee : Sir Edwin Herbert.

454

Penrose, E. Monopoly and competition in the international petroleum industry. *Yr bk wld affairs,* 18, 1964, pp 150–177.

Well presented short survey of main problems.

455

Political and Economic Planning. A fuel policy for Britain : [report by a group of experts]. [1966]. [1], iii, 236 p.

A survey of Britain's energy problems, and of her fuel industries. Energy forecasts, fuel policy in general and coal policy in particular are critically reviewed.

456

United States. *Federal Trade Commission.* The international petroleum cartel : staff report to the . . . commission, submitted to the Subcommittee on monopoly of the Select committee on small business, United States Senate, August 22, 1952. Washington, Gov't. Print. Off., 1952. xii, 378 p.

Transport

General

457

Dear, D. M. Some thoughts on the comparative costs of road and rail transport. *Bull. Oxf. Univ. Inst. Statist.,* 24 (1), Feb. 1962, pp 61–72.

458

Foster, C. D. The transport problem. Blackie, 1963. xiii, 354 p.

Discusses competition and co-ordination, price policies of public enterprise, subsidisation and cross-subsidisation, also choice of criteria for a transport policy. Useful references.

459

House of Commons. *Select committee on nationalised industries (1964/65).* Report from the Select committee . . . London Transport. HMSO, 1965. 2 v. (HC 313, 313-I, sess. 1964/65).

Vol. 1, Report and proceedings, includes chapters on capital structure and financial results, research and development, and paying for an adequate service. Vol. 2, Minutes of evidence, appendices and index, includes memoranda submitted by London Transport Board, Ministry of Transport, Treasury, Greater London Council, Transport Tribunal and British European Airways. Observations of the London Transport Board are in *Second special report from the Select committee . . .,* 1965 (HC 14, sess. 1965/66).

460

Institute of Municipal Treasurers and Accountants and Institute of Cost and Works Accountants Joint Committee. Transport costing. Gee, 1953. 23 p.

Investigates costs and costing procedures in road haulage, including costs incurred in investment, repairs, and fuel.

461

Journal of transport economics and policy. Vol. 1 1967+ London School of Economics.

Published 3 times a year.

462

Meyer, J. R. *and others.* Economics of competition in the transportation industries. Cambridge (Mass.), Harvard Univ. Pr., 1959. 359 p. (Harvard economic studies, vol. 107).

463

Milne, A. M. The economics of inland transport. Pitman, 1955. 292 p.

464

Ministry of Transport. Reorganisation of the nationalised transport undertakings. HMSO, 1960. 14 p. (Cmnd. 1248).

465

Ministry of Transport. Traffic in towns : a study of the long term problems of traffic in urban areas. Reports of the Steering group and Working group . . . HMSO, 1963. 224 p.

Chairman of Working group : Colin Buchanan.

466

Ministry of Transport. The transport needs of Great Britain in the next twenty years. HMSO, 1963. 27 p.

Report of a group under the chairmanship of Sir Robert Hall. Contains forecasts of rail and road traffic up to 1980. Emphasises importance of relating transport policies to policies for investment, location, education, town planning, car ownership, etc. Advocates more research into the nature of transport demands.

467

Ministry of Transport. Transport policy. HMSO, 1966. iii, 36 p. (Cmnd. 3057).

468

Ministry of Transport. *Committee of inquiry into the major ports of Great Britain.* Report of the Committee . . . HMSO, 1962. 264 p. (Cmnd. 1824).

Chairman of committee : The Viscount Rochdale.

469

Munby, D. L. The roads as economic assets. *Bull. Oxf. Univ. Inst. Statist.,* 22 (4), Nov. 1960, pp 273-297.

470

Ray, G. F. *and* **Crum,** R. E. Transport : notes and comments. *Natn. Inst. econ. rev.,* (24), May 1963, pp 23–41.

471

Sargent, J. R. British transport policy. Oxford, Clarendon Pr., 1958. xi, 164 p.

Examines post-war costs and charges for transport by road and rail. Special attention is paid to problems of indirect costs and unremunerative services. A short chapter on conclusions and recommendations. Useful references.

472

Sharp, C. H. The allocation of goods traffic between road and rail. *J. ind. econ.,* 7 (3), July 1959, pp 206–213.

473

Sharp, C. H. The problem of transport. Oxford, London, Pergamon Pr., 1965. [2], 202 p. (Commonwealth and international library. Commerce, economics and administration division).

474

Stewart, J. M. W. A pricing system for roads. Oliver & Boyd, 1965. v, 80 p. (Univ. of Glasgow social and economic studies. Occasional papers, no. 4).

475

Walker, G. Competition in transport as an instrument of policy. *Econ. j.,* 66 (263), Sept. 1956, pp 409–418.

476

Walker, G. Transport policy before and after 1953. *Oxf. econ. pap.,* new ser. 5 (1), March 1953, pp 90–116.

Railways

477

Beesley, M. E. Financial criteria for investment in railways. *Bull. Oxf. Univ. Inst. Statist.,* 24 (1), Feb. 1962, pp 31–50.

478

British Railways Board. The reshaping of British Railways. HMSO, 1963. 2 v.

The Beeching report.

479

Calvert, R. The future of Britain's railways. Allen & Unwin, 1965. 175 p.

Focuses on wide-spread bias in favour of road transport and against rail transport in questions of financial principles and improvements. Compares developments in Britain with those in US, France, and Germany.

480

Foster, C. D. Some notes on railway costs and costing. *Bull. Oxf. Univ. Inst. Statist.,* 21 (1), Feb. 1962, pp 73–104.

481

Glassborow, D. W. The comparison of partial productivity ratios for national railway systems. *Bull. Oxf. Univ. Inst. Statist.,* 24 (1), Feb. 1962, pp 148–153.

482

House of Commons. *Select committee on nationalised industries (1959/60).* Report from the Select committee . . . together with the proceedings of the Committee. British Railways. HMSO, 1960. cvi, 505 p. (HC 254, sess. 1959/60).

Observations of the British Transport Commission and of the Minister of Transport are in *Special report from the Select committee . . .*, 1961 (HC 163, sess. 1960/61).

483

Mills, G. *and* **Howe,** M. On planning railway investment. *Bull. Oxf. Univ. Inst. Statist.,* 24 (1), Feb. 1962, pp 51–59.

484

Ministry of Transport. Railway policy. HMSO, 1967. [1], 69 p. (Cmnd. 3439).

Includes, as an annex, a policy review submitted by a joint Ministry of Transport and British Railways Board steering group, assisted by consultants. Reviews outline plans for financial and managerial reconstruction of British Railways. Divides services into sections which are or can be made profitable and those unprofitable but socially necessary. Measures recommended refer to : creation of an acceptable basis for costing, pricing and financial control ; keeping railways competitive ; financing investment programme ; criteria for investment appraisal. Includes information on work in progress commissioned by the steering group, on pricing policy, unremunerative services, etc., which will result in further reports.

485
Munby, D. L. Economic problems of British Railways. *Bull. Oxf. Univ. Inst. Statist.,* 24 (1), Feb. 1962, pp 1–29.

486
Munby, D. L. The productivity of British Railways. *Bull. Oxf. Univ. Inst. Statist.,* 24 (1), Feb. 1962, pp 113–145.

487
Munby, D. L. The reshaping of British Railways. *J. ind. econ.,* 11 (3), July 1963, pp 161–182.

488
Oort, C. J. Costing and rate-setting in the Netherlands railway system. *Bull. Oxf. Univ. Inst. Statist.,* 24 (1), Feb. 1962, pp 105–112.

489
Wickham, S. The development of the French railways under the French four-year plans. *Bull. Oxf. Univ. Inst. Statist.,* 24 (1), Feb. 1962, pp 168–184.

Shipping

490
Ferguson, A. R. *and others.* The economic value of the United States merchant marine. Evanston (Illinois), Northwestern Univ. Transportation Center, 1961. xxii, 545 p.

Contains much material relevant for ocean transport in general. Six contributors deal with various aspects of the economics of shipping, such as the factors determining costs and prices, the economics of subsidies, the character of liner markets and the optimal size of liner firms. Many data, up to 1957. Eight-page bibliography.

491
Frihagen, A. Linjekonferanser og Kartell-Lorgivning. Oslo, Universitetsforlaget, 1963.

English summary. A lawyer's exploration of comparative law on shipping conferences.

492
Goss, R. O. The regulation of international transport. 1. Transport by sea. *Wld today,* 21 (10), Oct. 1965, pp 410–418.

493
Goss, R. O. USA legislation and the foreign shipowner. *J. ind. econ.,* 12 (1), Nov. 1963, pp 1–19.

Regulation of shipping competition by the USA.

494
Grossman, W. L. Ocean freight rates. Cambridge (Md.), Cornell Maritime Pr., 1956. x, 214 p.

Thorough investigation into competitive and discriminatory forces determining ocean freight rates. Interesting

appendices give texts of conference and exclusive patronage agreements, and extracts of conference tariffs.

495
Kojima, S. The effects of shipping competition on freight rates : a review of the normal price theory. *Kyoto Univ. econ. rev.,* 2 (1), July 1927, pp 63–88.

496
Kojima, S. Shipping combinations as seen from the viewpoint of freight theory. *Kyoto Univ. econ. rev.,* 1 (1), July 1926, pp 91–110.

497
McLachlan, D. L. The price policy of liner conferences. *Scott. j. political economy,* 10 (3), Nov. 1963, pp 322–335.

Suggests strong correlation between liner costs and liner freight rates.

498
McLachlan, D. L. Pricing in ocean transportation. 1959. (Ph.D. thesis, University of Leeds).

499
Marx, D. International shipping cartels : a study of industrial self-regulation by shipping conferences. Princeton (NJ), Princeton Univ. Pr. ; London, Oxford Univ. Pr., 1953. xiii, 323 p.

Description and analysis of shipping conferences. Among subjects discussed : effects of tramp-rationalization schemes, non-conference liner competition, tying arrangements such as deferred rebates and exclusive patronage contracts ; regulation of international ocean transport.

500
Marx, D. Regulation of international liner shipping and 'freedom of the seas'. *J. ind. econ.,* 16 (1), Nov. 1967, pp 46–62.

501
Royal commission on shipping rings (1906-09). Report of the . . . commission . . . HMSO, 1909. iv, 120 p. (Cd. 4668).

Chairman of Commission : Arthur Cohen. A primary source.

502
Sprigings, P. V. C. The effect of American legislation on liner conferences. *Inst. transp. j.,* 31 (3), March 1965, pp 104–106.

503
Sturmey, S. G. British shipping and world competition. Athlone Pr., 1962. x, 436 p.

History of industry. Causes for decline. Of special importance : chap. VIII, Enemies of competition in the post-war years ; chap. IX, Flags of convenience ; chap. XIII, The conference system. Bibliography.

504

Sturmey, S. G. On the pricing of tramp ship freight service. Bergen, Institute for Shipping Research, [1965]. 20 p.

505

Sturmey, S. G. Shipping in the 1960's. Bergen, Institute for Shipping Research, 1965.

Lecture delivered at the Institute. Deals with problems connected with developments in passenger shipping, cargo liners, large-size ships, tanker fleets and the possible expansion in the use of canals and in the size of container ships and ports.

506

Svendsen, A. S. Sea transport and shipping economics. Bremen, Institut für Schiffahrtsforschung, 1958. 473 p. (Weltschiffahrts-archiv, 5).

Text in German and English. Collection of lectures on shipping economics. Of special relevance : Chapters VII-IX on determination of freight rates under free competition ; objects and methods of limiting competition ; problem of second hand tonnage. Bibliography.

507

Thorburn, T. Supply and demand of water transport : studies in cost and revenue structures of ships, ports and transport buyers with respect to their effects on supply and demand of water transport of goods. Stockholm, School of Economics, Business Research Institute, 1960. x, 235 p.

Basic book for shipping economics. Stimulating appendix : competition between shipowners, railway companies and road transport undertakings for transport of goods ; based on a model. Bibliography.

508

Thornton, R. H. British shipping. 2nd ed. Cambridge Univ. Pr., 1959. viii, 274 p. (English institutions ; ed. by Sir George Barnes).

509

United States. *Congress. House. Committee on the Judiciary (87th Cong., 2nd sess.).* The ocean freight industry : report of the Antitrust subcommittee (Subcommittee no. 5) of the Committee . . . Washington, Gov't. Print. Off., 1962. xii, 399 p.

The 'Celler report'.

Air transport

510

Caves, R. E. Air transport and its regulations ; an independent study. Cambridge (Mass.), Harvard Univ. Pr., 1962. 479 p. (Harvard economic studies, vol. 120).

511

Gill, F. W. *and* **Bates,** G. L. Airline competition : a study of the effects of competition on the quality and price of airline service and the self-sufficiency of the United States domestic airlines. Boston, Harvard Univ. Division of Research, 1949. xv, 704 p. (Harvard Univ. Graduate School of Business Administration, George F. Baker Foundation publication).

512

House of Commons. *Select committee on nationalised industries (1958/59).* Report from the Select Committee . . . together with the proceedings of the Committee, minutes of evidence and appendices. The air corporations. HMSO, 1959. lxxvi, 369 p. (HC 213, sess. 1958/59).

Includes competition with independent airlines and future developments in civil air transport. Replies of the corporations and comments of the Minister of Aviation are in *Special report from the Select committee* . . . 1960. (HC 339, sess. 1959/60). See also item 448.

513

House of Commons. *Select committee on nationalised industries (1963/64).* Report from the Select committee . . . British Overseas Airways Corporation. HMSO, 1964. 2 v. (HC 240, 240-I, sess. 1963/64).

Vol. 1, Report and proceedings ; v. 2, Minutes of evidence, appendices and index, including memoranda submitted by BOAC and Ministry of Aviation. Observations of BOAC and the Minister of Aviation are in *First special report from the Select committee* . . . 1965 (HC 12, sess. 1965/66).

514

House of Commons. *Select committee on nationalised industries (1966/67).* Second report from the Select committee . . . together with further proceedings of the Committee, minutes of evidence and appendices. British European Airways. HMSO, 1967. lxxiii, 376 p. (HC 673, sess. 1966/67).

Appendices contain memoranda submitted by Board of Trade, Treasury, Ministry of Technology, BEA, Air Transport Licensing Board, British Independent Air Transport Association, and Hawker-Siddeley Aviation Ltd.

515

International Civil Aviation Organization. Air freight : trends and developments in the world air freight industry ; a preliminary study and forecast. Montreal, 1962. iv, 111 p.

Based on data for 1951-1961. Forecasts for 1965, 1970, 1975. Includes sample list of commodities carried by air.

516

Masefield, P. G. Air transport : a statistical and general review of its economic problems. Manchester, Manchester Statistical Society, 1954. 27 p.

517

Masefield, P. G. Some economic factors in air transport operation. *Inst. Transp. j.,* 24 (3), March 1951, pp 79–108.

518

Ministry of Aviation. *Air freight working party.* Report of the . . . working party. HMSO, 1963. [1], ii, 14 p. (C.A.P. 192).

519

Sealy, K. R. *and* **Herdson,** P. C. L. Air freight and Anglo-European trade : a sample study. 1961. 87 p.

Empirical study of competitive position of air transport industry ; compares total cost of distribution when related to air and surface transport.

520

Wheatcroft, S. F. The economics of European air transport. Manchester, Manchester Univ. Pr., 1956. xxii, 358 p.

Problems of size (of aircraft and of airline operation). Part II : competition and regulation. Questions of parallel airlines, of pooling, of tariff regulation.

521

Wheatcroft, S. F. The use and interpretation of air transport statistics. *Trans. Manchr Statist. Soc.,* June 1951, pp 11–18.

Gives principal sources of air transport statistics and surveys methods of measurement.

Distribution

522

Adelman, M. A. A & P ; a study in price-cost behavior and public policy. Cambridge (Mass.), Harvard Univ. Pr. ; London, Oxford Univ. Pr., 1959. 537 p. (Harvard economic studies vol. 113).

This study of the Great Atlantic & Pacific Tea Co. is an important contribution to the scarce literature on the economics of distribution.

523

Anglo-American Council on Productivity. Retailing : report of a productivity team representing British retailing which visited the United States of America in 1952. 1952. 82 p.

524

Bartels, R., *ed.* Comparative marketing : wholesaling in fifteen countries. Homewood (Illinois), Irwin, 1963. xii, 317 p.

Sponsored by the American Marketing Association.

525

Bellamy, R. [Study of retail distribution : summary report of an enquiry]. *Bull. Oxf. Univ. Inst. Statist.,* 8, 1946 : [part 1], The changing pattern of retail distribution, (8), Aug. 1946, pp 237–260 ; [pt. 2], Size and success in retail distribution, (10), Oct. 1946, pp 324–339 ; [pt. 3], Private & social cost in retail distribution, (11), Nov. 1946, pp 345–351.

526

Board of Trade. Census of distribution and other services 1950. HMSO, 1953-55. 3 v.

Contents: Vol. 1, Retail and service trades, area tables ; v. 2, Retail and service trades, general tables ; v. 3, Wholesale trades.

527

Board of Trade. Report on the census of distribution and other services, 1957. HMSO, 1959. 83 p.

Additional data have been published in the following articles in the *Board of Trade journal:*
Rapid growth of mail order trading (19 June 1959, pp 1389–1390).
Automatic machine trading (19 June 1959, pp 1390–1391).
Analysis of credit trading in 1957 (21 Aug. 1959, pp 73–79).
Report on self-service trading (4 Sept. 1959, pp 213–217).
Analysis of retail sales, 1950 and 1957 (2 Oct. 1959, pp 425–427. Correction, 23 Oct. 1959, p 590).
Department store trading (30 Oct. 1959, pp 629–634).
Further analyses of retail shops (5 Aug. 1960, pp 295–298).
Structure and growth of multiple retail enterprises (9 June 1961, pp 1333–1341).

528

Board of Trade. Report on the census of distribution and other services, 1961. HMSO, 1963-64. 14 parts.

Contents: Part 1, Establishment tables (contains an introduction) ; pts 2-13, Area tables ; pt 14, Organisation tables. Additional data have been published in the following articles in the *Board of Trade journal:*
Manufacturers' direct sales to the public in 1961 (15 Feb. 1963, p 383).
Sales by mail order (31 May 1963, pp 1249–1251).
Sales from mobile shops (19 July 1963, pp 133–134).
Analyses of retail establishments (20 Sept. 1963, pp 622–627).
Department store trading (4 Oct. 1963, pp 742–744).
Instalment credit trade (22 Nov. 1963, pp 1152–1157).
Self-service trading (20 Dec. 1963, pp 1372–1377).
Retail trade in main shopping centres (17 Jan. 1964, pp 83–87).
Analyses of retail organizations (7 Feb. 1964, pp 263–269).
The regional pattern of retailing (30 Apr. 1965, pp 942–950).

529

British Productivity Council. [A review of productivity in] retailing. [1957]. 63 p. (British productivity review, 28).

530

European Productivity Agency. Productivity in the wholesale trade. Paris, 1956. 157 p. (EPA project no. 153).

531

Fulop, C. Buying by voluntary chains and other associations of retailers and wholesalers. Allen & Unwin, 1962. 160 p.

532
Fulop, C. Competition for consumers : a study of the changing channels of distribution. Deutsch, 1964. xii, 323 p.

Published for the Institute of Economic Affairs. Deals mainly with recent developments and innovations at the retail end ; a few pages on wholesale-retail integration and wholesale self-service. Bibliography.

533
Fulop, C. Revolution in retailing. Barrie and Rockliff, 1961. 47 p. (Hobart papers, 9).

Published for the Institute of Economic Affairs. Reprinted, with a postscript, in *Ancient or modern ? Essays in economic efficiency and growth,* edited by Ralph Harris. (Institute of Economic Affairs, 1965. Hobart papers, Collected editions, v. 2).

534
George, K. D. Productivity in distribution. Cambridge Univ. Pr., 1966. 107 p. (Univ. of Cambridge Department of Applied Economics. Occasional papers, 8).

Based on the census of distribution. 1961.

535
Hall, M. Developments in British retailing since 1957. *Lond. Camb. econ. bull.,* (new ser. 48), Dec. 1963, pp viii–xi.

536
Hall, M., **Knapp,** I. *and* **Winsten,** C. B. Distribution in Great Britain and North America ; a study in structure and productivity. Oxford Univ. Pr., 1961. xv, 231 p.

Deals with retail and wholesale trade.

537
Hall, M. Distributive trading : an economic analysis. Hutchinson, 1950. 203 p. (Hutchinson's university library).

538
Hill, S. R. The distributive system. Oxford, London, Pergamon Pr., 1966. ix, 166 p. (The Commonwealth and international library. Social administration, training, economics and production division).

539
Holton, R. H. Price discrimination at retail : the supermarket case. *J. ind. econ.,* 6 (1), Oct. 1957, pp 13–32.

540
Hood, J. *and* **Yamey,** B. S. Imperfect competition in retail trade. *Economica,* new ser. 18 (70), May 1951. pp 119–137.

541
Hughes, J. D. *and* **Pollard,** S. Gross margins in retail distribution. *Oxf. econ. pap.,* new ser. 9 (1), Feb. 1957, pp 75–87.

Based on census of distribution, 1950.

542
Jefferys, J. B. The distribution of consumer goods : a factual study of methods and costs in the United Kingdom in 1938 . . . Cambridge Univ. Pr., 1950. xix, 430 p. (National Institute of Economic and Social Research. Economic and social studies, 9).

543
Jefferys, J. B. Retail trading in Britain, 1850-1950 : a study of trends in retailing, with special reference to the development of co-operative, multiple shop and department store methods of trading. Cambridge Univ. Pr., 1954. xvii, 497 p. (National Institute of Economic and Social Research. Economic and social studies, 13).

544
Jefferys, J. B. *and* **Knee,** D. Retailing in Europe : present structure and future trends. Macmillan. 1962. xiv, 177 p.

545
Lewis, W. A. Competition in retail trade. *Economica,* new ser. 12 (48), Nov. 1945, pp 202–234.

546
McNally, A. P. Investment and productivity in retailing. *J. ind. econ.,* 15 (1), Nov. 1966, pp 1–15.

An appendix includes estimated productivity 'scores' for 175 towns in Great Britain.

547
McClelland, W. G. Costs and competition in retailing. Macmillan, 1966. xvii, 334 p.

548
McClelland, W. G. Economics of the supermarket. *Econ. j.,* 72 (285), March 1962, pp 154–170.

549
McClelland, W. G. Studies in retailing. Oxford, Blackwell, 1963. ix, 182 p.

Collection of essays. Shows changing structure of retail trade, using results of 1961 census of distribution. Discusses problems of price and investment policies and of size.

550
Organisation for Economic Co-operation and Development. Analysis and evaluation of distribution structures and distribution channels in selected consumer goods industries. [Paris, 1963]. [1], 100 p.

Report on a research project. Includes summaries of selected papers given at an international conference in Rome, 1963, and summary reports on three model studies of distribution (beer in Italy ; footwear in France ; radio and television sets in Scandinavian countries). Covers wholesale and retail trade.

551
Organisation for European Economic Co-operation. Productivity in the distributive trade in Europe : wholesale and retail aspects, [by] J. B. Jefferys [and others]. Paris, 1954. 118 p.

552

Pennance, F. G. and **Yamey,** B. S. Competition in the retail grocery trade, 1850-1939. *Economica,* new ser. 22 (88), Nov. 1955, pp 303–317.

553

Pollard, S. and **Hughes,** J. D. Costs in retail distribution in Great Britain, 1950-7. *Oxf. econ. pap.,* new ser. 13 (2), June 1961, pp 166–183.

554

Smith, H. Retail distribution : a critical analysis. 2nd ed. Oxford Univ. Pr., 1948. viii, 222 p.

555

Stacey, N. A. H. and **Wilson,** A. The changing pattern of distribution. Rev. ed. Oxford, London, Pergamon Pr., 1965. xiii, 427 p. (The Commonwealth and international library. Business management division).

556

Walrand, I. M. Productivity in distribution. 1964. (M. Sc. thesis, London School of Economics).

557

Yamey, B. S. The price policy of co-operative societies. *Economica,* new ser. 17 (65), Feb. 1950, pp 23–42.

Other industries

558

Anglo-American Council on Productivity. Fruit and vegetable utilisation : report of a visit to the USA in 1951 of a British productivity team on fruit and vegetable utilisation. 1952. xii, 56 p.

559

Anglo-American Council on Productivity. Packet foods : report of a visit to the USA in 1951 of a productivity team representing the British packet foods industry. 1951. xii, 71 p.

560

British Productivity Council. [A review of productivity in the brush industry]. [1956]. 24 p. (Productivity review, 25).

561

British Productivity Council. A review of productivity in the building industry. [1954]. 47 p.

562

British Productivity Council. A review of productivity in the cakes and biscuits industry. [1955]. 30 p.

563

Corlett, W. J. The economic development of detergents. Duckworth, 1958. 208 p. (Industrial innovation series).

564

Edwards, H. R. Competition and monopoly in the British soap industry. Oxford, Clarendon Pr., 1962. xi, 270 p.

The title of the book is misleading. Part 1 of the study deals with price and output formation in manufacturing industry in general. This part discusses the concepts of competition, monopoly, firm, industry, and works with a static and a dynamic model of price determination. Part 2 deals with the soap and detergent industry as a case study in oligopoly.

565

Evely, R. The battle of the detergents. *Cartel,* 1, Jan. 1954, pp 10–18.

566

House of Commons. *Select committee on nationalised industries (1966/67).* First report from the Select committee . . . The Post Office. HMSO, 1967. 2 v. (HC 340, 340-I, sess. 1966/67).

The first comprehensive enquiry by an outside body for over 30 years. In vol. 1, *Report and proceedings,* there are sections on productivity (chapters 4 and 16) ; finances (chapters 5, 15 and 16) ; paying for telecommunications services, including unremunerative services (chapter 12) ; research and development (chapter 14). Vol. 2, *Minutes of evidence, appendices and index,* includes memoranda on structure of the telecommunications industry ; manufacturing by the Swedish Telecommunications Administration ; and on the industrial activities of the Swedish Post Office. Observations of the Post Office are in *First special report from the Select committee . . .* 1967 (HC 576, sess. 1966/67).

567

National Economic Development Council. The construction industry. HMSO, 1964. vi, 22 p.

568

National Economic Development Office. *Economic Development Committee for Civil Engineering.* Efficiency in road construction : a report by a working party . . . HMSO, 1966. ix, 51 p.

Pleads for more concentration in this section of the civil engineering industry via amalgamation or jointly owned subsidiaries specialising in road construction.

569

National Institute of Economic and Social Research. Paper and board : trends and prospects. *Natn. Inst. econ. rev.,* (32) May 1965, pp 43–69.

570

Political and Economic Planning. The British film industry, 1958. *Planning,* 24 (424), 23 June 1958, pp 131–170.

571

Royal Commission on the Press (1947-49). Report. HMSO, 1949. v, 363 p. (Cmd. 7700).

572
Royal Commission on the Press (1961-62). Report.
HMSO, 1962. 239 p. (Cmnd. 1811).

573
Steele, H. Monopoly and competition in the ethical drug
market. *J. law econ.,* 5, Oct. 1962, pp 131–163.

574
Strauss, E. The structure of the English milk industry.
J. R. Statist. Soc., ser. A 125 (2), 1962, pp 232–242.

575
Sturmey, S. G. The economic development of radio.
Duckworth, 1958. 284 p. (Industrial innovation series).

576
Thomas, D. Competition in radio. 2nd ed. Institute of
Economic Affairs, 1966. 28 p. (IEA occasional papers, 5).

3 Restrictive practices

See also items 400, 452, 454, 456

3.1 Restrictive practices : general

This section deals with the general phenomenon of restrictive practices, their causes, implementation and effects. It includes G. B. Richardson's article (item 586) on the theory of restrictive practices. The 'per se' rule is examined by J. B. Heath (item 590) and A. Phillips (item 585). In two Canadian publications (items 577, 578) evidence on loss-leader selling is made available. Publications concerned with two special types of restrictive practice—information agreements and resale price maintenance—are listed in sections 3.2 and 3.3 (pages 45-46). Further references to restrictive practices will be found in other parts of the bibliography, e.g. under *Entry* (page 28), *Specific Industries* (especially *Shipping*, page 38), *Prices and Costs* (page 55) and under *Regulation of Restrictive Practices* (page 46).

577
Canada. *Restrictive Trade Practices Commission.* Material collected by Director of investigation and research in connection with an inquiry into 'loss-leader' selling. Ottawa, Dept. of Justice, 1954. xvii, 308 p.

Based partly on questionnaires sent to manufacturers, trade associations, distributors and consumer groups, on nature and effect of loss-leader selling (including use of coupons). Also contains useful information collected from other sources.

578
Canada. *Restrictive Trade Practices Commission.* Report on an inquiry into loss-leader selling. Ottawa, Dept. of Justice, 1955. xxi, 278 p.

Based on public hearings conducted by the Commission in 1954.

579
Cuthbert, N. *and* **Black,** W. Restrictive practices in the food trades. *J. ind. econ.,* 8 (1), Oct. 1959, pp 33–57 ; 10 (1), Nov. 1961, pp 51–77.

580
General Agreement on Tariffs and Trade. *Contracting parties.* Restrictive business practices [by J. L'Huillier and C. A. Junod]. Geneva, 1959. 98 p.

Deals with causes and types of restrictive practices and with measures strengthening and weakening these practices.

581
Heath, J. B. Restrictive practices and after. *Manchr sch. econ. social stud.,* 29 (2), May 1961, pp 173–202.

Examines the consequences of abandonment of restrictive agreements that took place before mid-1959.

582
Heath, J. B. Still not enough competition ? Business restrictive practices re-examined. Institute of Economic Affairs, 1963. 47 p. (Hobart paper, 11).

First published 1961 as *Not enough competition ?* Reprinted with a postscript in *Ancient or modern ? Essays in economic efficiency and growth,* 2nd ed. (Institute of Economic Affairs, 1964).

583
Hutton, G., *ed.* Source book on restrictive practices in Britain . . . with a select bibliography by Jossleyn Hennessy. Institute of Economic Affairs, 1966. 71 p. (Research monographs, 7).

Part II gives examples of restrictive practices applied by labour.

584
Knox, F. *and* **Hennessy,** J. Restrictive practices in the building industry. Institute of Economic Affairs, 1966. v, 54 p. (Research monographs, 1).

585
Phillips, A. A critique of United States experience with price-fixing agreements and the 'per se' rule. *J. ind. econ.,* 8 (1), Oct. 1959, pp 13–32.

586
Richardson, G. B. The theory of restrictive trade practices. *Oxf. econ. pap.,* new ser. 17 (3), Nov. 1965, pp 432–449.

587
Sich, R. L. Evidence of detriment caused by restrictive trading agreements. *Oxf. econ. pap.,* new ser. 17 (3), Nov. 1965, pp 347–353.

588
Sich, R. L. Restrictive trading agreements and the public interest. *J. bus. law,* April 1962, pp 137–145.

589
Skeoch, L. A., *ed.* Restrictive trade practices in Canada : selected readings. Toronto, McClelland and Stewart, 1966. xi, 356 p.

Economists and lawyers assess problems of monopoly legislation, mergers, patents and RPM in the light of Canadian experience. Many references and documents.

590
Symposium on price competition and antitrust policy. *Northwestern Univ. law rev.,* 57 (2), May-June 1962, pp 137–205.

Concentrates on various aspects of price-fixing and price-fixing prosecutions. *Contents:* Price competition and the price fixing rule—preface and perspective, by J. A. Rahl ; The frequency of price fixing : an indication ; The 'per se' rule in the light of British experience, by J. B. Heath ; The impact of the Robinson-Patman act on pricing flexibility, by H. L. Shniderman ; Do administered prices involve an antitrust problem ? by R. B. Heflebower.

3.2 Information agreements

See also items 626, 660

The bibliography does not contain any major work concentrating on information agreements. However, valuable articles have been published by J. B. Heath (item 591), D. P. O'Brien and D. Swann (item 592). References to information agreements in the few books listed are not necessarily indexed there under this heading but rather under 'collusion', 'restrictive arrangements', etc. Some publications entered in the section *Regulation of restrictive practices* (page 46) also contain relevant material. (*Information agreements, competition and efficiency,* by D. P. O'Brien and D. Swann (Macmillan, 1968. 248 p.) is a recent important addition to the literature on this topic.)

591
Heath, J. B. Some economic consequences [of restrictive practices legislation]. *Econ. j.,* 70 (279), Sept. 1960, pp 474–484.

Surveys the development of information agreements.

592
O'Brien, D. P. *and* **Swann,** D. Information agreements—a problem in search of a policy. *Manchr sch. econ. social stud.,* 34 (3), Sept. 1966, pp 285–306.

Describes the position of open price agreements in Great Britain since the Restrictive trade practices Act 1956. 'A further contribution' is in *Manchr sch. econ. social stud.,* 35 (3), Sept. 1967, pp 285–288.

593
Organisation for Economic Co-operation and Development. Information agreements. Paris, 1967. 57, vii p.

Surveys the historical development, nature, extent, effects of and legal attitudes towards information agreements (in OECD countries). The seven page bibliography includes many German references.

594
Peacock, P. D. The law of open pricing in the United States and Britain : a comparative analysis. *Int. comp. law q.,* 16 (3), July 1967, pp 613–629.

Uses case studies to compare British and American legal approach to information agreements.

595
Richardson, G. B. Price notification schemes. *Oxf. econ. pap.,* 19 (3), Nov. 1967, pp 359–369.

596
Whiteman, P. G. The new judicial approach to the Restrictive trade practices Act 1956. *Mod. law rev.,* 30 (4), July 1967, pp 398–425.

Thorough study of court cases dealing with information agreements, including post-notification agreements. Examines definition of 'agreement' and 'arrangement' ; surveys concepts emerging in judgements such as 'understanding', 'real intention', 'arousing of expectations', 'concerted action', 'observed conduct', 'similarity of behaviour', 'essential purpose'.

3.3 Resale price maintenance

Listed below are general works on resale price maintenance (RPM) dealing with the development and extent of RPM, its impact on the competitive process, on producers, retailers and consumers, with the effects of the abolition of RPM, the arguments and evidence used by advocates and opponents of RPM, and with the problems of public policy on RPM.

The most thorough treatment of the subject can be found in B. S. Yamey's publications (items 613–615). S. Gammelgaar's book (item 603) is a useful work for reference. Arguments used for and against RPM will also be found in the reports of cases brought before the Restrictive Practices Court (see Appendix 3, page 96). In view of the frequent use of Canadian data relating to the effects of abolishing RPM, L. A. Skeoch's article (item 611) is important.

597
Andrews, P. W. S. *and* **Friday,** F. A. Fair trade : resale price maintenance re-examined. Macmillan, 1960. 84 p.

For discussion see item 601.

598
Board of Trade. A statement on resale price maintenance : being a trade practice which prevents shopkeepers from reducing certain prices to the public. HMSO, 1951. 12 p. (Cmd. 8274).

599
Board of Trade. *Committee on resale price maintenance (1947/49).* Report of the committee . . . HMSO, 1949. vi, 122 p. (Cmd. 7696).

Chairman of committee : G. H. Lloyd Jacob.

600
Board of Trade. *Committee on resale price maintenance (1947/49).* Statement submitted by R. Cohen, R. F. Kahn, W. B. Reddaway and J. Robinson, to the Committee on resale price maintenance. *Bull. Oxf. Univ. Inst. Econ. Stat.,* 26 (2), May 1964, pp 113–121.

601
Borts, G. H. The recent controversy over resale price maintenance. *J. R. Statist. Soc.,* ser. A 124 (2), 1961, pp 244–249.

Reviews items 597 and 614.

602
Federation of British Industries. Resale prices Act 1964 : a guide for the industrialist. 1964. [1], iii, 67 p.

603
Gammelgaard, S. Resale price maintenance. Paris, European Productivity Agency, 1958. 114 p. (EPA project no. 238).

Useful descriptive reference book : characteristics, types, techniques, extent of RPM ; legislation in nine countries ; arguments in favour of RPM ; economic effects on trade and industry.

604
Gould, J. R. *and* **Preston,** L. E. Resale price maintenance and retail outlets. *Economica,* 32 (127), Aug. 1965, pp 302–312.

Constructs model to demonstrate that when market demand depends on volume of retail service and number of outlets, increased profit margin achieved through RPM might increase either or both.

605
Heath, J. B. Free prices—what progress ? *Banker,* 110 (408), Feb. 1960, pp 107–111.

606
Korah, V. The Resale prices Act 1964. *J. bus. law,* Jan. 1965, pp 6–14, 123–129.

607
Leyland, N. H. Comment on resale price maintenance. *J. ind. econ.,* 8 (3), June 1960, pp 290–292.

608
Macdonald, I. A. Resale price maintenance. Butterworths, 1964. xxi, 247 p. (Also, Supplement, 1965 (vi, 21 p.)).

A lawyer's case guidance to the law. One section on the laws of other countries, including Common Market.

609
Pickering, J. F. The enforcement of resale price maintenance 1955-64. *Pub. law,* Autumn 1965, pp 221–236.

610
Pickering, J. F. Resale price maintenance in practice. Allen & Unwin, 1966. 236 p.

611
Skeoch, L. A. The abolition of resale price maintenance : some notes on Canadian experience. *Economica,* new ser. 31 (123), Aug. 1964.

Discusses, with examples, misconceptions about Canadian experience.

612
United States. *Federal Trade Commission.* Report . . . on resale price maintenance. Washington, Gov't. Print. Off., 1945. lxiv, 872 p.

613
Yamey, B. S. The economics of resale price maintenance. Pitman, 1954. ix, 182 p.

614
Yamey, B. S. Resale price maintenance and shopper's choice. 4th ed. Institute of Economic Affairs, 1964. 58 p. (Hobart paper, 1).

For discussion see item 601.

615
Yamey, B. S., *ed.* Resale price maintenance : studies . . . Weidenfeld and Nicolson, 1966. vii, 303 p.

Studies, by various authors, of RPM in Canada, USA, Sweden, Denmark, EEC, Ireland and the UK ; edited and introduced by B. S. Yamey. Describes development and effects of RPM and of laws relating to it. Analyses arguments for and against RPM.

3.4 Regulation of restrictive practices

3.41 Regulation of restrictive practices : general

See also items 9, 24, 26, 31, 35, 43, 44, 51, 182, 209, 328, 585, 589, 975, 1117

Only a small fraction of the extensive literature on anti-monopoly legislation in various countries, especially in the USA, can be accommodated in a selective bibliography. Publications by the British Institute of International and Comparative Law (item 618), the *Proceedings* of the International conference on control of restrictive business practices (item 623), H. L. Pinner's encyclopaedia (item 628), the OECD *Guide to legislation* (item 627), and other international surveys, e.g. by the US Department of State (item 632) and by Japan's Fair Trade Commission (item 624), provide ample information.

An analysis of the working of the US antitrust laws can be found in C. D. Edwards' (item 621), A. D. Neale's (item 626) and S. N. Whitney's (item 634) work. Many law journals, as listed in Appendix 1, page 89, publish articles on legal aspects and court cases. The *Antitrust bulletin* contains many articles of general interest and a special section on foreign countries.

616

Bernhard, R. C. The law and the economics of market collusion in Europe, Great Britain and the United States : an American point of view. *J. ind. econ.,* 14 (2), April 1966, pp 101–123.

A critical appraisal of different countries' approach to restrictive practices.

617

Celler, E. What's wrong with 'what is wrong with the antitrust laws'. *Antitrust bull.,* 8 (4), July-Aug. 1963, pp 571–593. (Rejoinder by M. Handler, pp 595–596).

The Chairman of the Committee on the Judiciary, US House of Representatives, answering criticism of antitrust laws, quotes examples of large-size USA industries—steel, cars, shoes—being less innovating than smaller-sized European industries.

618

Colloquium on comparative aspects of restrictive trade practices, *1960, Southampton.* Comparative aspects of restrictive trade practices : a report of a colloquium organised by the United Kingdom National committee of comparative law . . . British Institute of International and Comparative Law, 1961. iv, 91 p. (*International and comparative law quarterly* supplementary publication no. 2, 1961. An edition for the general public was published by Stevens & Sons).

Includes *The United Kingdom approach to restrictive business agreements: some observations,* by B. S. Yamey (pp 21–27). The colloquium also covers practices and legislation in France, Italy, Germany, Belgium and Switzerland.

619

Commerce Clearing House. Trade cases. New York.

An annual compilation, from the Commerce Clearing House's *Trade regulation reports,* of texts of decisions of federal and state courts throughout the US in cases involving antitrust, antimerger, Federal Trade Commission, and other trade regulation law problems, with table of cases and indexes.

620

Conference on comparative aspects of anti-trust laws in the United States, the United Kingdom and the European Economic Community, *1963, Enstone.* Comparative aspects of anti-trust laws . . report of a conference held on June 14-16, 1963 . . . Stevens, 1963. v, 153 p. (*International and comparative law quarterly* supplementary publication no. 6 1963. Published under the auspices of the British Institute of International and Comparative Law).

621

Edwards, C. D. Control of cartels and monopolies : an international comparison. Dobbs Ferry (N.Y.), Oceana Publications, 1967. ix, 380 p. (Studies in comparative law).

Published under the auspices of the Institute of Comparative Law, New York Univ. School of Law. A thorough, comparative study, based mainly on primary sources, of 13 European countries, Israel, Japan, New Zealand and South Africa, with information up to 1966. Surveys restrictive and anti-restrictive attitudes and practices. Part II deals with possibilities and problems of international collaboration based on experience of European Coal and Steel Community and of European Common Market. Useful summary tables.

622

Friedmann, W. Foreign investment and restrictive trade practices. *J. bus. law,* April 1960, pp 144–150.

Examines the problems of a possible clash between private foreign investors and restrictive trade practices legislation.

623

International conference on control of restrictive business practices, *1958, Chicago.* Proceedings [of the] International conference . . Glencoe (Illinois), Free Press, 1960. xix, 380 p.

Conference sponsored by the Graduate School of Business, University of Chicago. Lectures, papers, discussions, surveys, bibliographies on relevant policies in the UK, Netherlands, Norway, Germany, Austria, Belgium, Canada, Denmark, France, Ireland, Japan, Sweden. 140 pages of appendices containing major legislation enactments 1954-1957 and Articles 85–90 of the Treaty setting up the EEC, Rome 1957.

624

Japan. *Fair Trade Commission.* Antitrust legislation of the world (as of 1960). Tokyo, Eibun-horei-sha, [1960]. viii, 789 p.

A useful reference book containing antitrust laws, constitutional provisions against monopoly, and extracts from international treaties.

625

Kilgour, D. G. Restrictive trade practices. *Antitrust bull.,* 8 (1), Jan.-Feb. 1963, pp 101–112.

Compares differences in approach to and effectiveness of monopoly legislation in Canada, USA and UK.

626

Neale, A. D. The antitrust laws of the United States of America ; a study of competition enforced by law. Cambridge Univ. Pr., 1960. xvi, 516 p. (National Institute of Economic and Social Research. Economic and social studies, 19).

The case studies, many of them dealing with borderline cases, provide a guide for anti-monopoly legislation in other countries. They emphasise the problems of defining concepts such as 'restraint of trade', 'collusion', 'intent', 'conspiracy', 'injury', 'monopolistic practices', etc. Various types of agreements relating to prices, markets, information, boycotts, as well as problems of patents, oligopoly, mergers, vertical integration, resale price maintenance, are discussed in the light of antitrust laws. The author examines the problem of escape clauses in anti-monopoly law. Select bibliography.

627
Organisation for Economic Co-operation and Development. Guide to legislation on restrictive business practices : texts, explanatory notes, decisions, bibliography. Paris, 1960- 5 v. (loose-leaf).

Kept up to date by supplements.

628
Pinner, H. L., *ed.* World unfair competition law : an encyclopaedia. Leyden, Sijthoff, 1965. 2 v. (1008 p.). (The protection of intellectual and industrial property throughout the world ; a library of encyclopaedias).

Eighty two types of unfair competition ; relevant legislation (in 32 countries). Arranged in alphabetical order. One section deals with international aspects, including the Common Market, multilateral and bilateral conventions. The encyclopaedia also provides, for each country, a list of major acts, judgments and publications dealing with legislation.

629
Skeoch, L. A. The Combines investigation Act ; its intent and application. *Can. j. econ. political sci.*, 22 (1), Feb. 1956, pp 17–37.

Not limited to Canadian conditions. Author examines critically the concept of workable competition and the arguments — innovation and economies of scale — advanced in defence of concentration.

630
Trescher, K. The new German cartel law : a milestone in modern economic development. *Cartel,* 8 (1), Jan. 1958, pp 12–17.

631
United Nations. *Economic and Social Council.* Restrictive business practices : analysis of governmental measures relating to restrictive business practices. New York, 1953. 68 p. (Economic and Social Council official records, 16th sess. Supplement no. 11A).

631A
United States. *Attorney General. National committee to study the antitrust laws.* Report of the . . . Committee . . . Washington, Gov't. Print. Off., 1955. xiii, 393 p.

Co-chairmen of committee : S. N. Barnes and S. C. Oppenheim. A comprehensive report of a committee (including among its sixty members J. M. Clark, E. V. Rostow, Sumner H. Slichter, and G. J. Stigler) which was 'to evaluate the antitrust laws in their fundamental aspects' in relation to the competitive process and was 'to prepare

the way for modernizing and strengthening' these laws. A dissenting minority criticizes the majority report as too complacent about the competitive situation in the US. For discussion see item 10.

631B
United States. *Congress. Senate. Committee on the judiciary (89th Cong., 2nd sess.).* International aspects of antitrust : hearings before the Subcommittee on antitrust and monopoly . . . 1966. Washington, Gov't. Print. Off., 1967. 2 v. (1356 p.).

Includes statements by C. D. Edwards, C. P. Kindleberger, M. S. Massel, L. Skeoch and others.

632
United States. *Department of State.* Foreign legislation concerning monopoly and cartel practices : report to the Subcommittee on monopoly of the Select committee on small business, US Senate, 82nd Congress, 2nd sess. Washington, Gov't. Print. Off., 1952. v, 253 p.

633
United States. *Library of Congress. Legislative Reference Service.* Congress and the monopoly problem : history of congressional action in the antitrust field, 1890-1966. Washington, Gov't. Print. Off., 1966. xiv, 566 p.

Prepared for the Select committee on small business, House of Representatives, 89th Congress, 2nd session. A reference book of outstanding value. It surveys :
1) the provisions of the major antitrust statutes including supplemental Acts (e.g. Small business Act 1958 ; Bank merger Act 1960 and 1966), also the statutory bodies enforcing the Acts.
2) summary of legislative proposals arranged chronologically, by Congressional Session, from 1890.
3) excerpts from the Final Report and recommendations of the Temporary National Economic Committee (77th Congress) relating to antitrust laws and to topics such as technological progress, restriction of output, investment, price discrimination, mergers, together with a list of TNEC Monographs.
4) subject index of Laws and Bills.
5) statistics on antimonopoly law enforcement (appropriations for and number of staff employed on antimonopoly case work ; number and results of civil and criminal cases).

634
Whitney, S. N. Antitrust policies : American experience in twenty industries. New York, Twentieth Century Fund, 1958. 2 v.

Contents: Vol. 1, Meat packing, petroleum, chemical manufactures, steel, paper, bituminous coal, automobiles, cotton textiles ; v. 2, Cast iron pipe, tobacco products, anthracite, aluminium, shoe machinery, motion pictures, tin cans, farm machinery, corn refining, cement, Pullman cars, insurance. Both volumes contain summaries of the main characteristics of the case studies and of the type and effects of antitrust action. In an extensive appendix experts give dissenting comments on each case.

3.42 Regulation of restrictive practices: Great Britain

General

See also items 596, 739

Publications listed here cover, as the heading suggests, general aspects and problems of British post-war II anti-monopoly legislation. Case studies arising from legal proceedings will be found under the headings *Monopolies Commission* (page 50) and *Restrictive Practices Court* (page 51). A. Hunter's *Competition and the law* (item 648), P. H. Guénault's *Control of monopoly in the United Kingdom* (item 643), the *Midland Bank review* article (item 659) and the reports of the Registrar of Restrictive Trading Agreements (item 660) serve as useful guides to British legislation and its background. So do articles contained in the symposia on restrictive practices legislation published in the *Economic Journal* 1960 (items 591, 656, 664), the *Journal of Industrial Economics* 1959 (items 328, 579, 585, 695), and *Oxford Economic Papers* 1965 (items 640, 688, 690, 691, 694).

635
Baker, P. V. Restraint of trade at petrol filling stations. *Law q. rev.,* 83, Oct. 1967, pp 478–481.

A note on the case Esso Petroleum Co. v. Harper's Garage Ltd. when the House of Lords held that the doctrine of restraint of trade extends to 'solus' agreements. The first case of a report of the Monopolies Commission (*Petrol: a report on the supply of petrol to retailers in the United Kingdom.* 1965) contributing to a House of Lords judgment, the importance of public interest rather than the interests of the parties concerned being emphasised. See also items 653, 667, 674.

636
Beacham, A. The Restrictive trade practices Act 1956. *Yorks. bull. econ. social res.,* 11 (2), Dec. 1959, pp 79–85.

637
Board of Trade. Monopolies and restrictive practices Acts . . . annual report by the Board of Trade. 1949 + HMSO.

From 1965 entitled *Monopolies and mergers Acts . . . annual report by the Board of Trade.*

638
Board of Trade. Monopolies, mergers and restrictive practices. HMSO, 1964. [1], 8 p. (Cmnd. 2299).

639
Campbell, A. Restrictive trading agreements : some practical problems. *J. bus. law,* Jan. 1957, pp 38–44.

Outlines situations which may be claimed not to fall within the terms of the 1956 Act.

640
Cook, P. L. Effects of the Restrictive trade practices Act : analysis of the effects of ending price agreements. *Oxf. econ. pap.,* new ser. 17 (3), Nov. 1965, pp 450–460.

641
Dennison, S. R. The British Restrictive trade practices Act of 1956. *J. law econ.,* 2, Oct. 1959, pp 64–83.

642
Dennison, S. R. Restrictive practices and the Act of 1956. *Lloyds Bank rev.,* (59), Jan. 1961, pp 35–52.

643
Guénault, P. H. *and* **Jackson,** J. M. The control of monopoly in the United Kingdom. Longmans, 1960. ix, 197 p.

644
Hall, M. The new look in monopoly policy. *Bull. Oxf. Univ. Inst. Statist.,* 18 (4), Nov. 1956, pp 373–386.

Survey of British anti-monopoly legislation including 1956 Act.

645
Harbury, C. D. *and* **Raskind,** L. J. The British approach to monopoly control. *Q. j. econ.,* 67 (3), Aug. 1953, pp 380–406.

646
Heath, J. B. The 1956 Restrictive trade practices Act : price agreements and the public interest. *Manchr sch. econ. social stud.,* 27 (1), Jan. 1959, pp 72–103.

Examines the Act in the light of reports of the Monopolies Commission.

647
Hunter, A. Competition and the law. *Manchr sch. econ. social stud.,* 27 (1), Jan. 1959, pp 52–71.

Discusses some aspects of monopoly legislation in Great Britain with special reference to the 1948 and 1956 acts. Includes useful references.

648
Hunter, A. Competition and the law. Allen & Unwin, 1966. 328 p. (Univ. of Glasgow social and economic studies, new series, 7).

649
Hunter, A. The control of monopoly. *Lloyds Bank rev.,* (42), Oct. 1956, pp 19–34.

650
Hunter, A. The progress of monopoly legislation in Britain : a commentary. *Scott. j. political econ.,* 2 (3), Oct. 1955, pp 193–217.

651
Jewkes, J. British monopoly policy, 1944-1956. *J. law econ.*, 1, Oct. 1958, pp 1–19.

Draws special attention to the lack of evidence, in the Monopolies Commission's reports, for the hypothesis that largest producers show lowest costs.

652
Johnson-Davies, K. C. Trade associations and the Restrictive trade practices Act. *Br. j. adm. law*, 3 (1), Winter 1956, pp 12–15.

653
Koh, K. L. Contract doctrine of restraint of trade. *Camb. law j.*, Nov. 1967, pp 151–154.

Comment on the important House of Lords judgment on solus agreements. See also items 635, 667, 674.

654
Korah, V. The reform of the Restrictive trade practices Act 1956. *J. bus. law*, July 1967, pp 210–222.

655
Livesey, F. The Restrictive trade practices Act, 1956 : a review of certain judgments. *Scott. j. political econ.*, 7 (2), June 1960, pp 147–162.

Discusses the Restrictive Practices Court judgments on the yarn spinners', blanket manufacturers', water-tube boilermakers' and the Chemists' Federation's agreements.

656
Lloyd, A. Restrictive practices legislation : the lawyer's point of view. *Econ. j.*, 70 (279), Sept. 1960, pp 467–473.

657
McLachlan, D. L. *and* **Swann,** D. Next steps in monopoly policy. *Scott. j. political econ.*, 11 (2), June 1964, pp 3–8.

658
Martin, A. Restrictive trade practices and monopolies. Routledge, 1957. xii, 264 p.

Study of and guide to Restrictive trade practices Act 1956.

659
Midland Bank. Monopoly legislation in Britain. *Midl. Bank rev.*, Nov. 1965, pp 13–22.

660
Office of the Registrar of Restrictive Trading Agreements. Restrictive trading agreements : report of the Registrar ... 1956/59+ HMSO.

Title varies. Published at irregular intervals, as Command papers. Report covering 1963/66 (Cmnd. 3188, 1967) draws attention to the spread of information agreements.

661
Robinson, E. A. G., **Downie,** J. *and* **Montrose,** J. L. How should we control monopoly. *Econ. j.*, 66 (264), Dec. 1956, pp 567–586.

Shortened versions of three addresses given at a meeting of the Royal Economic Society, June 1956.

662
Sich, R. L. Progress under the Restrictive trade practices Act 1956. *Brd Trade j.*, 177 (3262), 25 Sept. 1959, pp 367–370. (Also pub. in *Yorks. bull. econ. and social res.*, 11 (2), Dec. 1959, pp 116–124).

663
Wilberforce, R. O., **Campbell,** A. *and* **Elles,** N. The law of restrictive trade practices and monopolies. 2nd ed. Sweet & Maxwell, 1966. xxxv, 841 p.

664
Wiseman, J. Restrictive practices legislation : economic analysis and public policy. *Econ. j.*, 70 (279), Sept. 1960, pp 455–466.

665
Yamey, B. S. Restrictive agreements and the public interest : a critique of the legislation. *Pub. law*, Summer 1960, pp 152–169.

Examines the seven possible grounds, specified in the Restrictive trade practices Act 1956, on which restriction may be allowed.

666
Yamey, B. S. Some issues in our monopolies legislation. *Three banks rev.*, June 1962, pp 3–19.

Monopolies Commission

In addition to the reports of the Monopolies Commission (see Appendix 2, page 94), which, by now, provide an extensive primary source, the study of the Monopolies Commission's work by C. H. Rowley (item 673), the M.Sc. thesis by D. W. McKenzie (item 670) and E. A. G. Robinson's article (item 672) are of considerable value.

667
Dixon, D. F. The Monopolies Commission report on petrol : a comment. *J. ind. econ.*, 15 (2), April 1967, pp 128–142.

Comments on the report and on the Barna—Townsend controversy (see item 674). See also items 635, 653.

668
Hunter, A. The Monopolies Commission and economic welfare. *Manchr sch. econ. social stud.*, 23 (1), Jan. 1955, pp 22–40.

669
Kilroy, *Dame* Alix. The task and methods of the Monopolies Commission. (In *Trans. Manchr Statist. Soc.*, session 1952-53. 25 p).

670

McKenzie, D. W. A critique of the reports of the Monopolies Commission. 1963. (M. Sc. thesis, London School of Economics).

A well-written examination of some 13 reports of the Monopolies Commission with special emphasis on problems of costs, prices and profits.

671

'Public interest' and the calico printing industry ; a review of the Monopolies and Restrictive Practices Commission's judgment in the report on the process of calico printing. *J. ind. econ.,* 6 (1), Oct. 1957, pp 64–75.

672

Robinson, E. A. G. Some thoughts on monopoly. *Scott. j. political econ.,* 14 (2), June 1967, pp 97–109.

Examines several cases on which the Monopolies Commission has reported ; discusses criteria for their decisions and possible future policy.

673

Rowley, C. K. The British Monopolies Commission. Allen & Unwin, 1966. 394 p.

Studies the historical background, structure, constitution, scope, authority and procedure of the Monopolies Commission. Discusses the role of trade associations and of dominant firms in the competitive process. The chapters on the measurement of economic performance—unit production costs and prices, and rate of return on capital—are followed by an outline of recommendations made by the Monopolies Commission and of their economic consequences. Pleads for greater powers being given to Board of Trade to implement recommendations, especially with regard to mergers and to the publication of price lists. Appendices : List of members of Monopolies Commission ; A case study of procedure of enquiry : Imperial Tobacco. 5 page bibliography. Very critical review by Ruth Cohen in *Econ. j.,* 76 (304), Dec. 1966, pp 902–904, deploring lack of references and of evidence for some of the statements made.

674

Townsend, H. Exclusive dealing in petrol : some comments. *Economica,* new ser. 32 (128), Nov. 1965, pp 410–423.

Discusses T. Barna's 'Note of dissent' in the Monopolies Commission report on the supply of petrol (Sess. 1964/65 HC 264). A reply by Barna is in *Economica,* 33 (130), May 1966, pp 226–233. See also items 635, 653, 667.

675

Tyre Manufacturers Conference. The pneumatic tyre industry of Britain ; some notes in anticipation of the Monopolies Commission's report. 1956. 32 p.

676

Yamey, B. S. The Monopolies Commission report on cigarettes and tobacco. *Mod. law rev.,* 24 (6), Nov. 1961, pp 747–756.

Restrictive Practices Court

In this important field of anti-monopoly legislation J. B. Heath (items 686, 687), A. Sutherland (items 693-696) and B. S. Yamey (items 698-702) have greatly contributed to a critical examination of the problems involved. The Incorporated Council of Law Reporting for England and Wales publishes reports of Restrictive Practices Court cases (see Appendix 3, page 96). Comments on interesting cases, by Valentine Korah, are published in the *Journal of business law* (see Appendix 1, page 91).

677

Andrews, P. W. S. In Mr. Sutherland's bad books ? *Solicitor q.,* 3 (1), Jan. 1964, pp 63–69.

Discusses item 693 ; see also item 696.

678

Barker, R. E., *ed.* Books are different : an account of the defence of the net book agreement before the Restrictive Practices Court in 1962. Edited by R. E. Barker and G. R. Davies ... with ... a commentary on the economic aspects by P. W. S. Andrews and Elizabeth Brunner ... Macmillan, 1966. xx, 938 p.

Documents and full account of the judgment and the hearings including statements by Professor C. F. Carter and P. W. S. Andrews.

679

Beacham, A. Some thoughts on the cement judgment. *Econ. j.,* 72 (286), June 1962, pp 335–343.

Discusses the judgment of the Restrictive Practices Court in 1961 on the Cement Makers' Federation agreement. See also items 685, 687.

680

Cairns, J. P. Benefits from restrictive agreements : the British experience. *Can. j. econ. political sci.,* 30 (2), May 1964, pp 228–240.

Five cases when restrictive agreements were approved by the Restrictive Practices Court.

681

Cairns, J. P. The Restrictive Practices Court and reasonable prices. *J. ind. econ.,* 12 (2), March 1964, pp 133–141.

A comment by A. Sutherland and a reply by the author are in 13 (2), March 1965, pp 168–175.

682

Cook, P. L. Orderly marketing and competition ? (The blanket manufacturers' agreement). *Econ. j.,* 71 (283), Sept. 1961, pp 497–511.

683

Dennison, S. R. The Restrictive Trade Practices Court in action. *Yorks. bull. econ. social res.,* 11 (2), Dec. 1959, pp 100–108.

684
Gould, J. R. The cement makers' agreement : risk and prices. *Mod. law rev.,* 24 (5), Sept. 1961, pp 632–637.

Criticises the economic arguments behind the judgment of the Restrictive Practices Court.

685
Gould, J. R. Some further thoughts on the cement judgment. *Econ. j.,* 73 (290), June 1963, pp 352–354.

See also items 679, 687.

686
Heath, J. B. The Restrictive Practices Court on competition and price restrictions. *Manchr sch. econ. social stud.,* 28 (1), Jan. 1960, pp 1–18.

687
Heath, J. B. Some further thoughts on the cement judgment. *Econ. j.,* 73 (290), June 1963, pp 350–352.

See also items 679, 685.

688
Hope, M. A manufacturer in the Restrictive Practices Court. *Oxf. econ. pap.,* new ser. 17 (3), Nov. 1965, pp 376–384.

689
Howe, M. The Restrictive Practices Court and the definition of the market. *Manchr sch. econ. social stud.,* 34 (1), Jan. 1966, pp 41–61.

690
Leyland, N. H. Competition in the Court. *Oxf. econ. pap.,* new ser. 17 (3), Nov. 1965, pp 461–467.

Suggests criteria by which the Restrictive Practices Court might assess the consequences of the termination of agreements.

691
Macdonald, I. A. The Restrictive Practices Court : a lawyer's view. *Oxf. econ. pap.,* new ser. 17 (3), Nov. 1965, pp 354–375.

692
Stevens, R. B. *and* **Yamey,** B. S. The Restrictive Practices Court : a study of the judicial process and economic policy. Weidenfeld and Nicolson, 1965. xxi, 260 p.

Raises the problem of the limitation of the judicial process. Many case studies, references, tables of cases, restrictions involved, gateways pleaded, decisions of Court, dates of judgments up to December 1963.

693
Sutherland, A. Are books different ? *Solicitor q.,* 2 (4), Oct. 1963, pp 323–338.

For discussion see item 677 ; see also item 696.

694
Sutherland, A. Economics in the Restrictive Practices Court. *Oxf. econ. pap.,* new ser. 17 (3), Nov. 1965, pp 385–431.

695
Sutherland, A. The Restrictive Practices Court and cotton spinning. *J. ind. econ.,* 8 (1), Oct. 1959, pp 58–79.

696
Sutherland, A. Whose bad books ? *Solicitor q.,* 3 (1), Jan. 1964, pp 69–72.

A reply to item 677 ; see also item 693.

697
Worswick, G. D. N. On the benefits of being denied the opportunity to 'go shopping'. *Bull. Oxf. Univ. Inst. Statist.,* 23 (3), Aug. 1961, pp 271–279.

Examines the argument that a price agreement among manufacturers may spare the purchaser time and expense.

698
Yamey, B. S. Competition and collaboration in industry. *Mod. law rev.,* 26 (2), March 1963, pp 185–191.

Restrictive Practices Court judgment on the Standard Metal Window Group's agreement (1962).

699
Yamey, B. S. The high costs of buying a trivial element. *Mod. law rev.,* 24 (4), July 1961, pp 488–493.

A study of the Restrictive Practices Court's judgment in the case of the Black Bolt and Nut Association's agreement.

700
Yamey, B. S. The net book agreement. *Mod. law rev.,* 26 (6), Nov. 1963, pp 691–699.

701
Yamey, B. S. The transformers agreement. *Mod. law rev.,* 24 (6), Nov. 1961, pp 762–768.

702
Yamey, B. S. Water-tube boilers : contradictions and a paradox. *Mod. law rev.,* 23 (1), Jan. 1960, pp 79–88.

3.43 Regulation of restrictive practices: European Economic Community (Common Market)

See also items 608, 615, 618, 620, 621, 1029-1054

Several publications listed in Section 3.41 (page 46) refer also to regulations of restrictive trade practices in the EEC. Of studies published in English and dealing only with regulations and developments within the Common Market, J. Houssiaux's book (item 709) as well as R. O. Wilberforce's (item 719), D. McLachlan's and D. Swann's publications (items 711, 712, 716, 717) are of special relevance.

703

Campbell, P. Restrictive trade agreements in the Common Market : texts, commentaries. Stevens, 1964. xv, 228 p.

704

Conference on legal problems of the European Economic Community and the European Free Trade Association, *1960, London.* Legal problems of the European Economic Community . . . report of a Conference held on September 29-30, 1960 . . . British Institute of International and Comparative Law, 1961. viii, 100 p. (*International and comparative law quarterly* supplementary publication no. 1, 1961).

Conference held under the auspices of Federal Trust for Education and Research, British Institute of International and Comparative Law and the Institute of Advanced Legal Studies. Includes *Rules of competition and restrictive trade practices* by P. Verloren van Themaat (pp 76–88), an important paper by the then Director-General for Competition of the EEC Commission.

705

de Boysson, X. E. Regulations on restrictive practices (European Economic Community). *J. bus. law,* April 1962, pp 207–209.

706

Deringer, A. Some practical aspects of the antitrust provisions of the treaty of Rome. British Institute of International and Comparative Law, 1962. [2], 34 p.

707

Graupner, R. The rules of competition in the European Economic Community : a study of the substantive law on a comparative law basis, with special reference to patent licence agreements and sole distributorship agreements. The Hague, Nijhoff, 1965. xxxvi, 283 p.

Written by a solicitor. Deals with rules laid down by the Rome Treaty.

708

Groeben, H. von der. Competition policy as part of economic policy in the Common Market. *Antitrust bull.,* Sept./Dec. 1965, pp 911–931.

709

Houssiaux, J. International trade and antitrust regulations : a European viewpoint. *Economia int.,* 19 (3), Aug. 1966, pp 443–456.

An interesting survey of recent monopoly and antitrust developments in Europe, including the problems raised by multinational companies, especially by the entry of large American firms into European markets.

710

Kelleher, G. W. The Common Market antitrust laws : the first ten years. *Antitrust bull.,* 12, Winter 1967, pp 1219–1252.

711

McLachlan, D. L. *and* **Swann,** D. Competition policy in the Common Market. *Econ. j.,* 73 (289), March 1963, pp 54–79.

712

McLachlan, D. L. *and* **Swann,** D. Competition policy in the European Community : the rules in theory and practice. Oxford Univ. Pr., 1967. xvii, 482 p.

Issued under the auspices of the Royal Institute of International Affairs. The authors deal with the Community as a whole and with the individual member countries. They attempt to cover a wide field : problems arising from customs unions ; the impact of and on fiscal policy ; the role of public purchasing, of private information agreements and market arrangements and of Community-wide industrial federations ; the conflicts between national and supernational policies, between the potential misuse of monopoly power and the need for economies of scale, between the needs of integration and excessive official dirigisme, between the British and American approach to the control of mergers and monopoly, mirrored in the rules of EEC and ECSC.

713

Markham, J. W. Antitrust trends and new constraints. *Harv. business rev.,* 41 (3), May/June 1963, pp 84–92.

714

Political and Economic Planning. Cartel policy and the Common Market. *Planning,* 28 (464), Aug. 1962, pp 201–296.

715

Skeoch, L. A. Anti-combine legislation : does it prevent rationalisation ? (In *Problems and policies in Canadian manufacturing; a symposium.* Montreal, National Industrial Conference Board Canadian Office, 1964).

716

Swann, D. *and* **McLachlan,** D. L. Concentration or competition : a European dilemma ? Research Publications, 1967. [2], 59 p. (European series, no. 1).

Issued jointly by Chatham House (RIIA) and PEP. 'An essay on antitrust and the quest for a "European "size of company in the Common Market'.

717

Swann, D. *and* **McLachlan,** D. L. Programming and competition in the European communities. *Econ. j.,* 74 (293), March 1964, pp 85–100.

718

Waer, D. K. Common Market antitrust : a guide to the law, procedure and literature. The Hague, Nijhoff, 1964. [7], 67 p.

Kept up to date by supplements.

719
Wilberforce, R. O. Restrictive trade practices in the
European Common Market. *J. bus. law,* April 1958,
pp 120–130.

Articles 85-89 of the Rome Treaty are reproduced as an
appendix.

4 Forms of competition

4.1 Prices and costs

See also item 104

The determinants of price, the function of the price mechanism and the relation between costs and prices—all essential for an understanding and evaluation of competition—remain topics of considerable controversy. The field is dominated by collective publications : the three studies of the American NBER, *Cost behavior and price policy* (item 773), *Business concentration and price policy* (item 772) and *Measuring international price competitiveness* (item 759) ; the *Oxford studies in the price mechanism* (item 797) ; *Price formation in various economies* (item 754) ; and the OECD publication *Non-wage incomes and prices policy* (item 777). Of individual contributions the important study of the determinants of consumer demand in the US 1929-1970, by H. S. Houthakker and L. D. Taylor (item 751), and the work of P. W. S. Andrews (items 720, 721), I. M. D. Little (item 762), S. Nelson (item 793), A. R. Oxenfeldt (item 778) and P. J. D. Wiles (item 796) should be mentioned. Results of empirical studies in British industry can be found in articles by W. A. H. Godley (items 745, 746), G. B. Richardson (item 781), R. M. Shone (item 785) and S. G. Sturmey (item 788), also in the reports of the National Board for Prices and Incomes (item 771). There are also useful publications by the Institute of Cost and Works Accountants (item 753), and contributions towards finding a common language between economists and accountants can be found in *The journal of accounting research* (see Appendix 1, page 90). The monthly journal *Which ?*, published by the Consumers' Association, contains valuable information on the relation between quality and price.

720
Andrews, P. W. S. Industrial analysis in economics, with especial reference to Marshallian doctrine. In *Oxford studies in the price mechanism*, ed. by Thomas Wilson and P. W. S. Andrews (Oxford, Clarendon Pr., 1951), pp 139–172.

A condensed version of *Manufacturing business* (item 721). The author defends Marshallian theory of price determination and business behaviour ; emphasizes importance of industrial research ; and pleads for more empirical research.

721
Andrews, P. W. S. Manufacturing business. Macmillan, 1949. xviii, 308 p.

For discussion see item 782.

722
Association of Certified and Corporate Accountants. Working party reports : some accounting and economic aspects. [1948]. 72 p.

723
Backman, J. The causes of price inflexibility. *Q. j. econ.,* 54 (2), May 1940, pp 474–489.

724
Backman, J. Economic concentration and price inflexibility. *Rev. econ. and statist.,* 40, Nov. 1958, pp 399–406.

Argument with Blair, Means, Neal, Tucker, Thorp about data used and significance of findings.

725
Bain, J. S. Price and production policies. In *A survey of contemporary economics,* vol. 1, ed. by H. S. Ellis (Homewood (Illinois)., Irwin, 1948. Published for the American Economic Association), pp 129–173.

Includes comments by J. P. Dean and D. H. Wallace.

726
Bain, J. S. Price theory. New York, Holt, 1952. xv, 461 p.

727
Balkin, N. Prices in the clothing industry. *J. ind. econ.,* 5 (1), Nov. 1956, pp 1–15.

728
Bank charges symposium. *Bankers mag.,* 204, Aug. 1967, pp 61–74.

Discussion of the National Board for Prices and Incomes report on bank charges (HMSO, 1967. Report no. 34 ; Cmnd. 3292), which dealt with the banks' alleged monopolistic price-fixing practices. Contributions by Aubrey Jones, H. G. Johnson, C. G. Tether and G. Maynard.

729
Barback, R. H. The pricing of manufactures. Macmillan, 1964. x, 177 p.

Surveys P. W. S. Andrews' and G. L. S. Shackle's empirical works. Reports results of his own research on the pricing process of seven manufacturing firms. One chapter on calculating profit margins from official statistics.

730

Beacham, A. Price policy in the coal industry. *J. ind. econ.,* 1 (2), April 1953, pp 140–154.

731

Bellamy, J. M. Flour pricing and the miller's margin. *J. ind. econ.,* 5 (3), July 1957, pp 202–219.

732

Bhatawdekar, M. V. Economic aspects of basing point price systems. 1956. (Ph. D. thesis, London School of Economics).

733

Board of Trade. International comparisons of cost and prices. *Econ. trends,* (163), May 1967, pp xxii–xxxii.

Comparisons of costs and prices in manufacturing industries in the UK and other industrial countries.

734

Bower, R. S. Decreasing marginal cost in brick production. *J. ind. econ.,* 13 (1), Nov. 1964, pp 1–10.

735

Brown, W. B. D. *and* **Jaques,** E. Product analysis pricing : a method for setting policies for the delegation of pricing decisions and the control of expense and profitability. Heinemann, 1964. xii, 148 p.

736

Business International. Solving international pricing problems. New York, 1965. [1], 50 p. (B.I. research report, 65–7).

Based on experience of international companies. Outlines problems of suitable export prices including intracorporate and intercorporate pricing.

737

Department of Economic Affairs. Public purchasing and industrial efficiency. HMSO, 1967. 8 p. (Cmnd. 3291).

Prepared jointly with the Treasury.

738

Dhrymes, P. J. On the measurement of price and quality changes in some consumer capital goods. *Am. econ. rev.,* 57 (2), May 1967, pp 501–521.

Examines possibilities and difficulties of constructing quality corrected price indices. Contribution to discussion by G. M. Kipnis.

739

Electrical Industry Public Relations Committee. Agreed prices in the heavy electrical plant industry. [Editorial Services Ltd., 1956]. 19 p.

Summary of the industry's submission to the Monopolies Commission in connection with the reference concerning certain electrical machinery and allied plant. Pleads that price agreements contribute to stable employment, reasonable profits, future capital needs and to the Chancellor's revenue. They also provide an 'assured income' for research, development and education.

740

Fog, B. How are cartel prices determined ? *J. ind. econ.,* 5 (1), Nov. 1956, pp 16–23.

Comments on existing theory in the light of interviews with members of Danish cartels.

741

Frank, H. J. Crude oil prices in the Middle East : a study in oligopolistic price behaviour. New York, London, Praeger, 1966. xi, 209 p. (Praeger special studies in international economics and development).

742

Gabor, A. *and* **Granger,** C. W. J. On the price consciousness of consumers. *Appl. statist.,* 10 (3), Nov. 1961, pp 170–188.

743

Gabor, A. *and* **Granger,** C. W. J. Price as an indicator of quality : report of an enquiry. *Economica,* 33, 1966, pp 43–70.

An important price-attitude survey, among about 4,000 Nottingham consumers. Suggests that many consumers have pre-conceived ideas about the price-range beyond which they will not buy, suspecting, at the lower end, the quality of the product. Buyers' resistance grew when a Wilton carpet worth 72s. per sq. yd. was offered at 40s./50s. and then at 20s./30s. Description of sample method used. A few interesting references.

744

Gates, T. R. *and* **Linden,** F. Costs and competition : American experience abroad. [New York, National Industrial Conference Board, 1961]. [6], 226 p. (Studies in business economics, no. 73).

Examines how various components of manufacturing and selling costs of US firms compare with those of other countries and regions and of US subsidiaries in other countries. Compares also productivity, profit margins, scale and capacity ratios of operations.

745

Godley, W. A. H. *and* **Gillion,** C. Pricing behaviour in manufacturing industry. *Natn. Inst. econ. rev.,* (33), Aug. 1965, pp 43–47.

746

Godley, W. A. H. *and* **Gillion,** C. Pricing behaviour in the engineering industry. *Natn. Inst. econ. rev.,* (28), May 1964, pp 50–52.

747

Gold, B. New perspective on cost theory and empirical findings. *J. ind. econ.,* 14 (2), April 1966, pp 164–197.

Author suggests that empirical findings do not fit any generally valid theory of costs. Wide variations in cost curves could be more easily explained by managerial preferences than by economic laws. List of references.

748

Hall, R. L. [Sir Robert Hall] *and* **Hitch,** C. J. Price theory and business behaviour. *Oxf. econ. pap.,* (2), May 1939, pp 12–45.

Also in *Oxford studies in the price mechanism,* ed. by Thomas Wilson and P. W. S. Andrews (Oxford, Clarendon Pr., 1951), pp 107–138. Well known sample survey of firms' pricing methods.

749

Haynes, W. W. Pricing decisions in small business ; prepared by the University of Kentucky under the Small Business Administration management research grant program. Lexington, Univ. of Kentucky Pr., 1962. 152 p.

750

House of Commons. *Select committee on nationalised industries (1966-67). Sub-committee A. Ministerial control of the nationalised industries.* Minutes of evidence, Wednesday, 26th July, 1967. HMSO, 1967. [43] p. (HC 440-XIII, Session 1966-67).

Also published in *First report from the Select committee . . . session 1967-68, vol. 2, Minutes of evidence* (HC 371-II, session 1967-68), pp 588–630. An important document on pricing and investment policies of public enterprise. Memoranda by D. L. Munby on 'Prices, investment and financial objectives' ; J. R. Sargent on 'Pricing policy and financial objectives' ; J. Wiseman on 'The organisation and control of nationalised industries'. See also item 98.

751

Houthakker, H. S. *and* **Taylor,** L. D. Consumer demand in the United States, 1929-1970 : analysis and projections. Cambridge (Mass.), Harvard Univ. Pr., 1966. x, 214 p. (Harvard economic studies, vol. 126).

Analyses 83 components of private consumption expenditure. Projection for 1970 based on hypothesis that demand for any product group is determined more by total private consumption expenditure than by price.

752

Hultgren, T. Cost, prices, and profits : their cyclical relations. New York, National Bureau of Economic Research, 1965. xxvi, 229 p. (NBER studies in business cycles, 14).

753

Institute of Cost and Works Accountants. The problem of selling and distribution cost accounting. 3rd ed. 1962. 40 p.

Useful pamphlet on definition and analysis of selling costs, including advertising, transportation, communication, information, etc.

754

International Economic Association. Price formation in various economies : proceedings of a conference held by the . . . Assocation, edited by D. C. Hague. Macmillan, 1967. xviii, 281 p.

Proceedings of a conference held at Jerusalem, March 1964. Papers on pricing under capitalism and socialism, private and public enterprise, on relation between pricing and investment decisions, and between price level and full employment.

755

Jackson, C. I. *and* **Bird,** P. A. Water supply—the transformation of an industry. *Three banks rev.,* March 1967, pp 23–35.

Discusses possibilities of influencing growing demand for water by new pricing policy.

756

Johnston, J. Statistical cost analysis. New York, London McGraw-Hill, 1960. 197 p. (Economics handbook series).

757

Kaplan, A. D. H. Pricing in big business : a case approach. Washington, Brookings Institution, 1958. xiv, 344 p.

Based on interviews. Part I examines pricing of 11 selected groups of products, and five different types of pricing policy as followed by twenty giant companies. Part II analyses the results of the enquiry. The appendix gives the questionnaire for the interviews, the price recommendation form of US Steel, and the pricing systems for different products of one company—Du Pont.

758

Kravis, I. B. *and* **Lipsey,** R. E. Comparative prices of non-ferrous metals in international trade, 1953-1964. New York, National Bureau of Economic Research, 1966. viii, 56 p. (NBER occasional paper 98).

759

Kravis, I. B., **Lipsey,** R. E. *and* **Bourque,** P. J. Measuring international price competitiveness : a preliminary report. New York, National Bureau of Economic Research, 1965. [8], 40 p. (NBER occasional paper 94).

A preliminary report on an important study. The authors discuss the problems connected with possible methods for measuring competitiveness, e.g. market shares, prices and costs. Gives details of a special study of domestic and export prices of iron and steel products in different countries. See also *A report on the study of international price competitiveness,* by I. B. Kravis and R. E. Lipsey (*Am. econ. rev.,* 57 (2), May 1967, pp 482–491).

760

Langholm, O. Cost structure and costing method : an empirical study. *J. accounting res.,* 3 (2), Autumn 1965, pp 218–227.

761
Lerner, A. P. Employment theory and employment policy. *Am. econ. rev.,* 57 (2), May 1967, pp 1–18.

An important re-appraisal of Keynesian theory, discussing the possibilities of developing wage and price guide posts to replace those parts of the price mechanism paralysed by monopoly.

762
Little, I. M. D. The price of fuel. Oxford, Clarendon Pr., 1953. xiv, 197 p.

Critical survey of pricing policies for coal, gas and electricity. Argues in favour of price being not less than marginal cost. Compares cost of gas, electricity and coal for domestic use.

763
Loescher, S. M. Imperfect collusion in the cement industry. Cambridge (Mass.), Harvard Univ. Pr., 1959. xi, 331 p. (Harvard Univ. series on competition in American industry, 4).

Examines collusion resulting from basing point pricing system. Bibliography.

764
Markham, J. W. The nature and significance of price leadership. *Am. econ. rev.,* 41 (5) pt 1, Dec. 1951, pp 891–905.

Discussion by A. R. Oxenfeldt in *Am. econ. rev.,* 42 (3) pt 1. June 1952 pp 380–384 ; reply by Markham in 43 (1) pt 1, March 1953, pp 152–154. Important controversy about effectiveness or ineffectiveness of price leadership.

765
Mason, E. S. Price and production policies of large scale enterprise. *Am. econ. rev.,* 29 (1 pt 2, suppl.), March 1939, pp 61–74.

766
Means, G. C. Industrial prices and their relative inflexibility ; letter transmitting . . . report [entitled 'NRA, AAA, and making of industrial policy'] relating to subject of industrial prices and their relative inflexibility. Washington, Gov't. Print. Off., 1935. v, 38 p. (74th Cong., 1st sess., Senate doc. 13).

767
Means, G. C. Notes on inflexible prices. *Am. econ. rev.,* 26, March 1936, pp 23–35.

768
Meek, R. L. An application of marginal cost pricing : the 'green tariff' in theory and practice. *J. ind. econ.,* 11 (3), July 1963, pp 217–236.

Comments on the 'first serious attempt ever made to engage in marginal cost-pricing', undertaken by the French electricity supply industry.

769
Melverda, H. A. A. de. The illusion of fixed costs. *Int. econ. pap.,* 2, 1952, pp 155–177.

Translation of 'Illusie der vaste kosten', published in *De Ingenieur,* no. 14/15, 1950.

770
Mund, V. A. Identical bid prices. *J. political econ.,* 68 (2) April 1960, pp 150–169.

Argues against the doctrine that identical bidding is consistent with effective competition.

771
National Board for Prices and Incomes. Reports. No. 1- HMSO, 1965-

Published as Command papers. To July 1968, 77 reports had been published, including *General report, April 1965 to July 1966* (Report no. 19 ; Cmnd. 3087), *Second general report, July 1966 to August 1967* (Report no. 40 ; Cmnd. 3394) and *Third general report, August 1967 to July 1968* (Report no. 77 ; Cmnd. 3715). As well as summarising the conclusions reached in individual reports, and recording action taken to implement their recommendations, these general reports describe the economic background to the movement of prices and incomes, and the criteria guiding the NBPI. The third general report includes a chapter on the relation between prices and efficiency and, as an appendix, 'a preliminary study of the effects of incomes policy', which stresses the importance of directly influencing price increases. Up to July 1968 reports dealing with prices of the following goods and services had been published :
Aluminium semi-manufactures. 1967. (Report no. 39. Cmnd. 3378).
Bank charges. 1967. (Report no. 34. Cmnd. 3292).
Batteries, mercury hearing-aid. 1968. (Report no. 64. Cmnd. 3625).
Batteries, secondary. 1968. (Report no. 61. Cmnd. 3597).
Beer. 1966. (Report no. 13. Cmnd. 2965).
Bread and flour. 1965. (Report no. 3. Cmnd. 2760).
Bricks, fletton and non-fletton. 1967. (Report no. 47. Cmnd. 3480).
Building society mortgage interest rates. 1966. (Report no. 22. Cmnd. 3136).
Butyl rubber. 1968. (Report no. 66. Cmnd. 3626).
Cement. 1967. (Report no. 38. Cmnd. 3381).
Chocolate and sugar confectionery. 1968. (Report no. 75. Cmnd. 3694).
Coal. 1966. (Report no. 12. Cmnd. 2919).
Coal distribution. 1966. (Report no. 21. Cmnd. 3094).
Compound fertilisers. 1967. (Report no. 28. Cmnd. 3228).
Distributors' margins. 1968. (Report no. 55. Cmnd. 3546).
Electricity and gas. 1965. (Report no. 7. Cmnd. 2862).
Electricity, bulk supply tariff. 1968. (Report no. 59. Cmnd. 3575).
Flour. 1968. (Report no. 53. Cmnd. 3522).
Fruit and vegetables. 1967. (Report no. 31. Cmnd. 3265).
Gas. 1968. (Report no. 57. Cmnd. 3567).
Hoover domestic appliances. 1968. (Report no. 73. Cmnd. 3671).
Laundry and dry cleaning charges. 1966. (Report no. 20. Cmnd. 3093).
Milk distributors. 1967. (Report no. 46. Cmnd. 3477).

Motor repairing and servicing. 1967. (Report no. 37. Cmnd. 3368).

Newsprint. 1967. (Report no. 26. Cmnd. 3210).

Printing. 1965. (Report no. 2. Cmnd. 2750).

Radio, television rental and relay. 1968. (Report no. 52. Cmnd. 3520).

Road haulage. Interim report, 1965. (Report no. 1. Cmnd. 2695). Final report, 1966. (Report no. 14. Cmnd. 2968). Report, 1967. (Report no. 48. Cmnd. 3482). Statistical supplement. 1968. (Report no. 48, supplement. Cmnd. 3482-1).

Soaps and detergents. 1965. (Report no. 4. Cmnd. 2791).

In reports dealing with prices attention is given to special features, according to the case under review. Price agreements are dealt with in the reports on bank charges, building society mortgage interest rates, cement, road haulage ; marketing and distribution in the reports on bread and flour, coal distribution, fruit and vegetables ; investment criteria and target rates of return on new investment in public enterprise in the reports on electricity and gas, coal ; advertising and promotion in the report on soap and detergents ; concentration and integration in the reports on bread and flour, newsprint (and in *Wages in the bakery industry*. 1966. Report no. 17 ; Cmnd. 3019) ; technology and research in the report on aluminium semi-manufactures ; tied systems in the reports on the brewery industry, motor repairing and servicing. Distributors' margins are dealt with not only in the report no. 55 but also in the reports on secondary batteries, on mercury hearing-aid batteries and on milk distributors. The report on chocolate and sugar confectionery contains data on advertising expenditure and a 'note on the justification for the industry's level of expenditure on advertising and other promotional activities'. Other reports deal with incomes, but also contain information on structure of the relevant industry, on productivity, on costs and rates of return.

772
National Bureau of Economic Research, *New York.* Business concentration and price policy ; a conference of the Universities—National Bureau Committee for economic research . . . Princeton, Princeton Univ. Pr., 1955. x, 511 p. (Special conference series, no. 5).

For annotation see item 216.

773
National Bureau of Economic Research, *New York.* Cost behavior and price policy. New York, 1943. 356 p. (Conference on price research. Price studies, no. 4).

Report of the Committee on price determination established by the Conference on price research. Members of the Committee included J. M. Clark, J. T. Dunlop and E. S. Mason. Empirical investigation into aspects of cost behaviour such as relation between size of firm and cost, between cost and price ; problem of different costing methods. No analysis of impact of monopolistic/ oligopolistic conditions.

774
Neal, A. C. Industrial concentration and price inflexibility. Washington, American Council on Public Affairs, 1942. 173 p.

775
Neild, R. R. Pricing and employment in the trade cycle : a study of British manufacturing industry, 1950–61. Cambridge Univ. Pr., 1963. viii, 73 p. (National Institute of Economic and Social Research. Occasional paper, 21).

776
Nevin, E. The cost structure of British manufacturing, 1948-61. *Econ. j.,* 73 (292), Dec. 1963, pp 642–664. (Correction, 74 (295), Sept. 1964, p 743).

777
Organisation for Economic Co-operation and Development. Non-wage incomes and prices policy : supplement to the report. Paris, 1965. 159 p.

Papers for an international trade union seminar, published as a supplement to *Non-wage incomes and prices policy: trade union policy and experience. Background report,* prepared by D. Robinson (Paris, OECD, 1966). In Part II various authors contribute to problem of prices policy : E. Defossez on 'Special types of price setting and problems of control of prices' quotes case where a manufacturer's reduction of price which was based partly on reduced profit margin of distributor led to loss of sales.

778
Oxenfeldt, A. R. Industrial pricing and market practices. New York, Prentice-Hall, 1951. xii, 602 p.

A textbook on price formation in a free-enterprise economy. Describes structure and functional characteristics of economic environment. Distinguishes between intra-firm, inter-firm, inter-industry, and government influence on price. Two extensive case studies of whisky prices and steel prices. Suggests possible remedies for industrial disorders.

779
Paul, M. E. Covering costs by receipts. *Bull. Oxf. Univ. Inst. Statist.,* 22 (4), Nov. 1960, pp 299–311.

780
Purchasing Officers Association. Memorandum for submission to National Incomes Commission on the effect of the engineering pay award on prices. 1964. [2], 38 leaves.

781
Richardson, G. B. The pricing of heavy electrical equipment : competition or agreement ? *Bull. Oxf. Univ. Inst. Econ. Statist.,* 28 (2), May 1966, pp 73–92.

782
Robinson, E. A. G. The pricing of manufactured products. *Econ. j.,* 60 (240), Dec. 1950, pp 771–780.

Discusses *Manufacturing business,* by P. W. S. Andrews (item 721). A comment by Aubrey Silberston is in *Econ. j.,* 61 (242), June 1951, pp 426–429 ; with a rejoinder by Robinson (*The pricing of manufactured products and case against imperfect competition*) on pp 429–433.

783
Rostas, L. Productivity, prices and distribution in selected British industries. Cambridge Univ. Pr., 1948. xiii, 199 p. (National Institute of Economic and Social Research. Occasional papers, 11).

Investigates 37 British and American industries. Discusses significance, problems and methods of productivity comparisons. Calculates changes in productivity during the period 1907–1939 and analyses the factors affecting differences in productivity, including market factors, concentration and standardisation. Four page bibliography.

784
Schultze, C. L. *and* **Tryon,** J. L. Prices and costs in manufacturing industries. Washington, Gov't. Print. Off., 1960. viii, 58 p. (United States. Congress. Joint Economic Committee. Studies of employment, growth, and price levels. Study paper no. 17).

A valuable study. Describes methods for collecting and calculating cost and price data for different industries. Raises problems of aggregate series when product-mix and technology change, or when ratios between salaried and wage-earning employees change (for calculating unit labour costs) or when raw material prices change. Also problem of effect of recession and recovery.

785
Shone, R. M. Steel price policy. *J. ind. econ.,* 1 (1), Nov. 1952, pp 43–54.

For discussion see item 790.

786
Stocking, G. W. Basing point pricing and regional development : a case study of the iron and steel industry. Chapel Hill (N.C.), Univ. of North Carolina Pr., 1954. vii, 274 p.

787
Stones, F. Price policy in a nationally administered industry. *J. ind. econ.,* 1 (1), Nov. 1952, pp 32–42.

For discussion see item 790.

788
Sturmey, S. G. Cost curves and pricing in aircraft production. *Econ. j.,* 74 (296), Dec. 1964, pp 954–982.

The author believes that in the complicated competitive situation of the aircraft industry, costs of developing and testing aircraft have to be set against gains in the development and production time cycle. The fiction of competition in production should be ended and replaced by specialisation of factories. Among other problems, those of launching and overhead costs, and of the costs of 'the learning curve'.

789
Tucker, R. S. The reasons for price rigidity. *Am. econ. rev.,* 28, March 1938, pp 41–54.

For discussion see item 798.

790
Tyndall, D. G. Price policy in a nationally administered industry : an alternative view. *J. ind. econ.,* 4 (1), Oct. 1955, pp 62–73.

A controversy with Shone and Stones (see items 785 and 787).

791
United Nations. *Economic Commission for Europe.* The price of oil in Western Europe. Geneva, 1955. [4], 64 p.

792
United States. *Congress. Senate. Committee on the judiciary (85th Cong., 2nd sess.).* Administered prices ; hearings before the Subcommittee on antitrust and monopoly ... pursuant to S. Res. 231. Pt 6 [and] 7, Automobiles ... Washington, Gov't. Print. Off., 1958. 2 v.

Part 6, Hearings, Jan. 28–31, Feb. 4–10, 20, Apr. 29, 30, May 1, 2 & 6, 1958 ; pt 7, Appendix.

793
United States. *Congress. Temporary National Economic Committee.* Investigation of concentration of economic power ... Monograph no. 1, Price behavior and business policy. Washington, Gov't. Print. Off., 1941. xxv, 419 p.

Study made by S. Nelson and W. G. Keim under the auspices of the Bureau of Labor Statistics.

794
Walters, A. A. Production and cost functions : an econometric survey. *Econometrica,* 31 (1–2), Jan.-April 1963, pp 1–66.

Author examines and tabulates types and results of studies of cost curves. He discusses their shortcomings in the light of problems such as joint costs, multi-product firms, cross section analysis, and draws attention to the limitations of the engineering approach and of single equation-least square methods in industry studies. The extensive bibliography (345 items) covers econometric and non-econometric publications on production and cost functions, productivity, investment, growth, programming, economies of scale, input-, output-, and technological coefficients, rates of return, and innovation.

795
Whittle, J. *and others.* Central purchasing by local and public authorities : a research study. Institute of Municipal Treasurers and Accountants, [1963]. 142 p.

A valuable study based on questionnaires and interviews which included local authorities, public boards and the hospital services. Reviews merits of different methods of joint or central purchasing and contracting and the possibilities of influencing price and quality. A very short bibliography reveals the neglect of this field of research.

796

Wiles, P. J. D. Price, cost and output. Oxford, Blackwell, 1956. xi, 302 p.

Examines actual price and output policies in the light of welfare theory. Classifies and discusses five market forms : primitive higglers ; price-takers ; full cost chargers ; discontinuous producers ; marginal cost chargers. Important chapter on definitions.

797

Wilson, T. *and* **Andrews,** P. W. S., *ed.* Oxford studies in the price mechanism. Oxford, Clarendon Pr., 1951. xv, 274 p.

See also items 720 and 748.

798

Wood, R. C. Dr. Tucker's 'reasons' for price rigidity. *Am. econ. rev.,* 28, Dec. 1938, pp 663–673.

Discusses item 789.

4.2 Information

See also item 832

Literature on information agreements will be found in section 3.2 (page 45). The works listed below are concerned with the role of information in competition ; they examine the effect of knowledge or ignorance on the perfection/imperfection of the market. One of the most interesting books in this area is G. B. Richardson's *Information and investment* (item 805). Attention should also be drawn to paras. 607-611 of *The law of restrictive trade practices and monopolies,* by R. O. Wilberforce and others (item 663).

799

Clabault, J. M. Practicalities in competitors exchanging price information. *Antitrust bull.,* 12, 1967, pp 65-72.

800

Jenner, R. A. An information version of price competition. *Econ. j.,* 76 (304), Dec. 1966, pp 786-805.

According to the author it is the consumer who ultimately dominates production by informing the producer of his preferences. The exchange of information between producer and consumer is tested in the market transaction. Monopolies tend to become insensitive to information about consumer needs and thus create a favourable climate for better informed new competitors to establish themselves.

801

Lyon, L. S. *and* **Abramson,** V. Economics of open price systems. Washington, Brookings Institution, 1936. xii, 165 p. (Institute of Economics, publication no. 71).

802

Oxenfeldt, A. R. Consumer knowledge : its measurement and extent. *Rev. econ. statist.,* 32 (4), Nov. 1950, pp 300-314.

A sample enquiry into consumer satisfaction. Compares the informed consumer with the average consumer. Pleads for more product information.

803

Ozga, S. A. Imperfect markets through lack of knowledge. *Q. j. econ.,* 74 (1), Feb. 1960, pp 29-52.

804

Richardson, G. B. Equilibrium, expectations and information. *Econ. j.,* 69 (274), June 1959, pp 223-237.

805

Richardson, G. B. Information and investment : a study in the working of the competitive economy. Oxford Univ. Pr., 1960. [11], 226 p.

Examines the assumption of 'perfect knowledge', suggests that firms' expectations depend on information which depends on market structure. Discusses the problems of market information, imperfections, uncertainty, collusion, etc.

806

Scottish Council (Development and Industry). Report on a survey of small and medium engineering firms in Scotland, with special reference to their needs for information and the flow of information. [Edinburgh], 1957. [4], 174 leaves.

807

Shubik, M. Information, risk, ignorance and indeterminacy. *Q. j. econ.,* 68 (4), Nov. 1954, pp 629-640.

Advertising and promotion

The growing importance of advertising and promotion in creating, maintaining and increasing demand for a given product, in competition with other products, has failed to produce research of appropriate magnitude on the economic problems involved. The relation between large scale advertising and promotion expenditure, competition and monopoly, the relation between price and non-price competition (with its borders more and more blurred) remain fields wide open to a major research effort.

The two standard works are still those by N. H. Borden (item 811) and by N. Kaldor and R. Silverman (item 825). Additional information can be found in the reports of the Royal Commission on the Press (items 571, 572), the reports of the Monopolies Commission on tobacco and detergents (see Appendix 2, pages 94, 95), in the Reith report (item 828), in the *Journal of advertising research* (1960 + New York, Advertising Research Foundation) and in the *Journal of marketing* (see Appendix 1, page 91). Useful contributions by W. Taplin, L. G. Telser, and J. Treasure (items 833-839).

808
Advertising Association. Advertising expenditure.
1948+

Published every 4 years ; kept up to date by annual series
in the *Advertising quarterly,* first published in no. 8,
Summer 1966, pp 67-75. Expenditure classified by media
and main groups of advertisers.

809
Backman, J. Is competition in advertising anti-
competitive ? *Advertising q., (13),* Autumn 1967
pp 23-36.

Defends advertising by balancing beneficial against
harmful effects, and suggests that other anti-competitive
factors are more decisive.

810
Board of Trade. *Committee on consumer protection.*
Final report...HMSO, 1962. vii, 331 p. (Cmnd. 1781).

Chairman of committee : J. T. Molony. References to
advertising, sales practices, bargain pricing, brand names,
RPM.

811
Borden, N. H. The economic effects of advertising.
Chicago, Irwin, 1942. xl, 988 p.

A standard work, still widely used.

812
Comanor, W. S. *and* **Wilson,** T. A. Advertising, market
structure and performance. *Rev. econ. statist.,* 49 (4),
Nov. 1967, pp 423-440.

The enquiry, based on the same set of industries and the
same data as those used by Telser (see item 836), suggests
that Telser's method (one simple correlation) and
conclusion (no inverse association between advertising
and competition) are unsatisfactory. Authors work with
multi-variate equations and examine effect of advertising
on entry barriers, market power and rates of return, and the
importance of product differentiation, growth of demand,
economies of scale, capital requirements. Useful references.

813
Day, R. L., *ed.* Marketing models ; quantitative and
behavioral. Scranton (Pa.), International Textbook Co.,
1964. 671 p.

Collection of published articles of uneven quality dealing
with many aspects and variables relating to marketing
models. Of special interest Part III, on problems of
devising and choosing promotional activity and
measuring its effects.

814
Dorfman, R. *and* **Steiner,** P. O. Optimal advertising and
optimal quality. *Am. econ. rev.,* 44 (5), Dec. 1954,
pp 826-836.

A theoretical approach.

815
Economists Advisory Group. The economics of
advertising : a study...Advertising Association, 1967. 94 p.

Director of the study, D. S. Lees. Group members included
J. H. Dunning, E. V. Morgan, A. T. Peacock, J. Wiseman.
See also H. G. Johnson's review article (item 823).

816
Else, P. K. The incidence of advertising in manufacturing
industries. *Oxf. econ. pap.,* new series 18 (1), March 1966,
pp 88-110.

Examines advertising expenditure and advertising/sale
ratios of 20 product groups. Discusses relation between
advertising expenditure and competitive conditions.

817
Export Council for Europe. Marketing and advertising in
Europe. 1967. 35 p.

Prepared jointly with the Institute of Practitioners in
Advertising. Contains a comparison of British advertising
expenditure in Europe with that of competitor countries.

818
Firestone, O. J. The economic implications of
advertising. Toronto, London, Methuen, 1967. xiii, 210 p.

Commissioned by Institute of Canadian Advertising ;
submitted to a Special Joint Committee of Canadian
Senate and House of Commons on consumer credit
(prices). Tends towards treating advertising as effect
rather than cause of monopolistic power. Draws attention
to lack of statistical evidence ; emphasises need for
extensive, independent, objective, adequately financed,
research. Surveys literature on advertising and collects
claims for 43 advantages and 33 disadvantages. An
appendix lists 20 areas of research in the field of advertising
for studying the effects on competition, costs, prices,
profits, growth, product quality, innovation, allocation of
resources, concentration, etc. Advocates more consumer
education and protection.

819
Harris, R. *and* **Seldon,** A. Advertising and the public.
Deutsch, 1962. xxiii, 304 p.

Published for the Institute of Economic Affairs. Part II,
'The economics of advertising', deals with the relation of
advertising to competition, oligopoly and innovation, etc.
Useful bibliography.

820
Harris, R. Growth, advertising and the consumer.
Institute of Economic Affairs, [1964]. [2], 24 p. (Institute of
Economic Affairs. Occasional paper, 2).

Comments on problems of forecasting consumer demand
and patterns of expenditure.

821
International Foundation for Research in the Field of Advertising. An appraisal of European advertising statistics : their sources and adequacy. Brussels, [1965]. 53 p. (IFRA occasional papers, 1).

822
Jastram, R. W. Advertising ratios planned by large-scale advertisers. *J. mktg,* 14, July 1949, pp 13-21.

The author classifies firms into advertisers of producer goods, consumer durables and consumer non-durables, and examines how advertising expenditure as a proportion of sales revenue is related to these groups of goods. He also investigates the relation between advertising ratios and size of advertising expenditure. The article is referred to in *Advertising and economic policy* by P. Doyle (*Dist. Bank rev.,* (164), Dec. 1967, pp 39-58).

823
Johnson, H. G. Economics of advertising : a review of the E[conomists] A[dvisory] G[roup] report. *Advertising q.,* (13), Autumn 1967, pp 9-15.

A critical summary of the main problems discussed in the report (item 815).

824
Kaldor, N. The economic aspects of advertising. *Rev. econ. stud.,* 18 (1), 1950, pp 1-27.

825
Kaldor, N. *and* **Silverman,** R. A statistical analysis of advertising expenditure and of the revenue of the press. Cambridge Univ. Pr., 1948. xiv, 200p. (National Institute of Economic and Social Research. Economic and social studies, 8).

A standard work although based mainly on 1935 (and a few later) data. A thorough enquiry ; explains definition and methods of estimation ; examines relations between advertising, manufacturers' net sales and consumers' expenditure. Comparisons with US. Classifies different types of advertising by commodities. Discusses problem of wastefulness. Authors plead for improved advertising statistics in censuses.

826
Mann, H. M., **Henning,** J. A. *and* **Meehan,** J. W. Advertising and concentration : an empirical investigation. *J. ind. econ.,* 16 (1), Nov. 1967, pp 34-45.

Sample enquiry of 42 American firms for three periods : 1952-56, 1957-61, 1962-65. Appendix gives details of four-firm concentration ratios and ratios of advertising to sales revenue.

827
Millar, R. The affluent sheep. Longmans, 1963. [5], 203 p.

Use of mass observation approach for critical appraisal of advertising and of new methods of distribution. Discusses problem of government's role in consumer protection.

828
Labour Party. *Commission of enquiry into advertising.* Report of a commission. . .1966. [3], 205 p.

Chairman of commission : Lord Reith. Of special relevance Chapter II, paragraphs 76-132 : role of advertising in the economy ; problems of private versus social cost/benefit, of price competition and economies of scale.

829
Packard, V. O. The hidden persuaders. Longmans, 1957. 275 p.

Quotes examples of misuse of advertising and undesirable effects of advertising industry. Journalistic treatment.

830
Rothchild, K. W. A note on advertising. *Econ. j.,* 52 (205), April 1942, pp 112-121.

Examines the effects of advertising under conditions of full employment and unemployment, and the impact on economic fluctuations.

831
Sherrard, A. Advertising, product variation, and the limits of economics. *J. political econ.,* 59 (2), April 1951, pp 126-142.

Argues that the scale of advertising and product differentiation cannot sufficiently be explained by the Marshallian approach or in terms of theories of monopolistic or imperfect competition.

832
Stigler, G. J. The economics of information. *J. political econ.,* 69 (3), June 1961, pp 213-225.

Comments on the costs and benefits of and limits to providing information to the buyer. Advertising seen as method of firms to spread information, and of buyers to acquire it. Low-price firms would react to well-informed buyers by increased advertising.

833
Taplin, W. Advertising : a new approach. Hutchinson, 1960. 208 p.

834
Taplin, W. Advertising appropriation policy. *Economica,* new series 26 (103), Aug. 1959, pp 227-239.

835
Taplin, W. Advertising in the economy. *Dist. Bank rev.,* (140), Dec. 1961, pp 22-36.

836
Telser, L. G. Advertising and competition. *J. political econ.,* 72 (6), Dec. 1964, pp 537-562.

Constructs advertising model with advertising as input. Compares concentration ratios with advertising outlays. Doubts inverse relation between advertising and competition. See also item 812.

837
Telser, L. G. How much does it pay whom to advertise ? *Am. econ. rev.,* 51 (2), May 1961, pp 194-205.

838
Telser, L. G. Supply and demand for advertising messages. *Am. econ. rev.,* 56 (2), May 1966, pp 457-466.

Discussion, with contributions by H. J. Barnett and H. H. Golden, pp 467-475.

839
Treasure, J. Advertising expenditure in 1961 : a re-appraisal. *Dist. Bank rev.,* (144), Dec. 1962, pp 19-34.

Estimates that 'net expenditure on consumer advertising', i.e. after allowing for the element of subsidy to press and tv, has been not £470 m. but £180 m.

4.3 Innovation and invention

See also items 29, 68, 73, 99, 214, 439, 617, 629, 922, 930, 969.

Extensive investigations into the relation between competition and technological progress have been carried out by C. F. Carter and B. R. Williams (items 845-848). Important contributions by C. Freeman (items 862-865) and J. B. Quinn (item 891). R. Johnston (item 875) reviews relevant theories and literature (including other reviews). In North America the work by E. Mansfield (items 331, 879, 880) and F. M. Scherer (items 900, 901) is outstanding in the field. The importance of research and development is reflected in the series of studies on research and innovation in the *National Institute economic review,* and in the surveys undertaken by W. Gruber and others (item 869) and by OECD (item 887).
See also Section *6.2, Productivity* (page 84').

840
Adams, W. *and* **Dirlam,** J. B. Big steel, invention and innovation. *Q. j. econ.,* 80 (2), May 1966, pp 167-189.

Deals with the American steel giants' failure in technological leadership. Discussed in *Big steel, invention and innovation reconsidered,* by A. K. McAdams (*Q. j. econ.,* 81 (3), Aug. 1967, pp 457-474), with a reply by Adams and Dirlam (pp 475-482).

841
Adams, W. *and* **Dirlam,** J. B. Steel imports and vertical oligopoly power. *Am. econ. rev.,* 54 (5), Sept. 1964, pp 626-655.

Controversy about rate of innovation of US steel industry. Comments by R. E. Slesinger, D. S. Schoenbrod and G. A. Hone in *Am. econ. rev.,* 56 (1), March 1966, pp 152-160 (reply by Adams and Dirlam pp 160-168) ; by G. Rosegger in 57 (4), Sept. 1967, pp 913-917 (reply by Adams and Dirlam pp 917-919).

842
Ames, E. *and* **Rosenberg,** N. Changing technological leadership and industrial growth. *Econ. j.,* 73 (289), March 1963, pp 13-31.

Comments on the thesis that innovating countries suffer and latecomers gain, on balance, and suggests lack of sufficient evidence.

843
Blaug, M. A survey of the theory of process-innovations. *Economica,* new ser. 30 (117), Feb. 1963, pp 13-32.

844
Brown, W. H. Innovation in the machine tool industry. *Q. j. econ.,* 71 (3), Aug. 1957, pp 406-425.

845
Carter, C. F. *and* **Williams,** B. R. The characteristics of technically progressive firms. *J. ind. econ.,* 7 (2), March 1959, pp 87-104.

846
Carter, C. F. *and* **Williams,** B. R. Industry and technical progress ; factors governing the speed of application of science. Oxford Univ. Pr., 1957. viii, 244 p.

Most relevant : Chapter 15, 'A favourable environment'. Effect of competition depends on type of competition (product and process development) and type of industry (expanding, defensively restrictive, 'competitive depressed'). Authors believe that it depends on many other factors what effect competition or lack of competition has on technical progress. No general statement possible ; case studies required.

847
Carter, C. F. *and* **Williams,** B. R. Investment in innovation. Oxford Univ. Pr., 1958. ix, 167 p.

Authors examine the problems affecting investment in new plant and equipment ; emphasize again that with some firms or industries more competition, with others less competition may stimulate innovation. List eleven other factors influencing decisions to invest in innovation.

848
Carter, C. F. *and* **Williams,** B. R. Science in industry : policy for progress. Oxford Univ. Pr., 1959. ix, 186 p.

Chapters 14 and 15 deal with the effects on innovation of competition, and of restrictive practices and their control. The authors plead for more research into the effect of protection from foreign competition on efficiency. This is one point in a 12 page summary of proposals.

849
Central Office of Information. Industrial research in Britain. 1961. [2], 42 p. (Reference document, R. 4631).

850
Cooper, A. C. R & D is more efficient in small companies. *Harv. bus. rev.,* 42 (3), May-June 1964, pp 75-83.

851
Cooper, A. C. Small companies can pioneer new products. *Harv. bus. rev.,* 44 (5), Sept./Oct. 1966, pp 162-179.

852
Croome, H. Human problems of innovation. HMSO, 1960. 36 p. (Department of Scientific and Industrial Research. Problems of progress in industry, 5).

Summarises results of a research project fully reported in *The management of innovation,* by T. Burns and G. M. Stalker (Tavistock Publications, 1961).

853
Domar, E. D. On the measurement of technological change. *Econ. j.,* 71 (284), Dec. 1961, pp 709-729.

854
Donnithorne, A. G. British rubber manufacturing : an economic study of innovations. Duckworth, 1958. 159 p. (Industrial innovation series).

Largely technical but important concluding chapter, and introduction by Prof. G. C. Allen. Author's conclusions : little evidence that monopolistic or competitive conditions influenced innovations. (This conclusion seems to contradict the statement on page 138 that the development of synthetic rubber had been stimulated by the cartel restrictions on natural rubber).

855
Dunning, J. H. Anglo-American research co-operation and industrial progress. *Dist. Bank rev.,* (118), June 1956, pp 3-22.

856
Dunning, J. H. Newer British industries and increasing productivity. *Dist. Bank rev.,* (110), June 1954, pp 16-25.

857
Eltis, W. A. Economic growth : an analysis and policy. Hutchinson, 1966. 173 p. (Hutchinson's university library, Economics series).

858
Eltis, W. A. Investment, technical progress and economic growth. *Oxf. econ. pap.,* new ser. 15 (1), March 1963, pp 32-52.

859
Fabian, Y. Note on the measurement of the output of research and development activities. [Paris], Organisation for Economic Co-operation and Development, 1963. 41 p. (DAS/PD/63.48).

Document prepared for a working meeting of the Directorate for Scientific Affairs, Frascati, June 1963.

860
Federation of British Industries. Industrial research in manufacturing industry, 1959-60 : results of a survey, including commentaries, and a statistical report. 1961. 129 p.

Statistical report prepared by the National Institute of Economic and Social Research, pp 29-112. Commentary by B. R. Williams, pp 21-28.

861
Fellner, W. J. The influence of market structure on technological progress. *Q. j. econ.,* 65 (4), Nov. 1951, pp 556-577. (Erratum, 66 (2), May 1952, pp 297-298).

862
Freeman, C., **Young,** A. *and* **Fuller,** J. K. The plastics industry : a comparative study of research and innovation. *Natn. Inst. econ. rev.,* (26), Nov. 1963, pp 22-62.

863
Freeman, C. Research and development : a comparison between British and American industry. *Natn. Inst. econ. rev.,* (20), May 1962, pp 21-39.

864
Freeman, C. *and* **Young,** A. The research and development effort in Western Europe, North America and the Soviet Union : an experimental international comparison of research expenditures and manpower in 1962. [Paris], Organisation for Economic Co-operation and Development, [1965]. 152 p.

865
Freeman, C., **Harlow,** C. J. E. *and* **Fuller,** J. K. Research and development in electronic capital goods. *Natn. Inst. econ. rev.,* (34), Nov. 1965, pp 40-91.

866
Gold, B. Industry growth patterns : theory and empirical results. *J. ind. econ.,* 13 (1), Nov. 1964, pp 53-73.

Examines the findings of A. F. Burns in *Production trends in the US since 1870* (NBER, 1934) in the light of more recent developments. List of references.

867
Grossfield, K. The interaction of scientific, technical and economic factors in the cable industry. 1956. (M. Sc. thesis, London School of Economics).

868
Grossfield, K. Inventions as business. *Econ. j.,* 72 (285), March 1962, pp 12-26.

Examines the activities of the National Research Development Corporation, the criteria used for developing and exploiting inventions, and difficulty of estimating profitability.

869
Gruber, W., **Mehta,** D. *and* **Vernon,** R. The R & D factor in international trade and international investment of United States industries. *J. political econ.,* 75 (1), Feb. 1967, pp 20-37.

An important article comparing 5 US industries with highest research effort and 14 other industries with regard to their export and foreign investment record in European and non-European countries. One table on R & D activity in US, UK, W. Germany, and France in 1962. Suggests strong relation between research content of goods, exports and the establishment of manufacturing subsidiaries. Statistical appendix, sources of data ; references.

870
Gustafson, W. E. Research and development, new products, and productive change. *Am. econ. rev.,* 52 (2), May 1962, pp 177-189.

871
Heath, J. B. British-Canadian industrial productivity. *Econ. j.,* 67 (268), Dec. 1957, pp 665-691.

Includes the results of an empirical study of British-Canadian industrial productivity in 1948. Examines differences in productivity, costs, prices, investment, their causes and effects. Suggests that, generally, under conditions of high productivity, equipment may be considered more quickly obsolescent when, relative to equipment, labour is expensive rather than cheap. An appendix describes methods of comparing gross and net output, materials and fuel used, employment, prices and investment.

872
Henderson, P. D., *ed.* Economic growth in Britain. Weidenfeld and Nicolson, 1966. 296 p.

Nine essays. Of special relevance : *The determinants of economic growth* by W. Beckerman (pp 55-83). Contributions by P. D. Henderson, R. G. Opie, P. Streeten, J. Vaizey and others.

873
Hilhorst, J. G. M. Monopolistic competition, technical progress and income distribution. Rotterdam, Rotterdam Univ. Pr., 1965. xii, 152 p. (Economic series, vol. 3).

874
Hitch, C. J. Character of research and development in a competitive economy. In *Proceedings of a conference on research and development and its impact on the economy* (Washington, Gov't. Print. Off., 1958), pp 129-139.

An important paper, given at a conference sponsored by the US National Science Foundation, which stresses the danger of too much centralisation and the need for multiple path research. Argues that the losses caused by the former outweigh those—duplication and waste—caused by the latter.

875
Johnston, R. E. Technical progress and innovation. *Oxf. econ. pap.,* new ser. 18 (2), July 1966, pp 158–176.

An informative review of recent literature on the subject. The author examines existing theories on technical progress (Kaldor, Arrow, Domar, etc.) and on innovation ; (Schumpeter, Galbraith, Bain, J. Robinson, Freeman, etc.) and quotes evidence for and against these theories. Problems discussed : how to measure effects of innovation ; factors affecting innovation, including the effect of economic and market structure, such as size, competition, protection, stability, risk and risk finance. 3 page bibliography and references.

876
Kennedy, C. Technical progress and investment. *Econ. j.,* 71 (282), June 1961, pp 292–299.

877
MacLaurin, W. R. The process of technological innovation : the launching of a new scientific industry. *Am. econ. rev.,* 40 (1), March 1950, pp 90–112.

878
Maddala, G. S. *and* **Knight,** P. T. International diffusion of technical change : a case study of the oxygen steel making process. *Econ. j.,* 77 (307), Sept. 1967, pp 531–558.

Authors examine determinants and diffusion of technical change, using as example a process developed in a small-sized country and first adopted in a small-size Canadian plant.

879
Mansfield, E. Industrial research and development expenditures : determinants, prospects, and relation to size of firm and inventive output. *J. political econ.,* 72 (4), Aug. 1964, pp 319–340.

880
Mansfield, E. Size of firms, market structure and innovation. *J. political econ.,* 71 (6), Dec. 1963, pp 556–576.

881
Markham, J. W. Market structure, business conduct and innovation. *Am. econ. rev.,* 55 (2), May 1965, pp 323–332.

882
Massell, B. F. Capital formation and technological change in United States manufacturing. *Rev. econ. statist.,* 42 (2), May 1960, pp 182–188.

883
Massell, B. F. A disaggregated view of technical change. *J. political econ.,* 69 (6), Dec. 1961, pp 547–557.

884
National Bureau of Economic Research, *New York.*
The rate and direction of inventive activity : economic and social factors. A conference of the Universities-National Bureau Committee for economic research and the Committee on economic growth of the Social Science Research Council. Princeton (NJ), Princeton Univ. Pr., 1962. xi, 635 p. (Special conference series, no. 13).

See also item 922.

885
Nelson, R. R. The economics of invention : a survey of the literature. *J. bus.,* 32, April 1959, pp 101–127.

886
Nelson, R. R., **Peck,** M. J. *and* **Kalachek,** E. D. Technology, economic growth and public policy. Washington, Brookings Institution, 1967. xiii, 238 p.

A Rand Corporation and Brookings Institution study. Based largely on United States data, with some international comparisons. Of special interest the chapters on the institutional structure of the 'inventions industry' ; the concentration of R & D in certain size-groups of firms, certain industries and certain product fields. Extensive bibliography (pp 212–228).

887
Organisation for Economic Co-operation and Development. The overall level and structure of R & D efforts in OECD countries. Paris, 1967. 66 p.

First report in a planned series resulting from the International statistical year for research and development. It analyses the scale and structure of R & D in 17 member countries in 1963/64. Includes classifications of countries by size of industrial sector ; by main sectors of economy ; by objectives ; by type of activity ; by selected industries. Of special interest : concentration of R & D expenditure ; comparison of R & D manpower ; comparison with the USA.

888
Organisation for Economic Co-operation and Development. Science, economic growth and government policy. Paris, 1963. 66 p.

889
Paige, D. C., **Blackaby,** F. T. *and* **Freund,** S. Economic growth : the last hundred years. *Natn. Inst. econ. rev.,* (16), July 1961, pp 24–49.

890
Phillips, A. Concentration, scale and technological change in selected manufacturing industries,1899-1939. *J. ind. econ.,* 4 (3), June 1956, pp 179–193.

Investigation into 28 US industries for which suitable data were available.

891
Quinn, J. B. Technological competition : Europe vs. US. *Harv. bus. rev.,* 44, July/Aug. 1966, pp 113–116.

An important contribution based on results of a research project.

892
Reddaway, W. B. *and* **Smith,** A. D. Progress in British manufacturing industries in the period 1948-54. *Econ. j.,* 70 (277), March 1960, pp 17–37.

893
Robertson, D. J. Economic effects of technological change. *Scott. j. political econ.,* 12 (2), June 1965, pp 180–194.

894
Rogers, E. M. Diffusion of innovations. New York, Free Press of Glencoe, 1962. 367 p.

895
Rosenberg, N. Capital goods, technology and economic growth. *Oxf. econ. pap.,* new ser. 15 (3), Nov. 1963, pp 217–227.

896
Rudd, E. Expenditure on scientific research and technical development in Britain and America. Department of Scientific and Industrial Research, 1956. 34 p.

Paper read to section F of the British Association, 4th September 1956. Based on two surveys.

897
Rudd, E. Scientific research and technical development in British industries. 1959. (Ph. D. thesis, Univ. of London).

898
Salter, W. E. G. Productivity and technical change. 2nd ed., with an addendum by W. B. Reddaway. Cambridge Univ. Pr., 1966. xiv, 220 p. (Cambridge Univ. Dept. of Applied Economics. Monograph no. 6).

899
Sayers, R. S. The springs of technical progress in Britain, 1919-1939. *Econ. j.,* 60 (238), June 1950, pp 275–291.

900
Scherer, F. M. Firm size, market structure, opportunity and the output of patented inventions. *Am. econ. rev.,* 55 (5 part 1), Dec. 1965, pp 1097–1125.

Tests the influence of size of firm, technological opportunity, market powers, R & D, liquidity and product differentiation, on patented inventions. According to author's findings only size and opportunity seem to produce some systematic relation to inventions.

901

Scherer, F. M. Market structure and the employment of scientists and engineers. *Am. econ. rev.,* 57 (3), June 1967, pp 524–531.

Critical examination of Schumpeter's theories (see items 54 and 55) on the relation between monopoly power and technological innovation, analysing two samples of American manufacturing industry groups.

902

Schmookler, J. Bigness, fewness and research. *J. political econ.,* 67 (6), Dec. 1959, pp 628–635.

A criticism of *Competition, oligopoly and research,* by H. H. Villard (item 909) with a reply by Villard, pp 633–635.

903

Schmookler, J. Technological change and economic theory, with a discussion by M. A. Adelman, Z. Griliches, R. A. Tybout. *Am. econ. rev.,* 55 (2), May 1965, pp 333–347.

904

Schon, D. A. Champions for radical new inventions. *Harv. bus. rev.,* 41 (2), March-April 1963, pp 77–86.

Describes those factors in military and non-military large-size organisation which are responsible for resistance to innovation.

905

Scott, C. The use of technical literature by industrial technologists : a study of technical information in the electrical industry. Central Office of Information Social Survey Division, [1958]. [3], 106 p. (SS 245).

A report on the findings of a sample enquiry. The report, which suggests that technical literature is used to a very limited extent by industrial technologists, is included in the bibliography in view of its relevance for maintaining competitive strength.

906

United Nations. *Economic Commission for Europe.* Some factors in economic growth in Europe during the 1950s. Geneva, 1964. 1 v. (various pagings).

Issued as part 2 of *Economic survey of Europe in 1961.* Chapter 1 discusses problems of measuring labour and capital inputs and economic growth. Chapter 5 deals with technical progress and the effects of scientific research. In a series of tables the R & D efforts of various countries during the period 1950-1960 are compared and related to the growth of output.

907

United Nations. *Statistical Office.* Patterns of industrial growth . . . 1938-1958. New York, 1960. viii, 471 p.

908

United States. *Department of Commerce. Panel on inventions and innovations.* Technological innovation : its environment and management. Washington, Gov't. Print. Off., 1967. vii, 83 p.

909

Villard, H. H. Competition, oligopoly and research. *J. political econ.,* 66 (6), Dec. 1958, pp 483–497.

Explores the relationship between research and progress, and offers some suggestions for improving research performance. For discussion see item 902.

910

Westfield, F. M. Technical progress and returns to scale. *Rev. econ. statist.,* 48 (4), Nov. 1966, pp 432–441.

911

Williams, B. R. Research and development in Britain. *Lond. Camb. econ. bull.,* new ser. (33), March 1960, pp iv–vi.

912

Williamson, O. E. Innovation and market structure. *J. political econ.,* 73 (1), Feb. 1965, pp 67–73.

913

Woodward, J. Management and technology. HMSO, 1958. 40 p. (Department of Scientific and Industrial Research. Problems of progress in industry, 3).

914

Worley, J. S. Industrial research and the new competition. *J. political econ.,* 69 (2), April 1961, pp 183–186.

Patents

Although references to the economic effects of patents can be found in a number of works on monopoly and industrial structure, not many specialised studies on developments in the UK are available. Of special relevance are the early work by P. Meinhardt (item 925) and the recent investigations by K. Boehm and A. Silberston (item 916). Reports of general validity have been published in the course of the United States Congressional hearings on patents, trade marks and copyrights (1956-1961) ; they include interesting papers by G. E. Frost (item 920), F. Machlup (item 923) and S. Melman (item 926).

915

Allen, J. W. Economic aspects of patents and the American patent system : a bibliography. Study [no. 14] of the Subcommittee on patents, trademarks and copyrights of the Committee on the judiciary, United States Senate, 85th Cong., 2nd sess. Washington, Gov't. Print. Off., 1958. v, 54 p.

916

Boehm, K. The British patent system, by Klaus Boehm in collaboration with Aubrey Silberston. Vol. 1, Administration. Cambridge Univ. Pr., 1967. x, 184 p. (Cambridge Univ. Dept. of Applied Economics. Monograph no. 13).

Analyses history, legislation (including Monopolies and restrictive practices Act) and methods of administration. The chapter 'A statistical profile of the British patent system' demonstrates difficulties of using present-day patent data for industrial analysis. Second volume on economic effects of the patent system will complete the work.

917
Edwards, V. L. Efforts to establish a statutory standard of invention : study [no. 7] of the Subcommittee on patents, trademarks and copyrights of the Committee on the judiciary, United States Senate, 85th Cong., 1st sess. Washington, Gov't. Print. Off., 1958. vi, 29 p.

918
The Encyclopedia of patent practice and invention management . . . edited by R. Calvert. New York, Reinhold Pub. Corp. ; London, Chapman & Hall, 1964. xix, 860 p.

Mainly legal-technical but useful sections, with short bibliographies, on antitrust laws and patents ; foreign licensing and antitrust laws ; foreign patents ; monopolies, inventions and section 103 of the US Patent Act 1952.

919
Fox, H. G. Monopolies and patents : a study of the history and future of the patent monopoly. Toronto, Toronto Univ. Pr., 1947. xxv, 388 p. (Toronto Univ. studies, Legal series).

920
Frost, G. E. The patent system and the modern economy ; study [no. 2] of the Subcommittee on patents, trademarks and copyrights of the Committee on the judiciary, United States Senate, 84th Cong., 2nd sess. Washington, Gov't. Print. Off., 1957. v, 77 p.

Contents: 1, The patent system as a stimulus to competitive effort ; 2, The patent system in relation to the competitive economy ; 3, Administration of the patent system.

921
Gilfillan, S. C. Invention and the patent system : materials relating to continuing studies of technology, economic growth and the variability of private investment, presented for consideration of the [Congress] Joint Economic Committee. Washington, Gov't. Print. Off., 1964. ix, 247 p.

922
Kuznets, S. Inventive activity : problems of definition and measurement. In *The rate and direction of inventive activity* (NBER, 1962—item 884), pp 19–51.

Includes a comment by J. Schmookler (pp 43–51).

923
Machlup, F. An economic review of the patent system : study [no. 15] of the Subcommittee on patents, trademarks and copyrights of the Committee on the judiciary, United States Senate, 85th Cong., 2nd sess. Washington, Gov't. Print. Off., 1958. vi, 89 p.

924
Maclaurin, W. R. Patents and technical progress : a study of television. *J. political econ.,* 58 (2), April 1950, pp 142–157.

925
Meinhardt, P. Inventions, patents and monopoly. 2nd ed. Stevens, 1950. xvi, 320 p.

One of the few British books paying special attention to the relation between patents and monopoly. Although mainly legal-technical, useful sections on the abuse and the prevention of abuse of patent monopoly. Bibliography.

926
Melman, S. The impact of the patent system on research : study [no. 11] of the Subcommittee on patents, trademarks and copyrights of the Committee on the judiciary, United States Senate, 85th Cong., 2nd sess. Washington, Gov't. Print. Off., 1958. vii, 62 p.

927
Monopoly and patents in the USA. *Cartel,* 7, 1957, pp 130–133.

928
Mueller, D. C. Patents, research and development and the measurement of inventive activity. *J. ind. econ.,* 15 (1), Nov. 1966, pp 26–37.

929
Penrose, E. T. The economics of the international patent system. Baltimore, Johns Hopkins Pr., 1951. xv, 247 p. (Johns Hopkins Univ. Studies in historical and political science. Extra vols., new ser. no. 30).

Bibliography of pre-1950 publications.

930
Schmookler, J. The level of inventive activity. *Rev. econ. statist.,* 36, May 1954, pp 183–190.

Tries to explain changes in patent applications in the USA, 1869-1938.

931
Silberston, A. The patent system. *Lloyds Bank rev.,* (84), April 1967, pp 32–44.

932
Sturmey, S. G. Patents and progress in radio. *Manchr sch. econ. social stud.,* 28 (1), Jan. 1960, pp 19–36.

933
United States. *Congress. Senate. Select committee on small business (88th Cong., 1st sess.).* Economic aspects of government patent policies : hearings before the Subcommittee . . . Impact of Government patent policies on economic growth, scientific and technological progress, competition, monopoly, and opportunities for small business. Washington, Gov't. Print. Off., 1963. v, 391 p.

5 International competition

5.1 International competition : General

See also items 176, 226

The bibliography does not contain general works on international trade ; literature relevant for competition in foreign trade, including studies relating to rates of exchange, would require a separate bibliography. The publications selected refer to special aspects, such as British imports and exports, and in particular to some of the major factors which influence export performance and competitiveness of British industry : prices—H. B. Junz and R. R. Rhomberg (item 953), and S. J. Wells (item 978) ; volume of home demand—R. J. Ball and others (item 934) ; other non-price factors—A. L. Ginsburg, and R. M. Stern (item 948) ; age of product—S. Hirsch (item 949) ; G. C. Hufbauer (item 950) ; rate of economic growth—A. Maizels (item 961) ; size of plant—G. F. Ray (item 226) ; productivity—R. M. Stern (item 976). Two short studies by the National Economic Development Council (items 965, 966) summarize the price and non-price elements at work.

934
Ball, R. J., **Eaton,** J. R. *and* **Steuer,** M. D. The relationship between United Kingdom export performance in manufactures and the internal pressure of demand. *Econ. j.,* 76 (303), Sept. 1966, pp 501–518.

Part of a research project undertaken for the Board of Trade. Explains methods used. Period chosen 1954-1964. Finds high correlation between volume of world trade and level of manufactured exports. Effect of pressure of home demand difficult to separate from other factors, among them the relatively low growth rate of UK economy. Authors warn that results must be interpreted with care.

935
Balogh, T. Unequal partners. Oxford, Blackwell, 1963. 2 v.

Essays on international economic affairs, 1930-60, covering a wide range of topics. Vol. 1 contains a section on investment and a theoretical introduction dealing with problems such as comparative and opportunity costs, technical progress, economic growth, economies of scale, in the context of international trade. In some essays export incentives, import substitution and non-price competition are discussed. Vol. 2 includes a chapter on the effects of the 1949 devaluation on Britain's competitive strength.

936
Bank for International Settlements. Export credit insurance and export credit. [4th ed.]. Basle, 1965. [2], 290 leaves.

Review of government-sponsored schemes in 14 industrial countries (11 European, and Canada, Japan, USA).

937
Board of Trade. Structure of international trade credit. *Brd Trade j.,* 188 (3555), 7 May 1965, pp 991–996.

Results of an enquiry into the structure of trade credit extended to, or received from, other countries in 1962 and 1963.

938
Board of Trade. United Kingdom and world exports of manufactures in 1966. xix p. (Insert in *Brd Trade j.,* 193 (3684), 27 Oct. 1967).

Analysis for the period 1956-1966, by countries (exporting and importing) and commodities.

939
Brechling, F. Anglo-German export competition. *Three banks rev.,* (41), March 1959, pp 3–20.

940
Chang, H. Relative movements in the prices of exports of manufactures : United States versus other industrial countries, 1953-59. *Int. Monetary Fund staff pap.,* 9 (1), March 1962, pp 80–106.

Comments on difficulties in comparing unit labour costs or costs of materials. Countries examined include the UK, Germany, and Japan.

941
Chipman, J. S. A survey of the theory of international trade. *Econometrica,* 33 (3), July 1965, pp 477–519 ; 33 (4), Oct. 1965, pp 685–760 ; 34 (1), Jan. 1966, pp 18–76.

Contents: Part 1, The classical theory ; pt 2, The neo-classical theory ; pt 3, The modern theory. Extensive references, including non-econometric publications.

942
Competition in export credits. *Banker,* 108 (390), July 1958, pp 440–443.

943
Conan, A. R. Sterling : the problem of diagnosis. *Westminster Bank rev.,* Aug. 1967, pp 2–13.

Argues that balance of payments deficit is not due to lack of competitiveness and domestic inflation but to heavy government overseas expenditure, large capital exports and sudden outflows of short-term capital.

944
Dyer, J. M. *and* **Dyer,** F. C. Export financing : modern US methods. Coral Gables, Univ. of Miami Pr., 1963. xiii, 180 p. (Univ. of Miami publications in economics, no. 6).

945
Dyson, B. H. *and* **Mayall,** W. H. Design and programming for world markets. British Productivity Council, [1964]. [9], 118 p.

946
Financial Advisory Panel on Exports. *Committee on invisible exports (1966/67).* Britain's invisible earnings : the report of the Committee . . . British National Export Council, 1967. 267 p.

Deplores discrimination in favour of visible exports, in the fields of statistics and incentives. Argues that aids and incentives provided for visible exports should be extended to invisibles, including credit, missions, Queen's Award to Industry, etc., to make invisibles more competitive.

947
General Agreement on Tariffs and Trade.
International Trade Centre. A bibliography of market surveys by products and countries . . . Geneva, 1967. xxi, 187 p.

948
Ginsburg, A. L. *and* **Stern,** R. M. The determination of the factors affecting American and British exports in the inter-war and post-war periods. *Oxf. econ. pap.,* new ser. 17 (2), July 1965, pp 263–278.

Discusses Sir Donald MacDougall's articles (items 958 and 959). Believes that MacDougall's assumption that price elasticity of substitution was constant for all commodities has to be modified. In addition to export price ratios other factors should be taken into account such as market proximity, quality differences, import demand. The authors classify the total by regions, according to location, economic importance and Commonwealth preference, and conclude that the regional effect, neglected in previous studies, is important.

949
Hirsch, S. The United States electronics industry in international trade. *Natn. Inst. econ. rev.,* (34), Nov. 1965, pp 92–97.

Analyses effect of age of a product on foreign demand, in terms of a 'product cycle' view of international competitiveness.

950
Hufbauer, G. C. Synthetic materials and the theory of international trade. Duckworth, 1966. 165 p.
Originally a Cambridge thesis, referred to in A. Shonfield's *Modern capitalism,* Appendix II (item 110). Hufbauer examines the average age of 56 synthetic products over the period 1910-1960 which entered international trade.

951
Institute of Bankers. The finance of international trade . . . [1965]. [3], 60 p.

Ernest Sykes memorial lectures, 1965. *Contents:* Short-term import and export finance, by B. S. Wheble ; Medium and long-term export credit, by C. P. Lunn ; Current aspects of foreign exchange, by E. G. Woolgar.

952
Jannaccone, P. Dumping and price discrimination. *Int. econ. pap.,* (5), 1955, pp 103–133.

First pub. as *Il 'dumping' e la discriminazione dei prezzi,* in *Riforma sociale,* March 1914. Major article treating dumping as part of price discrimination, local and international ; analyses forms and aims of dumping, conditions for its application, its relation to volume of output, costs of production, profits and welfare.

953
Junz, H. B. *and* **Rhomberg,** R. R. Prices and export performance of industrial countries, 1953-63. *Int. Monetary Fund staff pap.,* 12 (2), July 1965, pp 224–271.

An important contribution to the problems of measuring price competitiveness and price elasticities of demand for exports.

954
Kevork, C. The United Kingdom's demand for imports, 1946-1957 : a discussion of attempts to measure elasticities of selected commodities. 1959. (Ph. D. thesis, London School of Economics).

955
Letiche, J. M. Differential rates of productivity growth and international imbalance. *Q. j. econ.,* 69 (3) Aug. 1955, pp 371–401.

Examines whether long-term international imbalance of West European industrial countries vis-a-vis the US in the post-war period can be explained by different rates of change in productivity.

956
MacDougall, *Sir* G. D. A. Britain's bargaining power. *Econ. j.,* 56 (221), March 1946, pp 27–37.

957
MacDougall, *Sir* G. D. A. Britain's foreign trade problem. *Econ. j.,* 57 (225), March 1947, pp 69–113.

Comment by T. Balogh, *Econ. j.,* 58 (229), March 1948, pp 74–85 ; reply by McDougall, pp 86–98.

958

MacDougall, *Sir* G. D. A. British and American exports : a study suggested by the theory of comparative costs. *Econ. j.,* Part 1, 61 (244), Dec. 1951, pp 697–724 ; pt 2, 62 (247), Sept. 1952, pp 487–521.

For discussion see item 948.

959

McDougall, *Sir* G. D. A. *and others.* British and American productivity, prices and exports : an addendum. *Oxf. econ. pap.,* new ser. 14 (3), Oct. 1962, pp 297–304.

Addendum to *British and American productivity and comparative costs in international trade,* by Robert M. Stern (item 976). For discussion see item 948.

960

MacDougall, *Sir* G. D. A. Notes on Britain's bargaining power. *Oxf. econ. pap.,* new ser. 1 (1), Jan. 1949, pp 18–39.

961

Maizels, A. Industrial growth and world trade : an empirical study of trends in production, consumption and trade in manufactures from 1899-1959, with a discussion of probable future trends. Cambridge Univ. Pr., 1963. xxiv, 563 p. (National Institute of Economic and Social Research. Economic and social studies, 21).

This extensive study attempts an analysis of past and estimates of future relation between rate of economic growth of main industrial countries, imports and consumption of manufactured goods. 8 page bibliography. Based on the author's Ph. D. thesis (London School of Economics, 1962), *Industrialisation and international trade: a study of long-term trends in the world market for manufactured goods.*

962

Minchinton, W. E. The finance of exports. *Distr. Bank rev.,* (148), Dec. 1963, pp 35–51.

963

Moore, L. Factors affecting the demand for British exports. *Bull. Oxf. Univ. Inst. Econ. Statist.,* 27 (4), Nov. 1964, pp 343–359.

Calculates the effect of : relative export prices ; foreign exchange position of importing country ; relation between various countries' growth of real income and imports ; relation between volume of industrial production and imports ; relation between export proceeds and imports. Special calculations for chemicals, machinery and transport equipment.

964

Narvekar, P. R. The role of competitiveness in Japan's export performance, 1954-58. *Int. Monetary Fund staff pap.,* 8 (1), Nov. 1960, pp 85–100.

Analyses effect of factors such as expansion and change in the commodity and market pattern of world trade as distinct from increased competitiveness. Author examines consequences of scarcities, caused by an export-led boom, on exports.

965

National Economic Development Council. Export trends. HMSO, 1963. iv, 28 p.

Includes chapters on relative costs and prices and on reasons for UK's falling share in world exports.

966

National Economic Development Council. Imported manufactures : an inquiry into competitiveness. HMSO, 1965. iv, 40 p.

967

Nehrt, L. C. Financing capital equipment exports : a comparative study of medium-term export financing. Scranton (Pa.) ,International Textbook Co., 1966. [5], 122 p.

Compares credit facilities in the UK, Japan, France, Germany, Italy, and USA in the years 1964-1965. References to sources of information.

968

Patterson, G. Discrimination in international trade : the policy issues, 1945-1965. Princeton (NJ), Princeton Univ. Pr., 1966. xv, 414 p.

A useful research project on changes in attitudes towards discrimination and on the effects of discrimination and non-discrimination on the contracting parties and on third countries. Based largely on primary sources obtained at GATT headquarters. Many useful references.

969

Posner, M. V. International trade and technical change. *Oxf. econ. pap.,* new ser. 13 (3), Oct. 1961, pp 323–341.

Constructs a model for explaining trade in different products of similar industries between competing advanced nations. Discusses problem of 'imitation lag'.

970

Ray, G. F. British imports of manufactured goods. *Natn. Inst. econ. rev.,* (8), March 1960, pp 12–29.

Tries to examine, up to 1959, the role competitiveness plays in the increase of imported manufactures. Finds different causes for different commodities : cheapness of foreign lower quality textiles and clothing ; preference for foreign design in expensive consumer goods ; delivery dates in ships ; international specialization such as in machinery or high quality watches. General reasons : rise in international trade in manufactured goods ; relaxation of import controls ; increase in total demand for machinery and transport equipment relative to increase in national income. Comparing increase in imports of finished manufactures with increase of corresponding exports by Britain over the period 1899-1959 finds that in trade with USA and Western Europe net balance in Britain's favour. In a later article, *British imports of manufactures (Natn. Inst. econ. rev.,* (15), May 1961, pp 36–41), the examination is extended to 1960.

971

Ray, G. F. The competitiveness of British industrial products : a round up. Woolwich Polytechnic, 1966. 28 p. (Woolwich economic papers, no. 10).

Examines explanations given for Britain's falling share in world trade such as changes in the geographical and commodity pattern of trade, taxation, wage costs, stop-go policies, growth of subsidiary companies abroad, etc. Author draws attention to problems of standardisation, productivity, marketing and methods of export pricing.

972

Ray, G. F. Export competitiveness : British experience in Eastern Europe. *Natn. Inst. econ. rev.,* (36), May 1966, pp 43–60.

973

Romanis, A. Relative growth of exports of manufactures of United States and other industrial countries. *Int. Monetary Fund staff pap.,* 8 (2), May 1961, pp 241–273.

Compares competitiveness in different product classes and markets.

974

Scott, M. FG. A study of United Kingdom imports. Cambridge Univ. Pr., 1963. xvi, 269 p. (National Institute of Economic and Social Research. Economic and social studies, 20).

975

Skiold, A. Antitrust problems in international trade. *Antitrust bull.,* 10 (3), May–June 1965, pp 421–458.

Regulation and competition as alternatives.

976

Stern, R. M. British and American productivity and comparative costs in international trade. *Oxf. econ. pap.,* new ser. 14 (3), Oct. 1962, pp 275–296.

Critical addendum by Sir Donald MacDougall and others (see item 959).

977

United States. *Treasury.* Survey of export financing, prepared by P. P. Schaffner. [Washington, 1966]. x, 49 p.

A questionnaire-survey of 758 US manufacturing firms of various sizes at the end of 1965. Data collected and compiled by US Bureau of the Census.

978

Wells, S. J. British export performance : a comparative study. Cambridge Univ. Pr., 1964. xxiv, 235 p.

Compares prices of British exports with domestic prices and with export prices of other countries in selected industries.

5.2 Tariffs

See also items 64, 1152

Literature on tariffs is richly endowed with articles. Those by B. Balassa (items 979–981), J. Black (item 982), H. G. Johnson (items 1009–1012) and M. E. Kreinin (item 1014) should prove especially helpful. The important problem of measuring tariff levels is discussed by A. Loveday (item 1015) and G. F. Ray (item 1021). Among books those by F. K. Topping (item 1022A) and W. P. Travis (item 1024) and the symposium edited by G. D. N. Worswick (item 1027) should be mentioned. Reports of tariff investigations published by Australia, India, South Africa and the United States examine competitive conditions, by commodities. The *Board of Trade journal* records changes in tariffs and import regulations.

979

Balassa, B. The impact of the industrial countries' tariff structure on their imports of manufactures from less-developed areas. *Economica,* 34 (136), Nov. 1967, pp 372–383.

Critical examination of the discrimination practised by the advanced industrial countries in the structure of their tariffs, against imports of manufactures from less developed countries. Useful references.

980

Balassa, B. Tariff protection in industrial countries : an evaluation. *J. political econ.,* 73 (6), Dec. 1965, pp 573–594.

Discusses problems of measuring and comparing levels of tariffs and of assuming stable exchange rates. Elaborates distinction between nominal and effective rates of tariffs. Useful references.

981

Balassa, B. Trade liberalisation and 'revealed' comparative advantages. *Manchr sch. econ. social stud.,* 33 (2), May 1965, pp 99–123.

Examines long-term effects of lowering tariff barriers on allocation of resources. Works with dispersion of export performance and with export-import ratios.

982

Black, J. Arguments for tariffs. *Oxf. econ. pap.,* new ser. 11 (2), June 1959, pp 191–208.

Surveys arguments for tariffs and the circumstances in which they can be valid. Paragraphs 32–35 deal with the effect of tariffs on monopoly, size, and returns.

983

Board of Trade. Customs duties (dumping and subsidies) Act, 1957 : annual report by the Board of Trade. 1957/58+ HMSO. Published as a House of Commons paper.

984
Board of Trade. Import duties act 1958 : annual report by the Board. . .for the year ended 31st March. 1960+ HMSO.
Published as a House of Commons paper.

985
Board of Trade. Report on the Annecy tariff negotiations . . .HMSO, 1949. 12 p. (Cmd. 7792).

986
Board of Trade. The Kennedy round of trade negotiations, 1964–67. HMSO, 1967. 47 p. (Cmnd. 3347).

987
Board of Trade. Report on the Geneva tariff negotiations. . .HMSO, 1947. [1], vii, 46 p. (Cmd. 7258).

988
Board of Trade. Report on the Geneva tariff negotiations, 1956 ; with text of the sixth protocol of supplementary concessions to the General Agreement on Tariffs and Trade (Geneva, 23rd May, 1956). HMSO, 1956. 8 p. (Cmd. 9779).

989
Board of Trade. Report on the Geneva tariff negotiations, 1960–2, with texts of the final act and of the protocol to the General Agreement on Tariffs and Trade embodying results of the tariff conference (Geneva, 16th July, 1962). HMSO, 1962. 12 p. (Cmnd. 1804).

990
Board of Trade. Report on the Torquay tariff negotiations. . .HMSO, 1951. 18 p. (Cmd. 8228).

991
The British tariff system. *Three banks rev.,* Dec. 1965, pp 19–33.

An attempt to obtain an overall picture of relative tariff levels, protective and preferential, relating to Commonwealth, EEC, EFTA, and US. One table on effect of import surcharge.

992
Central Office of Information. Commonwealth preference. 1961. [2], 12 p. (Reference document, R.5155).

993
Central Office of Information. Rates of import duty and purchase tax in Britain. 1966. [1], 21 p. (Reference document, R. 5281/66).

994
Corden, W. M. The structure of a tariff system and the effective protective rate. *J. political econ.,* 74 (3), June 1966, pp 221–237.

995
Council of Europe. Low tariff club : a. . .study of the problem of lowering customs barriers as between member-countries. Strasbourg, 1952, 188 p.

Traces the post-1945 history of attempts to lower tariffs, from the Havana charter to the Schuman plan. Examines the implications of lowering tariffs.

996
Curzon, G. Multilateral commercial diplomacy : the General Agreement on Tariffs and Trade and its impact on national commercial policies and techniques. Michael Joseph, 1965. xiii, 367 p.

A thorough survey of the history, organisation, function and impact of GATT. Examines the tariff negotiations 1947–1962 including the 'Kennedy round', the problems of quantitative restrictions, of agriculture, state trading, economic regionalism. A 20-page bibliography lists the major GATT and other official documents, as well as relevant books and articles.

997
Customs and Excise. Protective duties : values or quantities of imported goods entered for home use in the United Kingdom, and receipts of duty. 1959–1965. HMSO.

Continues *Principal dutiable goods imported and retained for home use, receipts of duty and rates of duty charged,* pub. 1940–1958 as a supplement to vol. 2 of *Annual statement of the trade of the United Kingdom.* Information for 1966 and subsequent years may be obtained, on payment of a fee, from Bill of Entry Section (PD), Statistical Office, HM Customs and Excise, Portcullis House, 27 Victoria Avenue, Southend-on-Sea, Essex.

998
Diebold, W. Trade and payments in western Europe : a study in economic cooperation, 1947–51. New York, Harper, 1952. xvii, 488 p.

Published for the Council on Foreign Relations.

999
Economist Intelligence Unit. Britain and Europe : a study of the effects on British manufacturing industry of a free trade area and the Common Market. 1957. xv, 288, [16] p.

Estimates trade between Britain and Europe in 1970 for some 13 major industries, with and without Britain joining a European free trade area.

1000
Economist Intelligence Unit. A comparison of the United Kingdom tariff and the proposed tariff of the European Economic Community. 1959. 32 leaves.

Prepared for the Federal Trust for Education and Research.

1001
European Economic Community. Disparate aspects of selected tariff structures : a statistical comparison of the common external tariff of the EEC, the tariff of the United States of America and the tariff of the United Kingdom. . .by Marcel Mesnage. . .Brussels, 1964. 11 leaves. (Information memo P-6/64).

First published as *Comparison statistique du tarif douanier commun de la CEE...* in *Infs statist.,* (3), 1963, pp 101–123 (English summary p 123). Provides unweighted tariff averages.

1002
General Agreement on Tariffs and Trade. Review of the General Agreement on Tariffs and Trade : statement of policy with revised text of the agreement and related documents. HMSO, 1955. vii, 98 p. (Cmd. 9413).

1003
General Agreement on Tariffs and Trade. *Contracting parties.* Analytical index [to the general agreement]. (2nd revision). Notes on the drafting, interpretation and application of the articles of the general agreement. Geneva, 1966. [4], v, 184 p.

1004
General Agreement on Tariffs and Trade. *Contracting parties.* Basic instruments and selected documents. 1952+ Geneva.

Vol. 1, 1952, Text of the agreement and other instruments and procedures ; v. 1 (revised), 1955, Texts of the general agreement, as amended, and of the agreement on the Organization for Trade Cooperation ; v. 2, 1952, Decisions, declarations, resolutions, rulings and reports of working parties, etc. ; v. 3, 1958, Text of the general agreement in force 1958. Kept up to date by annual supplements containing protocols, decisions and reports.

1005
General Agreement on Tariffs and Trade. *Contracting parties.* Trends in international trade : report by a panel of experts. Geneva, 1958. [6], 143 p.

Chairman of the panel : Gottfried Haberler. Contains a chapter on protectionist policies.

1006
Green, R. W. Commonwealth preference : United Kingdom customs duties and tariff preferences on imports from the preference area. *Brd Trade j.,* 189 (3589), 31 Dec. 1965, pp 1551–1558.

Measures the height of preference.

1007
Green, R. W. Commonwealth preference : tariff duties and preferences on United Kingdom exports to the preference area. xix p. (Insert in *Brd Trade j.,* 188 (3560), 11 June 1965).

1008
International Customs Tariffs Bureau. Bulletin international des douanes. The international customs journal. [English ed.] 1891+ Brussels.

Publishes tariffs of all member states.

1009
Johnson, H. G. The cost of protection and the scientific tariff. *J. political econ.,* 68 (4), Aug. 1960, pp 327–345.

1010
Johnson, H. G. An economic theory of protectionism, tariff bargaining, and the formation of customs unions. *J. political econ.,* 73 (3), June 1965, pp 256–283.

1011
Johnson, H. G. The Kennedy round. *J. wld trade law,* 1 (4), July/Aug. 1967, pp 475–481.

A précis of the history and results of the Kennedy round and of the likely implications for the future of trade liberalisation.

1012
Johnson, H. G. Optimum tariffs and retaliation. *Rev. econ. stud.,* 21, 1953/54, pp 142–153.

1013
Krause, L. B. United States imports and the tariff. *Am. econ. rev.,* 49 (2), May 1959, pp 542–551.

Examines effects of tariff reductions agreed at Torquay in 1951 (item 990). Criticism by W. S. Hunsberger in discussion (pp 555–558).

1014
Kreinin, M. E. Effect of tariff changes on the prices and volume of imports. *Am. econ. rev.,* 51 (3), June 1961, pp 310–324.

Analyses effects of 1955/56 GATT negotiations on volume and prices of US imports. Compares his results with those of other authors. Useful references.

1015
Loveday, A. The measurement of tariff levels. *J. R. Statist. Soc.,* 92 (4), 1929, pp 487–529.

Paper and discussion. A major contribution.

1016
MacDougall, *Sir* G. D. A. *and* **Hutt,** R. Imperial preference : a quantitative analysis. *Econ. j.,* 64 (254), June 1954, pp 233–257.

1017
McGuire, E. B. The British tariff system. 2nd ed., rev. and enl. Methuen, 1951. vii, 365 p.

Describes the principles and administration of the British tariff system. Two chapters have been added to the first edition, published in 1939, in order to take account of development 1938-1950 (including GATT).

1018

Maizels, A., **Campbell-Boross,** L. F. *and* **Glover,** F. J. EEC and EFTA : tariffs on manufactures and our trade balance. *Natn. Inst. econ. rev.,* (23), Feb. 1963, pp 51-55.

Based on 1960 data. Compares effects of entering and not entering EEC.

1019

Political and Economic Planning. Atlantic tariffs and trade : a report...Allen & Unwin, 1962. xvii, 426 p.

Chiefly tables comparing, in detail, the tariffs of USA, Canada, the EEC and the EFTA countries.

1020

Political and Economic Planning. Tariffs and trade in Western Europe : a report...Allen & Unwin, 1959. xvi, 119 p.

Tables illustrate patterns of intra-European trade and compare in detail the tariffs of the 12 main industrial countries of western Europe and the planned external tariff of the Common Market. For the first time, the Brussels Classification is used for comparing like with like.

1021

Ray, G. F. Changes in the height of tariffs. National Institute of Economic and Social Research, 1957. 1v. (various pagings).

Typescript with many duplicated graphs and tables. Shows trend of duties pre and post war (1937 and 1955) in various countries and commodities. Discusses measurement of level of tariffs and problems arising from composition of individual commodities, different types of duty, extra charges, other restrictions, changes in prices and in countries of origin. Useful references.

1022

Steuer, M. D. *and* **Erb,** G. F. An empirical test of the "GATT hypothesis". *J. political econ.,* 74 (3), June 1966, pp 274–277.

'The "GATT hypothesis" asserts that, in a slump, imports of goods subject to high tariffs decline proportionately more than goods subject to low tariffs'.

1022A

Topping, F. K., *ed.* Comparative tariffs and trade : the United States and the European Common Market. New York, Committee for Economic Development, 1963. 2v. (1117 p.). (Committee for Economic Development supplementary paper no. 14).

A rearrangement of the US tariff according to the Brussels nomenclature showing for each item the tariff rate and imports for both the USA and EEC.

1023

Trade, growth and the balance of payments : essays in honour of Gottfried Haberler. Chicago, Rand McNally, 1965. viii, 267p.

Part 1, Trade and resource allocation, includes the following contributions : *Tariff-cutting techniques in the Kennedy round,* by R. E. Baldwin (pp 68–81) ; *On the equivalence of tariffs and quotas,* by J. Bhagwati (pp 53–67) ; *Optimal trade intervention in the presence of domestic distortions,* by H. G. Johnson (pp 3—24) ; *Some aspects of policies for freer trade,* by B. Ohlin (pp 82–92).

1024

Travis, W. P. The theory of trade and protection. Cambridge (Mass.), Harvard Univ. Pr., 1964. xiii, 296p. (Harvard economic studies, vol. 121).

In the course of elaborating his theory, the author discusses causes and effects of protective policies, compares tariff levels, capital-labour ratios, imports and home production of raw materials, etc. Many references to relevant literature.

1025

Wartna, J. A. Import duties inside and outside the European Economic Community. *Infs statist.,* (2), 1966, pp 11–54.

Originally published, in Dutch, by Netherlands Central Bureau of Statistics, 1965.

1026

Wemelsfelder, J. The short-term effect of the lowering of import duties in Germany. *Econ. j.,* 70 (277), March 1960, pp 94–104.

Refers to the years 1956 to 1958.

1027

Worswick, G. D. N., *ed.* The free trade proposals. Oxford, Blackwell, 1960. vii, 142p.

Comprises a reprint of a symposium on the European free trade area proposals, first pub. in *Bull. Oxf. Univ. Inst. Statist.,* 19 (1), Feb. 1957, with a further appraisal and an account of the Common Market. Contributions by T. Balogh, J. Black, A. C. L. Day, Sir Roy Harrod, H. G. Johnson, R. F. Kahn, J. R. Sargent, G. D. N. Worswick.

1028

Woytinsky, W. S. *and* **Woytinsky,** E. S. World commerce and governments : trends and outlook. New York, Twentieth Century Fund, 1955. lii, 907p.

Contents: Part 1, Trade ; pt 2, Transport ; pt 3, Governments. Chapter 6 of this encyclopaedic work deals with 'Tariffs, trade agreements and trade restrictions', with many tables on tariff levels in the US and Europe in the early 1950's. Short survey of methods of measuring tariff levels.

5.3 International competition:
European Economic Community (Common Market)

See also items 270, 703–719, 999, 1000, 1001, 1018, 1019, 1020, 1102

The many issues raised by the Common Market include those of competition, concentration and anti-monopoly legislation (see Section 3.43, page 52). In this section, Britain's potential gains and losses are dealt with in works by the Economist Intelligence Unit (item 1035), H. G. Johnson, U. W. Kitzinger, A. Lamfalussy, M. Lipton (items 1042–1045), J. E. Meade (item 1049), M. Shanks and T. Lambert (item 1051). Publications by J. F. Deniau (item 1034), EEC, I. Frank, J. Hennessy (items 1034–1041), R. L. Major (item 1047), and T. Scitovsky (item 270) deal with the structure and effects of the Common Market.

1029
American Economic Association. *Annual meeting, 75th, 1962, Pittsburgh.* Problems of regional integration [papers and discussion]. *Am. econ. rev.,* 53 (2), May 1963, pp 147–203.

Contents: European economic integration and the pattern of world trade, by E. Thorbecke ; European integration : problems and issues, by B. Balassa ; European economic integration and the United States, by L. B. Krause.

1030
Balassa, B. Trade creation and trade diversion in the European Common Market. *Econ. j.,* 77 (305), March 1967, pp 1–21.

1031
Blackburn, J. A. The British cotton industry in the Common Market. *Three banks rev.,* (56), Dec. 1962, pp 3–22.

1032
Britain and Europe [special issue of the *Political quarterly*]. *Polit. q.,* 34 (1), Jan./March 1963, pp 1–95.

Contributions include : The consequences for economic structure, by J. Pinder (pp 29–43) ; The consequences for economic planning, by A. C. L. Day (pp 44–54) ; The legal consequences, by D. G. Valentine (pp 88–95).

1033
Brown, A. J. Common Market criteria and experience. *Three banks rev.,* (57), March 1963, pp 3–18.

1034
Deniau, J. F. The Common Market. 3rd ed. Barrie and Rockcliff, 1962. vii, 167 p.

Examines the theory, history and economics of the 'large market'.

1035
Economist Intelligence Unit. If Britain joins : a guide to the economic effects of membership of the Common Market. 1961. 32 p.

1036
European Communities. Customs tariff of the European Communities. Provisional English edition. HMSO, 1961-1962. 11 parts.

Translation made by the Board of Trade.

1037
European Economic Community. Treaty setting up the European Economic Community, Rome, 25th March, 1957. HMSO, 1967. vi, 231p.

Unofficial translation prepared by the Foreign Office. Includes annexes to the treaty and amendments agreed up to 2nd March, 1960.

1038
European Economic Community. [Treaty establishing the European Economic Community . . .]. Index to the Treaty of Rome. Association of British Chambers of Commerce, 1961. 2v.

Contents: [Part I], Index to the treaty ; pt. 2, Index to the annexes.

1039
European Economic Community. *Commission.* General report on the activities of the Community. 1st, 1958+ Brussels.

Issued annually. Topics reported include freedom of establishment and common competition policy.

1040
Frank, I. The European common market : an analysis of commercial policy. Stevens, 1961. [7], 324 p. (The library of world affairs, no. 55).

Published under the auspices of the London Institute of World Affairs.

1041
Hennessy, J. The European common market ; what will it mean to you ? Westminster Chamber of Commerce, [1957]. [6], 38 p.

1042
Johnson, H. G. The economic gains from freer trade with Europe. *Three banks rev.,* (39), Sept. 1958, pp 3–19.

1043
Kitzinger, U. W. The challenge of the Common Market. 4th ed. Oxford, Blackwell, 1962. viii, 240 p.

1044
Lamfalussy, A. The United Kingdom and the six ; an essay on economic growth in Western Europe. Macmillan, 1963. xviii, 147 p.

1045
Lipton, M. The Common Market : the economic arguments examined. *Three banks rev.,* (58), June 1963, pp 17–36.

1046
McClellan, A. British business and the Treaty of Rome.
J. bus. law, 1962, pp 31–40.

1047
Major, R. L. The Common Market : production and trade.
Natn. Inst. econ. rev., (21), Aug. 1962, pp 24–36.

1048
Meade, J. E. *and others.* Case studies in European
economic union : the mechanics of integration. Oxford
Univ. Pr., 1962. viii, 425 p.

Issued under the auspices of the Royal Institute of
International Affairs. Studies the Belgo-Luxembourg
Economic Union, Benelux and the European Coal and
Steel Community. Bibliography, mainly of publications in
German and French.

1049
Meade, J. E. UK, Commonwealth and Common Market.
Institute of Economic Affairs, 1962. 52 p. (Hobart papers,
no. 17).

Bibliography.

1050
Political and Economic Planning. Trade diversion in
Western Europe. 1960. 49 p. (Britain and the European
market. Occasional paper no. 9).

1051
Shanks, M. *and* **Lambert,** J. Britain and the new Europe :
the future of the Common Market. Chatto & Windus, 1962.
253 p.

1052
**Union des Industries de la Communauté
Européenne,** *Brussels.* Certains aspects des disparités
dans les dimensions des plus grandes entreprises de la CEE
comparées avec leurs principaux concurrents des pays
tiers. Bruxelles, 1965. [49] leaves.

Includes annexes providing data on individual firms.

1053
Weil, G. L., *ed.* A handbook on the European Economic
Community. New York, London, Praeger, 1965. xiv,
479 p. (Praeger special studies in international economics).

Published in cooperation with the European Community
Information Service, Washington.

1054
Westminster Bank Ltd. The Common Market . . . and the
United Kingdom : a guide to the European Economic
Community and the possible effects of British membership.
4th ed. 1966. 60 p.

6 Performance

6.1 Profits and investment

See also items 48, 104, 171, 173, 177, 180, 222, 261, 292, 330, 879

The role investment and its profitability play in economic growth and in competitive strength remain major issues. Valuable contributions by T. Barna (item 1059), G. Dean (items 1074, 1075), V. R. Fuchs (item 261), A. Lamfalussy (item 1093), National Bureau of Economic Research (item 1104) and A. Shonfield (item 1116). Other important issues : the relation between concentration and rate of profit, I. P. Andren (item 1055), J. S. Bain (item 171), H. M. Mann (item 330), A. Merrett and A. Sykes (item 1099), A. Silberston and D. Solomons (item 1117), G. J. Stigler (item 1121) ; the choice between British investment at home and abroad, A. K. Cairncross (item 1069), W. B. Reddaway (item 1113) ; the effect of non-British investment at home, J. H. Dunning (items 1078, 1079), R. F. Mikesell (item 1102) ; factors determining investment decision, J. R. Meyer and E. Kuh (item 1101), OECD (item 48), R. W. Wright (item 1130) ; the definition and measurement of capital, depreciation, rates of return and overheads, T. Barna (items 1059, 1060), G. Dean (items 1074, 1075), H. Kendall (item 1092), C. L. Parker (item 1109), A. Silberston and D. Solomons (item 1117), G. D. N. Worswick and D. G. Tipping (item 1129).

1055
Andren, I. P. Monopoly investigation and methods for calculating the rate of return on capital employed. *J. ind. econ.,* 4 (1), Oct. 1955, pp 1–15.

Uses reports of Monopolies Commission on matches and electric lamps (see Appendix 2, p 94) to demonstrate that their methods of estimating 'reasonable' profits are unsatisfactory. Pleads for more information in published company reports.

1056
Appleby, R. Profitability and productivity in the United Kingdom, 1954-1964. British Institute of Management, [1967]. 79 p. 12 tables as insert.

Opening address to the BIM national conference, March 7 1967. Distinguishes between public and private sectors. Some comparisons of UK and US data. Discusses problem of taking profits as a measure of efficiency.

1057
Balogh, T. Differential profits tax. *Econ. j.,* 68 (271), Sept. 1958, pp 528–533.

Argues against the findings of the *Final report* of the Royal Commission on the taxation of profits and income (1951-55) (HMSO, 1955. Cmd. 9474), which suggested that a differential profits tax works against the most efficient use of resources.

1058
Balogh, T. *and* **Streeten,** P. P. Domestic versus foreign investment. *Bull. Oxf. Univ. Inst .Statist.,* 22 (3), Aug. 1960, pp 213–224.

1059
Barna, T. Investment and growth policies in British industrial firms. Cambridge Univ. Pr., 1962. viii, 71 p. (National Institute of Economic and Social Research. Occasional paper, 20).

An enquiry sponsored by the European Productivity Agency. Case studies of firms in the food processing and electrical engineering industries. Examines differences in investment behaviour between industries and within one industry. Describes method of enquiry and of choosing sample. Of special relevance : parts of chapter 4 (Pressures for investment) and of chapter 5 (Increase in competition). Appendix C provides a statistical test of differences between firms.

1060
Barna, T. The replacement cost of fixed assets in British manufacturing industry in 1955. *J. R. Statist. Soc.,* ser. A 120 (1), 1957, pp 1–36.

1061
Bates, J. A. The financing of small business. Sweet & Maxwell, 1964. xv, 230 p.

1062
Bates, J. A. The financing of small business. *Bull. Oxf. Univ. Inst. Statist.,* 20 (2), May 1958, pp 153–186.

1063
Baumol, W. J. Business behavior, value and growth. New York, London, Macmillan, 1959. xv, 164 p.

Attempts to explain oligopolistic behaviour in terms of a 'sales maximisation hypothesis' according to which firms maximise sales subject to a minimum profit constraint.

1064

Board of Trade. Capital expenditure of manufacturing industry, 1948-1962. *In* Central Statistical Office. *New contributions to economic statistics,* 3rd series (HMSO, 1964), pp 128–138.

Reprinted from *Econ. trends,* (115), May 1963.

1065

Board of Trade. Income and finance of quoted companies, 1949-1960. *In* Central Statistical Office. *New contributions to economic statistics,* 3rd series (HMSO, 1964), pp 33–48.

Reprinted from *Econ. trends,* (102), April 1962. The sixth in an annual series of articles, earlier ones of which covered pairs of years from 1954/55. Continued by *Income and finance of quoted companies, 1960-62,* in *New contributions to economic statistics,* 3rd series, pp 49–60 (reprinted from *Econ. trends,* (122), Dec. 1963) and by quarterly articles in *Board of Trade journal* (first in 183 (3429), 7 Dec. 1962, pp 1153–1155). Includes income/asset ratios of selected industries and expenditure on acquiring subsidiary companies. Global data for all manufacturing. Supplemented by *Summary and industrial group tables* (1954/55-1960. Issued by Statistics Division Board of Trade). The final issue of these tables gives figures for 1949 to 1960. Industry group tables supplementing the quarterly *Board of Trade journal* articles are published in the Department of Employment and Productivity's *Statistics on incomes, prices, employment and production* (published quarterly by HMSO ; to 1968 compiled by Ministry of Labour). Figures for 1961 first published in no. 3, Dec. 1962.

1066

Board of Trade. Non-quoted companies and their finance. *In* Central Statistical Office. *New contributions to economic statistics,* 4th series (HMSO, 1967), pp 32–45.

Reprinted from *Econ. trends,* (136), Feb. 1965.

1067

British Institute of Management. Efficiency comparisons within large organizations, with an analysis of efficiency and the factors affecting it in any manufacturing or selling unit or firm. 1962. vi, 38 p.

Report published jointly with the Centre for Interfirm Comparison.

1068

Burn, D. Why investment has fallen. *Lloyds Bank rev.,* (68), April 1963, pp 1–16.

Problem of 'bunching' investment. Importance of pattern of investment.

1069

Cairncross, A. K. Home and foreign investment, 1870-1913 : studies in capital accumulation. Cambridge Univ. Pr., 1953. xvi, 251 p.

1070

Clay, M. J. *and* **Walley,** B. H. Performance and profitability : a manual of productivity and cost reduction techniques for industry and commerce. Longmans, 1965. xvi, 610 p. (Management study series).

Instructive manual about methods such as performance analysis, interfirm comparison, productivity measurement, profit measurement, standard costing, operational research, competitive strategy (including game theory), sales promotion, etc. References.

1071

Conference on investment criteria and economic growth, *1954, Cambridge* (*Mass.*). Investment criteria and economic growth : papers presented at a conference sponsored jointly by the Center for International Studies and the Social Science Research Council, October 15, 16 and 17, 1954. Asia Publishing House, 1961. 161 p.

1072

Conference on scientific and technological developments in relation to investment and capital, *1963, London.* Science and the city : papers prepared for the conference . . . New Scientist, 1963. 77 p.

A conference sponsored by the *New Scientist* and Hambros Bank. The 14 contributions are based mainly on experience in British industry and provide interesting new information ; they vary in quality.

1073

Cooper, M. H. *and* **Parker,** J. E. S. Profitability ratios and foreign owned subsidiaries. *Bus. ratios,* 1 (3), Autumn 1967, pp 8–10.

Examines how far apparently greater profitability of foreign subsidiaries may be due to accounting practices. Compares, by industry groups, current liabilities as a percentage of assets.

1074

Dean, G. Fixed investment in Britain and Norway : an experiment in international comparison. *J. R. Statist. Soc.,* ser. A 127 (1), 1964, pp 89–107.

Raises the problem of definition and composition of investment ; whether investment is for replacement or expansion, whether repair is included and how far it contains improvements, etc. If the ratios of gross fixed investment to gross product are compared, this ratio would by 115 per cent higher for Norway than for the United Kingdom (1958 data) according to one set of definitions, but only 40 per cent above the British if an attempt is made to compare like with like.

1075

Dean, G. The stock of fixed capital in the United Kingdom in 1961. *J. R. Statist. Soc.,* ser. A 127 (3), 1964, pp 327–358.

States assumptions and describes difficulties and methods of making estimates for various dates. Examines nine groups of industries. Gives age-distribution of capital stock and estimates of capital consumption.

1076
De Paula, F. C. Return on investment : how should it be calculated ? *Accountancy,* 78 (888), Aug. 1967, pp 532–536 ; 78 (890), Oct. 1967, pp 667–673.

Describes, in detail, the difficulties and possible sources of error in determining return on investment.

1077
Dobson, R. W. Return on capital. *Mgmt accounting,* 45 (11), Nov. 1967, pp 438–447.

Analyses calculations of returns on capital and examines reasons why the percentages given by the Board of Trade, *The Times, Financial Times* and *Business Ratios* range from 14.4 per cent to 21.5 per cent for the same firm and year. Suggests alternative method.

1078
Dunning, J. H. American investment in British manufacturing industry. Allen & Unwin, 1958. 365 p.

1079
Dunning, J. H. US subsidiaries in Britain and their UK competitors : a case study in business ratios. *Bus. ratios,* 1 (1), Autumn 1966, pp 5–18.

Examines causes of differences in rates of return.

1080
Economic Research Group of the Amsterdam-Rotterdam Bank, Banque de la Société Générale de Belgique, Deutsche Bank, Midland Bank. Capital markets in Europe : a study of markets in Belgium, West Germany, the Netherlands, and the United Kingdom. 1966. 103 p.

1081
Edwards, E. O. The effect of depreciation on the output-capital co-efficient of a firm. *Econ. j.,* 65 (260), Dec. 1955, pp 654–666.

1082
Feinstein, C. H. Domestic capital formation in the United Kingdom, 1920-1935. Cambridge Univ. Pr., 1965. xii, 270 p. (Studies in the national income and expenditure of the United Kingdom, 4).

1083
Firestone, O. J. British investment in Canada. *Westminster Bank rev.,* Nov. 1967, pp 18–35.

Examines types of British investment, its sectoral and regional distribution and profitability. Analyses reasons why British investment when compared with investment from other countries obtains only half the rate of return.

1084
Foster, C. D. Surplus criteria for investment. *Bull. Oxf. Univ. Inst. Statist.,* 22 (4), Nov. 1960, pp 337–357.

1085
Goldsmith, R. W. The flow of capital funds in the postwar economy. New York, National Bureau of Economic Research, 1965. xxi, 317 p. (NBER Studies in capital formation and financing, 12).

1086
Hanson, W. C. Capital sources and major investing institutions. New York, Simmons-Boardman, 1963. 283 p.

1087
Hanson, W. C. *and* **Wang,** F. W., *eds.* Capital sources in the United Kingdom ; a directory. New York, Simmons-Boardman, 1966. 164 p.

1088
Harrington, C. T. Problems of using return on capital as a measure of success. Manchester, Manchester Statistical Society, 1961. [1], 37 p.

1089
Hart, P. E. Studies in profit, business saving and investment in the United Kingdom, 1920-1962. Vol. 1, with two chapters by James Bates. Allen & Unwin, 1965. 229 p. (Univ. of Glasgow social and economic studies, new series, 3).

Contents: Part 1, Profits and their appropriation in industries in the UK, 1920-1938 ; pt 2, The effects of the size of firm.

1090
Henderson, R. F. The new issue market and the finance of industry. Cambridge, Bowes & Bowes, 1951. xii, 172 p.

The developing role of the market in providing supplies of risk capital for industry.

1091
International conference on problems of capital formation and investment in industry, *1962, Istanbul.* Capital formation and investment in industry : a report of the International conference . . . sponsored by the Economic and Social Studies Conference Board. Istanbul, Economic and Social Studies Conference Board, 1963. 471 p.

1092
Kendall, H. The use of ratios in the printing industry. *Bus. ratios,* 1 (2), Summer 1967, pp 15–20.

A detailed scheme for examining a firm's performance with the aid of 32 different ratios relating profits, capital, output, sales, costs of production, distribution and administration, etc.

1093
Lamfalussy, A. Investment and growth in mature economies : the case of Belgium. Macmillan, 1961. xviii, 206 p.

1094

Lomax, K. S. The assessment of economic performance : an inaugural lecture. Leeds, Leeds Univ. Pr., 1965. 25 p.

Believes that methods of measurement have not kept in step with shift in economic aims towards growth. Balance sheets contain elements of estimation and 'pure speculation' (e.g. inventory, work in progress, fixed assets, goodwill, value of patents, depreciation ; allocation of overheads, taxes, research and development). Economic performance of the same firm may change owing to a change in input (materials, manpower, management) or type of output. Author pleads for more research so as to find adequate measurements related to major economic aims, i.e. competitive strength, growth and a sound balance of payments.

1095

Macrae, N. The London capital market : its structure, strains and management. Staples Pr., 1955. 285 p.

1096

Manser, W. A. P. The Reddaway report—not the last word on foreign investment. *Westminster Bank rev.,* Aug. 1967, pp 14–22.

Criticizes the Reddaway report (item 1113) for excluding large sections and examining only 'one aspect of a small part of UK's direct investment overseas'. See also item 1111.

1097

Marris, R. L. *and others.* The economics of capital utilisation : a report on multiple-shift work. Cambridge Univ. Pr., 1964. xviii, 267 p. (Univ. of Cambridge Dept. of Applied Economics. Monographs, 10).

A study undertaken by the Cambridge University Industrial Research Group on optimum utilisation of capital equipment. One of the assumptions on which the study is based is an industry in which there is sufficient competition and where the power of the firm to vary its price is limited. The case studies include : glass ; cement ; the 'kiln' industries, china and fireclay ; chemicals and allied trades ; paint and varnish ; soap ; candles and glycerine ; drugs and pharmaceuticals ; vehicles.

1098

Marris, R. L. Profitability and growth in the individual firm. *Bus. ratios,* 1 (2), Spring 1967, pp 3–12.

1099

Merrett, A. J. *and* **Sykes,** A. Calculating the rate of return on capital projects. *J. ind. econ.,* 9 (1), Nov. 1960, pp 98–115.

1100

Merrett, A. J. *and* **Sykes,** A. The finance and analysis of capital projects. Longmans, 1963. xx, 544 p.

Thorough treatment of methods and problems of investment appraisal, calculation of risk, time and scale of expansion. Authors explain difficulties in discounting estimated future cash flows. Occasional errors in calculation. Many references. Three growth tables for 1-50 years and 1 per cent—50 per cent rate of interest.

1101

Meyer, J. R. *and* **Kuh,** E. The investment decision : an empirical study. Cambridge (Mass.), Harvard Univ. Pr., 1957. xv, 284 p. (Harvard economic studies, vol. 102).

Carefully explained sample enquiry into 630 United States firms in 15 industries, 1946-1950. Uses multi-variate analysis. Extensive appendices ; 9 page bibliography. Concludes that the retention of market-share and of trade position will, in a world of oligopolistic markets, remain the 'central wellspring' of entrepreneurial action, but statistical evidence does not seem sufficiently conclusive for generalisations.

1102

Mikesell, R. F. Decisive factors in the flow of American direct investment to Europe. *Economia int.,* 20 (3), Aug. 1967, pp 431–456.

Investigates recent acceleration of US investment in Western Europe, especially in Common Market countries compared with UK. Author examines reasons for US firms preferring investment in foreign countries to exports. Suggests that desire for growth leads to competition in establishing multi-national enterprise and that possible cost/price advantages play a secondary role.

1103

Modigliani, F. *and* **Miller,** M. H. The cost of capital, corporation finance and the theory of investment. *Am. econ. rev.,* 48 (3), June 1958, pp 261–297.

An attempt to establish, with 'drastically simplified assumptions', a theory of the valuation of firms and a definition of 'cost of capital' which can serve as basis for a firm's rational investment decision. Useful references. Critical comments in *Am. econ. rev.,* 49 (4), Sept. 1959, by J. R. Rose (pp 638–639) and D. Durand (pp 639–655), with a reply by Modigliani and Miller (pp 655–669).

1104

National Bureau of Economic Research, *New York.* Capital formation and economic growth ; a conference of the Universities-National Bureau Committee for economic research . . . Princeton (NJ), Princeton Univ. Pr., 1955. xiii, 677 p. (Special conference series, no. 6).

Collection of papers referring to developed and developing countries. Emphasis on empirical data, international comparisons, importance of institutional factors.

1105

National Economic Development Council. Investment appraisal. 2nd ed. HMSO, 1967. iii, 18 p.

1106

National Institute of Economic and Social Research. Company income and finance, 1949-53. [1957]. 72 p.

'A summary of the accounts of 3,000 public companies . . . with an analysis of the sources and uses of their capital funds'.

1107
Nigam, R. K. The measurement of profits : a study in methods. Incorporated Accountants' Research Committee for the Stamp-Martin Professor of Accounting, 1956. 119 p. ('Reprint' series, no. 26).

Reprinted from *Accounting research,* 6 (3), July 1955 ; 6 (4), Oct. 1955 ; and 7 (1), Jan. 1956. Abridgment of a London School of Economics Ph.D. thesis, approved 1954.

1108
Paish, F. W. Business finance. 2nd ed. Pitman, 1961. ix, 158 p.

1109
Parker, C. L. Capital employed : the need for a definition of capital employed for use in measuring remuneration earned. *J. ind. econ.,* 3 (2), April 1955, pp 111–121.

1110
Parker, J. E. S. Profitability and growth of British industrial firms. *Manchr sch. econ. social stud.,* 32 (2), May 1964 pp 113–129.

1111
Potter, S. J. *and* **Taylor,** C. T. Foreign investment : a reply. *Westminster Bank rev.,* Nov. 1967, pp 50–62.

Answer to W. A. P. Manser's criticism (item 1096) of the Reddaway report (item 1113).

1112
Rayner, A. C. *and* **Little,** I. M. D. Higgledy piggledy growth again : an investigation of the predictability of company earnings and dividends in the UK, 1951-1961. Oxford, Blackwell, 1966. [7], 111 p.

Raises problem of how to judge performance when earnings are not predictable on basis of past record. See also item 1118.

1113
Reddaway, W. B. Effects of UK direct investment overseas. Cambridge Univ. Pr., 1967-1968. 2 v. (408 p.). (Univ. of Cambridge Dept. of Applied Economics. Occasional papers, 12 and 15).

[Vol. 1], Interim report ; [Vol. 2], Final report. Essential reading for controversy about short-term and long-term burdens and benefits of British overseas direct investment. Calculates additional annual exports arising from this type of investment. Subdivision by groups of industries and ranges of pre-tax profitability. Summary of interim report in *Economist,* 223 (6449), 1 April 1967, pp 58–60 ; of final report in *Economist,* 229 (6535), 23 Nov. 1968, pp 74–75. For criticism of interim report see items 1096 and 1111.

1114
Redfern, P. Net investment in fixed assets in the United Kingdom, 1938-1953. *J. R. Statist. Soc.,* ser. A 118 (2), 1955, pp 141–193.

1115
Rose, H. B. The economic background to investment. Cambridge Univ. Pr., 1960. xi, 661 p.

Published for the Institute of Actuaries and the Faculty of Actuaries. A textbook.

1116
Shonfield, A. British economic policy since the war. Harmondsworth, Penguin Books, 1958. 288 p. (Penguin special, S 170).

Argues that excess load of traditional commitments leads to recurrent balance of payments crises which detrimentally affect investment. Low level of investment at home becomes main barrier to growth and competitiveness.

1117
Silberston, A. *and* **Solomons,** D. Monopoly investigation and the rate of return on capital employed. *Econ. j.,* 62 (248), Dec. 1952, pp 781–801.

1118
Skinner, R. C. The maintenance of rates of return on capital. *Bull. Oxf. Univ. Inst. Econ. Statist.,* 28 (4), Nov. 1966, pp 231–240.

Investigates short-term and long-term relation between efficiency and profitability. Disagrees with Rayner's and Little's findings in item 1112.

1119
Stekler, H. O. Profitability and size of firm ; prepared under the Small Business Administration management research grant program. Berkeley, California Univ. Institute of Business and Economic Research, 1963. x, 112 p. (Small Business Administration management research report).

1120
Stern, E. H. Industrial production and profits in the United Kingdom and the United States. *Econ. j.,* 65 (259), Sept. 1955, pp 485–497.

1121
Stigler, G. J. Capital and rates of return in manufacturing industries. Princeton (NJ), Princeton Univ. Pr., 1963. xiii, 229 p. (National Bureau of Economic Research. General series, no. 78).

Period 1926-1958. Based on United States income tax reports. Chapter 3 examines relations between competition, concentration and rates of return. Appendices include description of data and of methods used.

1122
Tew, B. *and* **Henderson,** R. F., *eds.,* Studies in company finance ; a symposium on the economic analysis and interpretation of British company accounts. Cambridge Univ. Pr., 1959. xx, 301 p. (National Institute of Economic and Social Research. Economic and social studies, 17).

For annotation see item 162.

1123
Treasury. The financial and economic obligations of the nationalised industries. HMSO, 1961. 15 p. (Cmnd. 1337).

1124
Treasury. Nationalised industries : a review of economic and financial objectives. HMSO, 1967. 19 p. (Cmnd. 3437).

Important document which lays down how, in the light of changes in technology, in patterns of demand and investment, and in the size of the public sector, the principles set out in the nationalisation acts are to be applied to investment, pricing policies and financial objectives so that they correspond to the Government's economic and social aims (including prices and incomes policy). Problems of monopoly power, excess capacity, joint costs, cross-subsidisation, differential pricing systems, short-run and long-run marginal costs ; discounted cash flow techniques ; relation between maximum social return on all capital invested and one industry's financial return ; distinction between postponable-desirable and immediate-essential investment.

1125
Treasury. *Committee on the working of the monetary system.* Report. HMSO, 1959. vii, 375 p. (Cmnd. 827).

Also, *Principal memoranda of evidence.* HMSO, 1960. 3 v. Chairman of Committee : Lord Radcliffe.

1126
Twentieth Century Fund. *Corporation survey committee.* How profitable is big business ? New York, 1937. xviii, 201 p.

1127
Williams, B. R. International report on factors in investment behaviour. Paris, Organisation for Economic Co-operation and Development, [1962]. 1 v. (various pagings).

Sponsored by the European Productivity Agency. Covers six European countries including the UK. Two important pages in chapter 10 on 'impulses and pressures to invest', which include competitive pressure.

1128
Williams, B. R. Investment proposals and decisions. Allen & Unwin, 1965. 100 p. (Manchester Univ. Centre for Business Research publications).

Based on studies by the Manchester University Centre for Business Research.

1129
Worswick, G. D. N. *and* **Tipping,** D. G. Profits in the British economy, 1909-1938. Oxford, Blackwell, 1967. [7], 155 p. (Oxford Univ. Institute of Economics and Statistics. Monograph no. 8).

Estimate of trading profits and wear and tear allowances for some 100 trade groups and six separate years during period 1909-1938, based on inland revenue data. Important comment on interpretation of profit data. Of special value, table XII : index numbers for changes in gross true income.

1130
Wright, R. W. Investment decision in industry. Chapman & Hall, 1964. xiii, 170 p.

Discusses the problem of decision-making, the influence of uncertainty and the decision process. 4 page bibliography.

6.2 Productivity

See also items 104, 853, 955

In view of the fact that several bibliographies on productivity, as listed below, have been compiled, only a few publications of special relevance have been selected for this bibliography. The contributions of E. D. Domar (item 1134 ; see also 853), J. H. Dunning (items 1135, 1136), T. E. Easterfield (item 1137) and C. H. Feinstein (item 1131), of OEEC and OECD (items 1144-1146) deal with the vital problems of measurement and comparability.

As a result of the close relation between innovation and productivity, and between productivity and growth, suitable publications can be found under other headings such as *Industrial structure—General* (page 10), and *Innovation and Invention* (page 64).

Many additional publications will be found in the following bibliographies :
Select bibliography on productivity, by L. Rostas (Board of Trade. 1952) ; *Bibliography on productivity* (Paris, European Productivity Agency, 1954) ; *Bibliography on productivity* (Paris, European Productivity Agency, 1956. EPA project no. 233) ; *Productivity: a bibliography,* by the US Bureau of Labor Statistics : November 1957 (Bulletin no. 1226), and July 1966 (Bulletin no. 1514) (2 vols. Washington, Gov't. Print. Off.).

1131
Brown, M. On the theory and measurement of technological change. Cambridge Univ. Pr., 1966. xii, 214 p.

A thorough econometric study of the factors determining technological progress. Examines several production functions.

1132
Carter, C. F., **Reddaway,** W. B. *and* **Stone,** R. The measurement of production movements. Cambridge Univ. Pr., 1948. vii, 135 p. (Univ. of Cambridge Dept. of Applied Economics. Monographs, 1).

1133
David, P. A. Measuring real net output : a proposed index. *Rev. econ. statist.,* 48 (4), Nov. 1966, pp 419–425.

1134
Domar, E. D. *and others.* Economic growth and productivity in the United States, Canada, United Kingdom, Germany and Japan in the post-war period. *Rev. econ. statist.,* 46 (1), Feb. 1964, pp 33–40.

1135

Dunning, J. H. *and* **Utton,** M. A. Measuring changes in productivity and efficiency in UK industry, 1954-63. *Bus. ratios,* 1 (2), Summer 1967, pp 21–29.

Authors discuss various methods for measuring technical and economic progress and social efficiency of resource allocations ; application of one method to 12 industry groups in the years 1954, 1958, 1963. References.

1136

Dunning, J. H. *and* **Barron,** M. J. A productivity measure of business performance. *Bus. ratios,* 1 (3), Autumn 1967, pp 11–15.

Experimenting with various measures of productivity in seven industry groups authors suggest profitability as the best available proxy. 11 tables.

1137

Easterfield, T. E. Productivity measurement in Great Britain : a survey of recent work. Department of Scientific and Industrial Research, 1959. [1], ii, 79 p.

1138

Farrell, M. J. The measurement of productive efficiency. *J. R. Statist. Soc.,* ser. A 120 (3), 1957, pp 253–290.

1139

Feinstein, C. H. Production and productivity, 1920-1962. *Lond. Camb. econ. bull.,* (48), Dec. 1963, pp xii–xiv.

1140

Fourastié, J. Productivity, prices and wages. Paris, European Productivity Agency, 1957. 113 p. (EPA project no. 235).

A method for measuring long-term productivity trends ; published as a preliminary study to *Productivity measurement,* v. 3 (see item 1144).

1141

The Growth of productivity in Great Britain and abroad : three Cantor Lectures. *J. R. Soc. Arts,* 111 (5078), Jan. 1963, pp 96–143.

Contents: 1, Comparisons of gross national products, by J. A. C. Brown ; 2, Industrial comparisons, by J. A. C. Brown ; 3, A symposium : Productivity in Great Britain, by Sir Hugh Beaver ; Productivity—a trade union angle, by H. Douglass ; A principle of productivity, by Sir Walter Puckey.

1142

Matuszewski, T. I. Concepts and measurements of productivity. 1954. (M. Sc. thesis, London School of Economics).

1143

Nicholson, R. J. *and* **Gupta,** S. Output and productivity changes in British manufacturing industry, 1948-1954 : a study from census of production data. *J. R. Statist. Soc.,* ser A 123 (4), 1960, pp 427–459.

The authors compute index numbers for 138 manufacturing industries (in 15 industry groups), discuss methods and problems, examine how far changes in industrial structure influence overall productivity and conclude that the effect of re-distributing manpower is small.

1144

Organisation for Economic Co-operation and Development. Productivity measurement. Paris, 1955-1966. 3 v.

Vols. 1 and 2 issued by the European Productivity Agency, as project no. 235. *Contents:* Vol. 1, Concepts ; v. 2, Plant level measurements, methods and results ; v. 3, Global measurement of productivity for international comparisons at branch of industry level . . . See also item 1140.

1145

Organisation for European Economic Co-operation. Definitions and methods. 3rd ed. Paris, 1958-1960. (OEEC statistical bulletins).

Contents: I, Indices of industrial production ; II, Industrial commodities.

1146

Organisation for European Economic Co-operation. Measurement of productivity ; methods used by the Bureau of Labor Statistics in the USA. [Report by] Technical assistance missions, nos. 7, 10, 11. Paris, 1952.

1147

Paige, D. *and* **Bombach,** G. A comparison of national output and productivity of the United Kingdom and the United States. Paris, Organisation for European Economic Co-operation, 1959. 245 p.

Joint study by OEEC and the Cambridge Univ. Dept. of Applied Economics. Provides detailed estimates of production in the two countries for 1950, with extensions to 1954 and 1957.

1148

Paul, M. E. International productivity comparisons over time. *Bull. Oxf. Univ. Inst. Statist.,* 24 (1), Feb. 1962, pp 155–165.

1149

Rostas, L. International comparisons of productivity. Geneva, International Labour Organization, 1948. 23 p.

Reprinted from *Int. labour rev.,* 58 (3), Sept. 1948.

1150
Saunders, C. T. International comparisons of productivity growth in the 1950's. *J. R. Statist. Soc.,* ser. A 126 (2), 1963, pp 227–235.

Industries in France, Germany, United States and Great Britain are compared.

1151
Snow, E. C. The international comparison of industrial output. *J. R. Statist. Soc.,* ser. A 107 (1), 1944, pp 1–30. (Discussion, pp 30–55).

1152
Vaccara, B. M. Employment and output in protected manufacturing industries. Washington, Brookings Institution, 1960. 107 p.

7 Statistical sources

See also item 16

Publications concerned mainly with problems of
measurement will be found in the appropriate sections of
the bibliography. The few general works listed below may
facilitate the tracing and interpretation of economic data in
the fields of research covered by the bibliography. Most
British government statistical publications have been
omitted as they can be found in the Central Statistical
Office's *List of principal statistical series available* (item
1155). A more detailed guide to the census of production is
provided by *Guides to official sources, no. 6: Census of
production reports,* issued by the Interdepartmental
Committee on Social and Economic Research (HMSO,
1961). This includes a full bibliography of census reports
up to the 1958 census, with a subject index, and a
bibliography of associated publications. Of the vast
number of statistics published by international
organisations such as the European Productivity Agency,
the International Labour Organization, OEEC and OECD,
the United Nations agencies, etc. or by government
departments of foreign countries, especially the United
States Department of Commerce and the US Census
Office, only a very few, of special significance for the
subject matter of this bibliography, have been included.
Attention should be drawn to the attempts of the OECD to
make statistics (including industrial statistics) of different
countries as comparable as possible. From May 1968 the
Central Statistical Office is issuing *Statistical news*
(quarterly, HMSO), which provides information on current
statistical developments in all British government
departments.

1153
Board of Trade. Business monitor : production series.
1962+ HMSO.

Monthly or quarterly data on some 70 commodities or
groups of commodities (volume and value, home and
export).

1154
Carter, C. F. *and* **Roy,** A. D. British economic statistics ; a
report. Cambridge Univ. Pr., 1954. vii, 188 p. (National
Institute of Economic and Social Research. Economic and
social studies, 14).

1155
Central Statistical Office. List of principal statistical
series available ... HMSO, 1965. iv, 36 p. (Studies in
official statistics, no. 11).

Gives source and frequency of publications containing
original economic, financial and regional data. Provides
short commentaries on nature and coverage of data.

1156
Department of Education and Science. Statistics of
science and technology. 1967+ HMSO.

To be published annually. Compiled jointly with Ministry
of Technology. Includes statistics on research and
development, deployment of qualified manpower. 1967
issue gives figures mainly for period 1961-1965.

1157
Devons, E. An introduction to British economic statistics.
Cambridge Univ. Pr., 1956. vii, 256 p.

1158
General Agreement on Tariffs and Trade.
International Trade Centre. Compendium of sources :
international trade statistics. An analytical compilation of
foreign trade statistics published by the international
agencies and national governments the world over, with an
introduction on their use in market research. Geneva, 1967.
[3], v, 150 p.

1159
International Labour Organization. Year book of
labour statistics. 1, 1935/36+ Geneva.

Previously incorporated in *ILO year book.* Includes
international statistics—mainly indices—on labour
productivity, wages and consumer prices ; international
standard classification of industries and occupations ;
international references and sources.

1160
Mitchell, B. R. *and* **Deane,** P. Abstract of British
historical statistics. Cambridge Univ. Pr., 1962. xiv, 513 p.

Tables cover various periods mostly between 1800 and
1939.

1161
National Institute economic review. No. 1, Jan.
1959+ National Institute of Economic and Social
Research.

Quarterly (6 issues a year 1959-1961). Regular feature
'The economic situation' contains forecasts of investment,
employment, production and foreign trade. Statistical
appendix includes statistics of foreign countries (e.g. wage
costs, productivity), up-to-date estimates of British
statistical series and a special index of commodity prices.

1162
**Organisation for Economic Co-operation and
Development.** Sources of statistics for market research.
Paris, 1961-1964. 6 v.

Contents: Vol. 1, Radio sets ; v. 2, Footwear ; v. 3, General
statistics ; v. 4, Household appliances ; v. 5, Machine
tools ; v. 6, Pharmaceuticals. These volumes contain data on
production, trade and, when available, promotion. Vol. 3
contains general data relevant for market research, such as
population statistics.

1163
Organisation for European Economic Co-operation.
Industrial statistics, 1900-1959. Paris, 1960. [10], 180 p.
(OEEC statistical bulletins).

1164
United Nations. *Statistical Office.* Bibliography of
industrial and distributive-trade statistics. [3rd ed.]. New
York, 1965. [2], 75 p. (Statistical papers, series M, no. 36,
rev. 2).

The statistics are classified by countries grouped by
continents. The statistical sources quoted refer to mining,
manufacturing, construction, production and distribution
of electricity and gas, wholesale and retail trade and related
services. The entries cover many aspects : structure,
output, sales, consumption, employment, stocks, fixed
assets, investment, but exclude price and financial
statistics. It is intended to revise the bibliography at
intervals.

1165
United States. *Bureau of the Census.* Historical
statistics of the United States, colonial times to 1957.
Washington, Gov't. Print. Off., 1960. xi, 789 p.

Also, *Continuation to 1962 and revisions* (Washington.
Gov't. Print. Off., 1965. iv, 154 p.).

1166
Wasserman, P., **Allen,** E. *and* **Georgi,** C., *eds.* Statistics
sources : a subject guide to data on industrial, business,
social, educational, financial, and other topics for the
United States and selected foreign countries. [2nd ed.].
Detroit, Gale Research Co., 1965. 387 p.

Lists bibliographies, guides, almanacs, annuals, yearbooks,
censuses, books and periodicals, with emphasis on works
published in the United States and by international
organisations. Entries arranged by subjects in alphabetical
order (countries other than US being listed as subjects).
Sources of statistics on advertising, concentration ratios,
foreign, wholesale and retail trade, bankruptcies,
industries, investment, prices, transport, etc.

Appendix 1 Journals cited in the bibliography

This appendix gives the full titles and essential bibliographical details of the journals in which articles included in the bibliography have been published. The citations there incorporate an abbreviated form of journal title, and this list is therefore arranged in alphabetical order of those abbreviations. Apart from its use as a key to the abbreviated titles used in the bibliography, this list also gives an indication of the range of journals in which articles on the subjects of competition, monopoly and restrictive practices are likely to be found.

Advertising q.

Advertising quarterly. 1964+ Advertising Association.

Am. econ. rev.

American economic review. 1911+ Evanston (Illinois), American Economic Association. (Quarterly).

Am. j. comp. law

American journal of comparative law. 1952+ Baltimore, American Association for the Comparative Study of Law. (Quarterly).

Antitrust bull.

Antitrust bulletin. 1955+ New York, Federal Legal Publications. (Quarterly).

Appl. statist.

Applied statistics. 1952+ Royal Statistical Society. (3 issues a year).

Ban. Naz. Lav. q. rev.

Banca Nazionale del Lavoro quarterly review. 1947+ Rome.

Banker

Banker. 1962+ (Monthly).

Bankers' mag.

Bankers' magazine. 1844+ Waterlow & Sons. (Monthly).

Brd Trade j.

Board of Trade journal. 1886+ HMSO. (Weekly).

Brit. j. adm. law

British journal of administrative law. 1954-1957. (Incorporated in *Public law* from 1958).

Brit. j. ind. relations

British journal of industrial relations. 1963+ London School of Economics. (3 times a year).

Bull. Oxf. Univ. Inst. Econ. Statist.;
Bull. Oxf. Univ. Inst. Statist.

Bulletin of the Oxford University Institute of Economics and Statistics. 1939+ Oxford, Blackwell.
(Quarterly. To 1962 as *Bulletin of the Oxford University Institute of Statistics*).

Bus. ratios

Business ratios. 1966+ Dun & Bradstreet. (3 times a year).

Camb. law j.

Cambridge law journal. 1921+ Cambridge Univ. Pr. (2 issues a year. Published for the Faculty of Law, University of Cambridge).

Can. bar rev.

Canadian bar review. 1923+ Toronto, Osgoode Hall Law School. (Quarterly).

Can. chartered accountant

Canadian chartered accountant. 1911+ Toronto, Canadian Institute of Chartered Accountants. (Monthly).

Can. j. econ. political sci.	Canadian journal of economics and political science. 1933-1967. Toronto, Univ. of Toronto Pr. (Continued by *Canadian journal of economics* and *Canadian journal of political science*).
Cartel	Cartel : quarterly review of monopoly developments & consumer protection. 1950-1964. International Co-operative Alliance.
Common mkt law rev.	Common market law review. 1963+ Stevens. (Quarterly). (Issued in co-operation with the British Institute of International and Comparative Law and the Europa Instituut of the University of Leyden).
Dir.	Director. 1947+ Institute of Directors. (Monthly).
Dist. Bank rev.	District Bank review. 1926-1968. Manchester, District Bank Ltd. (Continued by *National Westminster Bank quarterly review*).
Econ. j.	Economic journal. 1891+ Macmillan. (Quarterly. Journal of the Royal Economic Society).
Econ. trends	Economic trends. 1953+ HMSO. (Monthly. Prepared by the Central Statistical Office).
Econometrica	Econometrica. 1933+ Amsterdam, North-Holland Pub. Co. (Quarterly).
Economia int.	Economia internazionale. 1948+ Genoa, Istituto di Economia Internazionale. (Quarterly).
Economica	Economica. 1921+ London School of Economics. (Quarterly).
Harv. bus. rev.	Harvard business review. 1922+ Boston (Mass.), Harvard Univ. Graduate School of Business Administration. (6 issues a year).
Infs statist.	Informations statistiques : cahiers trimestriels de l'intégration économique européenne. 1953+ Brussels, Statistical Office of the European Communities. (Title varies. To 1959 issued by the European Coal and Steel Community).
Inst. Transp. j.	Institute of Transport journal. 1920+ (6 issues a year).
Int. comp. law q.	International and comparative law quarterly. 1896+ Society of Comparative Legislation. (Title varies).
Int. econ. pap.	International economic papers. 1951+ Macmillan. (Published at irregular intervals. Translations prepared for the International Economic Association).
Int. labour rev.	International labour review. 1921+ Geneva, International Labour Office. (Monthly).
Int. Monetary Fund staff pap.	International Monetary Fund staff papers. 1950+ Washington. (Published at irregular intervals).
J. accounting res.	Journal of accounting research. 1963+ Chicago, Univ. of Chicago Institute of Professional Accounting. (Twice yearly).

J. Am. Statist. Ass.	Journal of the American Statistical Association. 1888+ Washington. (Quarterly. Title varies).
J. bus.	Journal of business. 1928+ Chicago, Univ. of Chicago Graduate School of Business. (Quarterly).
J. bus. law	Journal of business law. 1957+ Stevens. (Quarterly).
J. ind. econ.	Journal of industrial economics. 1952+ Oxford, Blackwell. (3 issues a year).
J. law econ.	Journal of law & economics. 1958+ Chicago, Univ. of Chicago Law School. (Annually).
J. mktg	Journal of marketing. 1936+ Chicago, American Marketing Association. (Quarterly).
J. political econ.	Journal of political economy. 1892+ Chicago, Univ. of Chicago Pr. (Quarterly).
J. R. Soc. Arts	Journal of the Royal Society of Arts. 1852+ (Monthly).
J. R. Statist. Soc.	Journal of the Royal Statistical Society, series A (general). 1838+ (Quarterly).
J. transp. econ. policy	Journal of transport economics and policy. 1967+ London School of Economics. (3 issues a year).
J. wld trade law	Journal of world trade law. 1967+ Vincent Pr. (6 issues a year).
Kyklos	Kyklos : international review for social science. 1947+ Basel, Kyklos-Verlag.
Kyoto Univ. econ. rev.	Kyoto University economic review. 1926+ Kyoto, Kyoto Univ. Faculty of Economics. (2 issues a year).
Law q. rev.	Law quarterly review. 1885+ Stevens.
Lloyds Bank rev.	Lloyds Bank review. 1917+ Lloyds Bank Ltd. (Quarterly. Title varies).
Lond. Camb. econ. bull.	London and Cambridge economic bulletin. 1923+ Times Pub. Co. (Quarterly ; title varies. 1952-1965 published as supplements to *Times review of industry.*)
Manchr sch. econ. social stud.	Manchester school of economic and social studies. 1930+ Manchester, Univ. of Manchester Department of Economics. (3 issues a year).
Mgmt accounting	Management accounting. 1965+ Institute of Cost and Works Accountants. (Monthly. Continues *The cost accountant*).
Mgmt decision	Management decision : the quarterly review of management technology. 1967+ Heywood-Temple Industrial Publications. (Continues *Scientific business*).
Midl. Bank rev.	Midland Bank review. 1919+ Midland Bank Ltd. (Quarterly).
Mod. law rev.	Modern law review. 1937+ Stevens. (6 issues a year).
Natn. Inst. econ. rev.	National Institute economic review. 1959+ National Institute of Economic and Social Research. (Quarterly).

Northwestern Univ. law rev.	Northwestern University law review. 1966+ Chicago, Northwestern Univ. School of Law. (6 issues a year).
Oxf. econ. pap.	Oxford economic papers. 1938+ Oxford, Clarendon Pr. (3 issues a year).
Planning	Planning. 1933+ Political and Economic Planning. (Frequency varies).
Pub. law	Public law. 1956+ Stevens. (Quarterly. From 1958 incorporates *British journal of administrative law*).
Q. j. econ.	Quarterly journal of economics. 1886+ Cambridge (Mass.), Harvard Univ. Pr.
Rev. écon.	Revue économique. 1950+ Paris, Librairie Armand Colin. (6 issues a year).
Rev. econ. statist.	Review of economics and statistics. 1919+ Cambridge (Mass.), Harvard Univ. Pr. (Quarterly. Title varies).
Rev. econ. stud.	Review of economic studies. 1933+ Edinburgh, Oliver and Boyd. (Quarterly. Journal of the Economic Study Society).
Scott. j. political econ.	Scottish journal of political economy. 1954+ Edinburgh, Oliver and Boyd. (3 issues a year. Journal of the Scottish Economic Society).
Solicitor q.	Solicitor quarterly. 1962+ Pitman. (Continues *Solicitor*).
Statist	Statist. 1878-1967. (Weekly).
Steel rev.	Steel review. 1956-1967. British Iron and Steel Federation. (Quarterly. Continued by *British steel,* published by British Steel Corporation).
Three banks rev.	Three banks review. 1949+ Glyn Mills & Co. (Quarterly. Published jointly with Royal Bank of Scotland and Williams Deacon's Bank).
Times rev. ind. technol.	Times review of industry and technology. 1963+ Times Pub. Co. (Monthly. Continues *Times review of industry and Technology*).
Trans. Manchr Statist. Soc.	Transactions of the Manchester Statistical Society. 1853+ Manchester. (Annually).
Urban studies	Urban studies. 1964+ Edinburgh, Oliver and Boyd. (3 issues a year).
Westminster Bank rev.	Westminster Bank review. 1920-1968. Westminster Bank Ltd. (Quarterly. Continued by *National Westminster Bank quarterly review*).
Wld today	World today. 1945+ Royal Institute of International Affairs
Yale econ. essays	Yale economic essays. 1961+ New Haven (Conn.), Yale Univ. Department of Economics. (Twice yearly).
Yale law j.	Yale law journal. 1891+ New Haven (Conn.), Yale Law Journal Co. (8 issues a year).

Yorks. bull. econ. social res.

Yorkshire bulletin of economic and social research. 1948+ Hull, Univ. of Hull Department of Economics. (2 issues a year. Issued jointly with the Departments of Economics of the Universities of Leeds and Sheffield).

Yr bk wld affairs

Year book of world affairs. 1947+ Stevens. (Published under the auspices of the London Institute of World Affairs).

Appendix 2 Monopolies Commission reports

This appendix lists, in chronological order of publication, the reports prepared by the Monopolies Commission (to 1956 known as the Monopolies and Restrictive Practices Commission) from its inception to the end of 1967. All the reports are published by HMSO as House of Commons papers or as Command papers.

1950
Report on the supply of dental goods. (1950-51, HC 18)

1951
Report on the supply of cast iron rainwater goods. (1950-51, HC 136)

Report on the supply of electric lamps. (1950-51, HC 287)

1952
Report on the supply of insulated electric wires and cables. (1951-52, HC 209)

Report on the supply of insulin. (1951-52, HC 296)

Report on the supply and export of matches and the supply of match-making machinery. (1952-53, HC 161)

1953
Report on the supply of imported timber. (1952-53, HC 281)

1954
Report on the process of calico printing. (1953-54, HC 140)

Report on the supply of buildings in the Greater London area. (1953-54, HC 264)

1955
Collective discrimination : report on exclusive dealings, collective boycotts, aggregated rebates and other discriminatory trade practices. (Cmd 9504)

Report on the supply and export of certain semi-manufactures of copper and copper-based alloys. (1955-56, HC 56)

Report on the supply and export of pneumatic tyres. (1955-56, HC 133)

Report on the supply of sand and gravel in Scotland. (1955-56, HC 222)

Report on the supply of hard fibre cordage. (1955-56, HC 294)

1956
Report on the supply of certain rubber footwear. (1955-56, HC 328)

Report on the supply of linoleum. (1955-56, HC 366)

Report on the supply of certain industrial and medical gases. (1956-57, HC 13)

Report on the supply of standard metal windows and doors. (1956-57, HC 14)

Report on the supply of tea. (1956-57, HC 15)

Report on the supply of electronic valves and cathode ray tubes. (1956-57, HC 16)

Report on the supply and export of electrical and allied machinery and plant. (1956-57, HC 42)

1958
Imported timber : report on whether and to what extent the recommendation of the Commission has been complied with. (1957-58, HC 274)

1959
Report on the supply of chemical fertilisers. (1958-59, HC 267)

1961
Report on the supply of cigarettes and tobacco and of cigarette and tobacco machinery. (1960-61, HC 218)

1963
Report on the supply of electrical equipment for mechanically propelled land vehicles. (1963-64, HC 21)

1964
Report on the supply of wallpaper. (1963-64, HC 59)

1965

Petrol : a report on the supply of petrol to retailers in the United Kingdom. (1964-65, HC 264)

The British Motor Corporation Ltd and the Pressed Steel Co. Ltd : a report on the merger. (1965-66, HC 46)

1966

Colour film : a report on the supply and processing of colour film. (1966-67, HC 1)

Ross Group Ltd and Associated Fisheries Ltd : a report on the proposed merger. (1966-67, HC 42)

Electrical wiring harnesses for motor vehicles : a report on whether uneconomic prices are quoted. (1966-67, HC 72)

The Times newspaper and the Sunday Times newspaper : a report on the proposed transfer to a newspaper proprietor. (1966-67, HC 273)

Household detergents : a report on the supply of household detergents. (1966-67, HC 105)

The Dental Manufacturing Co. Ltd or the Dentists' Supply Co. of New York and the Amalgamated Dental Co. Ltd : a report on the proposed mergers. (1966-67, HC 147)

Films : a report on the supply of films for exhibition in cinemas. (1966-67, HC 206)

Aluminium semi-manufactures : a report on a reference concerning the supply of aluminium semi-manufactures. (1966-67, HC 263)

1967

Infant milk foods : a report on the supply of infant milk foods. (1966-67, HC 319)

International motor insurance cards : a report on the provision of insurance in relation to the issue of international motor insurance cards. (1966-67, HC 487)

British Insulated Callender's Cables Ltd and Pyrotenax Ltd : a report on the proposed merger. (1966-67, HC 490)

Guest, Keen & Nettlefolds Ltd and Birfield Ltd : a report on the merger. (Cmnd 3186)

United Drapery Stores Ltd and Montague Burton Ltd : a report on the proposed merger. (Cmnd 3397)

Appendix 3 Restrictive trading agreements considered by the Restrictive Practices Court

This appendix provides a list of agreements on which the Restrictive Practices Court passed judgment up to the end of 1967. The agreements are classified in broad industrial groupings, generally corresponding to the orders of the Standard Industrial Classification. Most of the agreements were referred to the Court pursuant to section 20 (2) (a) of the Restrictive trade practices Act 1956. This permits the Registrar of Restrictive Trading Agreements to refer any registered agreement to the Court for a declaration that restrictions it contains are, or are not, contrary to the public interest. Other kinds of references are indicated where appropriate in the list below. The bibliographical citation following the name of each agreement identifies the report of the case published in *Reports of restrictive practices cases* (Vol 1, 1957/59+ Incorporated Council of Law Reporting for England and Wales). Thus, LR4RP, 169-239 refers to volume 4 of the *Reports*, pages 169–239. The periods covered by successive volumes are : vol. 1, 1957-1959 ; vol. 2, 1960-1961 ; vol. 3, 1961–1963 ; vol. 4, 1963-1964 ; vol. 5, 1964-1966 ; vol. 6, 1966-1968.

Fishing

Distant Water Vessels Development Scheme
LR6RP, 242–324

Food

Chocolate and sugar confectionery reference
LR6RP, 338–393 (Resale price maintenance ; reference made pursuant to section 6 (1) of Resale prices Act 1964)

Federation of Wholesale and Multiple Bakers' (Great Britain and Northern Ireland) agreement
LR1RP, 387–472

Wholesale and Retail Bakers of Scotland Association's agreement, and Scottish Association of Master Bakers' agreement
LR1RP, 347–386

Chemicals and Allied Industries

National Sulphuric Acid Association's agreement
[no. 1], LR4RP, 169–239
no. 2, LR6RP, 210–242 (application by the Registrar for the court to discharge the order made previously that the restrictions in the agreement were not against the public interest)

Phenol Producers' agreement
LR2RP, 1–48

Metal Manufacture

British Basic Slag Ltd's application. . .and Colville Ltd's application
LR3RP, 178–197 ; appeal, LR4RP, 116–156 (Application for cancellation of a registration. The agreement was concerned with arrangements for marketing basic slag, a by-product of steel manufacture, as a fertilizer)

British Heavy Steelmakers' agreement
LR5RP, 33–88

British Iron and Steel Federation and National Federation of Scrap Iron, Steel and Metal Merchants agreement
LR4RP, 299–360

Lead Sheet and Pipe Manufacturers' Federation agreement
LR3RP, 71–81

Mechanical Engineering

British Constructional Steelwork Association's agreement
LR1RP, 199–207

Water-tube Boilermakers' agreement
LR1RP, 285–346

Electrical Engineering

Associated Transformer Manufacturers' agreement
LR2RP, 295–345

Telephone Apparatus Manufacturers' application
LR3RP, 98–119 ; appeal, 462–495 (Whether registrable in view of Crown interest)

Other Metal Goods

Black Bolt and Nut Association's agreement
[no. 1], LR2RP, 50–102
no. 2, LR2RP, 433–447 ; appeal, LR3RP, 43–62
(Application by the Registrar for a declaration that an
agreement was "to the like effect" as a restriction
previously declared by the Court to be contrary to the
public interest)
no. 3, LR6RP, 1–47

Locked Coil Ropemakers Association's agreement,
Mining Rope Association's agreement, and Wire Rope
Manufacturers' Association's agreement
LR5RP, 146–218

Permanent Magnet Association's agreement
LR3RP, 119–177

Standard Metal Window Group's agreement LR3RP,
198–246

Textiles

Blanket Manufacturers' agreement
LR1RP, 208–261 ; appeal, LR1RP, 271–284

British Jute Trade Federal Council's agreements
LR4RP, 399–484 (Deals with seven agreements amongst
members of the Council's constituent associations)

Federation of British Carpet Manufacturers' agreements
LR1RP, 472–553

Yarn Spinner's agreement
[no. 1], LR1RP, 118–190
no. 2, LR2RP, 103–105 (Application by Yarn Spinners'
Association for release from part of undertaking)

Pottery, Glass, Cement

British Bottle Association's agreement
LR2RP, 345–392

Cement Maker's Federation agreement
LR2RP, 241–294

Glazed and Floor Tile Home Trade Association's
agreement
LR4RP, 239–299

Furniture

British Furniture Manufacturers' Federated Associations'
agreement
LR6RP, 185–210 (Preliminary point of law concerning
design copying)

Paper, Printing and Publishing

British Paper and Board Makers' Association's agreement
LR4RP, 1–29

British Waste Paper Association's agreement
LR4RP, 29–54

British Paper and Board Makers' Association's agreement
and British Waste Papers Association's agreement (no. 2)
LR6RP, 161–184 (Following recommendations made by
the Economic Development Committee for the Paper and
Board Industry the Associations applied to be released
from a previous undertaking)

Net Book agreement
[no. 1], LR3RP, 246–327
no. 2, LR4RP, 484–491

Other Manufacturing Industries

Linoleum Manufacturers' Association's agreement
LR2RP, 395–432

Mileage Conference Group of the Tyre Manufacturers'
Conference Ltd's agreement
LR6RP, 49–114 (Contempt case)

Tyre Trade Register agreement
LR3RP, 404–462

Construction

Birmingham Association of Building Trades Employers'
agreement
LR4RP, 54–116

National Federated Electrical Association's agreement
LR2RP, 447–452 (Contempt case)

Distributive Trades

Chemists' Federation agreement (no. 2)
LR1RP, 75–114

Doncaster and Retford Co-operative Societies' agreement
LR2RP, 105–129

Motor Vehicle Distribution Scheme agreement
LR2RP, 173–230

National Federation of Retail Newsagents', Booksellers'
and Stationers' agreement
LR5RP, 236–254 (Preliminary point—whether an
individual periodical title can be regarded as "goods")

Newspaper Proprietors' Association Ltd's and National
Federation of Retail Newsagents', Booksellers' and
Stationers' agreement
LR2RP, 453–500

Wholesale Confectioners Alliance's agreement
[no. 1], LR2RP, 135–165
no. 2, LR2RP, 231–241 (Application by the Registrar for
Court orders under sections 20 (3) and 20 (4) of the
Restrictive trade practices Act 1956)

Finance

Finance Houses Association Ltd's agreement
LR5RP, 366–436

Name index

All references are to item numbers in the bibliography

A

Abramson, A. G., 69, 801
Acton Society Trust, 274–276
Adams, W., 840, 841
Adelman, M. A., 168, 241, 277, 522, 903
Advertising Association, 808
Ady, P. H., 115, 116
Air Freight Working Party, 518
Air Transport Licensing Board, 514
Alberts, W. W., 278
Alexander, K. J. W., 310
Allen, E., 1166
Allen, E. G. W., 336
Allen, G. C., 3, 4, 28, 76, 77, 854
Allen, J. W., 915
Alpert, S. B., 230
American Council on Public Affairs
 Industrial concentration and price inflexibility, 774
 New firms and free enterprise, 334
American Economic Association
 Price and production policies, 725
 Problems of regional integration, 1029
American Marketing Association, 524
Ames, E., 842
Amey, L. R., 254
Andren, I. P., 1055
Andrews, P. W. S., 117, 597, 677, 678, 720, 721, 797
Anglo-American Council on Productivity
 Ammunition, 392
 Electricity supply, 440
 Fruit and vegetable utilisation, 558
 Gas, 441
 Metalworking machine tools, 417
 Packet foods, 559
 Retailing, 523
 Steel construction, 402
Appleby, R., 1056
Archibald, G. C., 5
Armstrong, A., 169
Arnfield, R. V., 310
Association of Certified and Corporate Accountants, 722
Aviation, Ministry of *see* Ministry of Aviation

B

Backman, J., 393, 723, 724, 809
Bain, J. S., 6, 7, 28, 34, 78, 170, 171, 324, 725, 726
Baker, P. V., 635
Balassa, B., 979, 980, 981, 1029, 1030
Baldwin, R. E., 100, 1023
Balkin, N., 727
Ball, R. J., 934

Balogh, T., 935, 957, 1027, 1057, 1058
Bank for International Settlements, 936
Banker, 942
Baran, P. A., 79
Barback, R. H., 729
Bareau, P., 95
Barker, R. E., 678
Barlow, M., 370
Barna, T., 196, 1059, 1060
Barnes, *Sir* G., 508
Barnes, S. N., 631A
Barnett, H. J., 838
Barron, M. J., 1136
Bartels, R., 524
Bates, G. L., 511
Bates, J. A., 172, 1061, 1062
Baumol, W. J., 118, 1063
Bayer Products Company, 400
Beacham, A., 636, 679, 730
Beaver, *Sir* H., 1141
Beckerman, W., 80, 872
Beesley, M. E., 337, 338, 477
Bellamy, J. M., 731
Bellamy, R., 525
Benishay, H., 173
Bennett, A., 403, 404
Berle, A. A., 137–139
Bernhard, R. C., 8, 9, 616
Bhagwati, J., 1023
Bhatawdekar, M. V., 732
Bird, P. A., 755
Black, J., 982, 1027
Black, W., 342, 579
Blackaby, F. T., 889
Blackburn, J. A., 1031
Blair, J. M., 174, 175, 241, 279, 724
Blaug, M., 843
Bo, D. Del, 280
Board of Trade
 Acquisitions and amalgamations of quoted companies.
  140, 141
 Business monitor, 1153
 Capital expenditure of manufacturing industry 1948-1962,
  1064
 Census of distribution and other services, 526, 527, 528
 Committee on consumer protection, final report, 810
 Committee on resale price maintenance:
  Report, 599
  Statement submitted . . . to the Committee, 600
 Company law committee report, 281
 Customs duties (dumping and subsidies) Act 1957
  annual report, 983
 Customs tariff of the European Communities, 1036

Ministry of Aviation
    Airfreight working party, 518
    Committee of inquiry into the aircraft industry, 426
Ministry of Fuel and Power, 453
Ministry of Health, 400
Ministry of Power, 447, 449
Ministry of Technology
    Memorandum on British European Airways, 514
    Statistics of science and technology, 1156
Ministry of Transport
    Committee of inquiry into the major ports of Great
        Britain, report, 468
    Observations on the Select committee on nationalised
        industries report on British Railways, 482
    Railway policy, 484
    Reorganisation of the nationalised transport undertakings,
        464
    Traffic in towns, 465
    The transport needs of Great Britain in the next twenty
        years, 466
    Transport policy, 467
Mireaux, L. A. Dicks-, 421
Mitchell, B. R., 1160
Modigliani, F., 46, 1103
Molony, J. T., 810
Monsen, R. J., 131
Montgomery, D. E., 112
Montmorency, S. F. G. de, 290
Montrose, J. L., 661
Moon, R. W., 308
Moore, F. T., 215, 230
Moore, L., 963
Morgan, E. V., 154, 163, 815
Moyle, J., 160
Mueller, D. C., 928
Munby, D. L., 469, 485–487, 750
Mund, V. A., 770
Munthe, P., 332

N
Narvekar, P. R., 964
Narver, J. C., 309
National Board for Prices and Incomes, 771
National Bureau of Economic Research
    Business concentration and price policy, 216
    Capital and rates of return in manufacturing industries,
        1121
    Capital formation and economic growth, 1104
    Comparative prices of nonferrous metal in international
        trade, 758
    Concentration in Canadian manufacturing industries, 228
    Corporate income retention, 147
    Cost behavior and price policy, 773
    Cost, prices, and profits, 752
    The flow of capital funds in the postwar economy, 1085
    Measuring international price competitiveness, 759
    Merger movements in American industry 1895-1956, 311
    The rate and direction of inventive activity, 884
National conference on company mergers and acquisitions,
    310

National Economic Development Council
    The construction industry, 567
    Efficiency in road construction, 568
    Electronics and the future, 427
    Export trends, 965
    Growth of the economy, 101
    Growth of the United Kingdom economy 1961-1966, 102
    Imported manufactures, 966
    Investment appraisal, 1105
National Industrial Conference Board, 217, 715
National Institute of Economic and Social Research
    A classified list of large companies engaged in British
        industry December 1955, 218
    Company income and finance, 1106
    Economic and social studies:
        6, A statistical analysis of advertising expenditure and
            of the revenue of the press, 825
        9, The distribution of consumer goods, 542
        13, Retail trading in Britain 1850-1950, 543
        14, British economic statistics, 1154
        15, The structure of British industry, 81
        16, Concentration in British industry, 185
        17, Studies in company finance, 162, 1122
        19, The antitrust laws of the USA, 626
        20, A study of UK imports, 974
        21, Industrial growth and world trade, 961
        22, The management of the British economy
            1945-60, 87
        23, The British economy in 1975, 80
    Factory location and industrial movement, 363
    Industrial research in manufacturing industry . . . a
        statistical report, 860
    National Institute economic review, 1161
    Occasional papers:
        14, The cost of industrial movement, 362
        19, Post-war investment, location and size of plant, 94
        20, Investment and growth policies in British industrial
            firms, 1059
        21, Pricing and employment in the trade cycle, 775
    Paper and board, 569
    Productivity, prices and distribution in selected British
        industries, 783
Neal, A. C., 724, 774
Neale, A. D., 626
Needleman, L., 428
Nehrt, L. C., 967
Neild, R. R., 775
Nelson, R. L., 219, 241, 263, 311
Nelson, R. R., 885, 886
Nelson, S., 793
Netherlands. Central Bureau of Statistics, 1025
Nevin, E., 365, 776
Newman, P. K., 348
New Scientist, 1072
Newton, W. L., 399
New York University Institute of Comparative Law, 621
Nicholson, R. J., 366, 1143
Niehans, J., 220
Nigam, R. K., 1107
Norris, W. G., 312
Northern Economic Planning Council, 383
Northern Ireland Government, 384
Northwestern University Transportation Center, 490
Nutter, G. W., 47

Subject index

All references are to item numbers in the bibliography.

A

Administered prices (USA), 590, 792
Advertising, 61, 90, 808–839
  chocolate and sugar confectionery, 771
  costing, 753
  economics, 815, 818–9, 823–4
  expenditure, 808, 816–7, 822, 825, 834, 837, 839
  nationalised industries, 98
  pharmaceutical industry, 400 ; USA, 32
  soap and detergents, 771
  statistics, 825 ; European, 821
Advertising and :
  capital requirements, 812
  competition, 324, 809, 812, 816, 819, 831, 836
  concentration, 826, 836
  consumers, 810
  demand, 812, 820
  employment, 830
  entry barriers, 812
  innovation, 819
  monopoly, 818
  oligopoly, 819
  product differentiation, 812, 831
  profits, 812
  sales revenue, 822, 826
  size, 812
  the press, 825
Agreements, Termination of : consequences, 690
Agricultural industries : structure, 81
Agricultural machinery industry, 430, 634
Agriculture and monopoly, 36
Air transport industry see Civil aviation industry
Aluminium casting industry : competition, 403–4
Aluminium industry (USA) : anti-trust action, 634
Aluminium semi-manufactures : NBPI Report no. 39, 771
Ammunition industry : productivity, 392, 395
Anthracite industry (USA) : anti-trust action, 634
Anti-trust
(see also Monopoly ; Restrictive practices)
  anti-trust vulnerability, 35
  international aspects, 631 B
Anti-trust and international trade, 975
Assets
  depreciation of, 1081
  fixed : investment, 1114 ; replacement cost, 1060
Assets-income ratios : UK companies, 1065
Assets-sales ratio see Sales-assets ratio
Australia : mergers, 285
Automatic machine trading, 527
Automobile industry see Motor vehicle industry
Aviation see Civil aviation

B

Bakery industry wages : NBPI report no. 17, 771
Balance of payments and :
  competitiveness, 943
  EEC and EFTA, 1018
  export demand, 963
  growth, 1023
  investment, 1116
Bank charges : NBPI report no. 34, 728, 771
Bank merger acts (USA), 633
Bargain pricing and consumers, 810
Basing point price systems, 732, 763, 786
Batteries
  mercury hearing-aid : NBPI report no. 64, 771
  secondary : NBPI report no. 61, 771
Beer
  distribution (Italy), 550
  NBPI report no. 13, 771
Belgium : investment and growth, 1093
Bids
(see also Take-over bids)
  identical, 770
Black bolt and nut industry : restrictive practices, 699
Blanket manufacturing industry : restrictive practices, 655, 682
Boiler industry : restrictive practices, 655, 702
Bolt and nut industry : restrictive practices, 699
Bones industry : concentration, 185
Book trade : restrictive practices, 677–8, 693, 696, 700
Boots Pure Drug Co., 91
Boycotts, 626
Branch factories : costs in alternative locations, 362–3
Brand names : pharmaceutical industry, 400
Brand names and consumers, 810
Brass casting industry : productivity, 405
Bread and flour industry
  concentration, 185, 771
  NBPI report no. 3, 771
Brewing industry
  finance, 162
  mergers, 289
Brick industry
  concentration, 185
  cost margins, 734
  NBPI report no. 47, 771
British Commonwealth see Commonwealth
British Motor Corporation/Pressed Steel merger, 301
British Oxygen Co., 90
British Railways, 98
(see also Rail, etc.)
Bronze casting industry : productivity, 405
Brown Shoe Co. Inc : mergers and competition, 298
Brush industry : productivity, 560

Jenkins Committee on company law, 142

Printed in England for Her Majesty's Stationery Office
by St. Clements Fosh & Cross Ltd, London
Dd. 152707 K24 10/69   SBN 11 510211 6